To Libby,
this only took
twenty-five
and you were
the beginning.
Much love
Rich

July 2003

Common Sense About Craziness

RICHARD F. CURRAN, M.D.

Hollis Publishing
95 Runnells Bridge Road
Hollis, NH 03049
603.889.4500

Copyright © 2003 by Richard F. Curran

All rights reserved. No part of this publication may be reproduced, translated, or transmitted in any form or by any means without permission in writing from the Hollis Publishing Company.

ISBN 1-884186-23-8

Printed in the United States of America

Table of Contents

Introduction i

Chapter One
    The Early Years 1

Chapter Two
    Adolescence 53

Chapter Three
    Young Adulthood 121

Chapter Four
    Marriage 173

Chapter Five
    Midlife 207

Chapter Six
    The Latter Years 235

Conclusion 243

Acknowledgements

Thanks,

- To Fred Lyford, the boss at Hollis Publishing Company, for his encouragement and guidance with the project;

- To Sarah Bruce, my editor, for her wisdom, patience, and sensitivity and for keeping me from wandering too far, especially with the stories;

- To My dearest wife of forty-five years, Suzanne, for allowing me to use her kitchen table as my desk for so many months and years;

- To My daughter, Laura Duffy, wife, mother, teacher, administrator, who somehow found the time to transfer the handwritten word into print;

- To My God, for so much;

- To My patients, for the precious gift of sharing.

For the Tortured Minds

For the Tender Hearts

For the Trusting Souls

Introduction

By the time this book is published I will have retired from forty years of practice as a psychiatrist in the historic town of Salem, Massachusetts. During these years, I have treated approximately forty thousand people suffering from mental illness in one form or another. Insurance companies and professional organizations have me listed as a general practitioner of psychiatry (GPP). I bear this title proudly and gratefully. Were it not for the warnings from my medical school mentors about the approaching age of specialization, I would have entered the general practice of medicine. I know now that the two careers are quite similar. Perhaps the common denominator is one's closeness to the patient. I have come to share the pains and pleasures, hope and despair, joys and sorrows, not just of individuals but of families, sometimes three generations of them.

These people have enriched my life enormously and have taught me about life itself. I intend to share with you some of those lessons as a small-town psychiatrist, but more importantly, as a fellow human being.

Each year, many well educated mental health providers enter the field. Like me four decades ago, they are bristling with theories and good intentions. My training in the Boston area was heavily influenced by the post–World War II disciples of Freudian psychoanalysis. But I found out over the years that the behavior of human beings does not fit into any one theory. Instead, we respond and adapt to a world of natural laws and try desperately to reconcile our thoughts, feelings, and behavior with the choices we have in this world through something that separates us from all other earthly matter and forms of life: our personal essence, our soul.

Along with death and taxes, change is inevitable in our lives. With change comes the challenge to adapt and to continue growing. Challenge invites choice. Some do not choose to adapt and have trouble growing. Others are simply too sick, bothered, or confused and need help along the way. Helping has been my work. By and large, my efforts have been focused on restoring a sense of trust—a trust in one's self and others.

Lacking a single theory, I present my observations of human behavior based on the inevitability of change and challenge in the natural order of living and of the single most critical ingredient in coping with the world and the people in it: trust.

A word about the book's format: I describe the most natural changes of our lives in sequence from birth to death. Borrowing from thousands of case histories, I hope to illustrate these flesh-and-blood experiences by use of stories. Confidentiality has been preserved by changing names and places, as well as taking license in the details. Each of the six chapters describes problems common to a phase of life, in three sections. The first section of each chapter, entitled "Change," explores age-related changes that are unavoidable in life. The second section, "Challenge," features the continuing story of children born to two separate families, from their earliest days until their deaths. The third section, called "Choice," reconciles the observations presented in the first section with the composite stories. Included are in-depth discussions of the most common illnesses.

Understanding mental illness need not be difficult. It takes an open mind willing to look at how life itself shapes our course. My hope is to humanize and de-spook the field of psychiatry and to present in an understandable way our common human experiences.

My colleagues and I have not done a very good job during the past century in explaining what makes us tick. This book is a modest remedy. Join me and trust above all in your own common sense.

Finally, at the risk of oversimplification, I offer a brief summary of the main messages of this book.

1. Very few people truly go crazy.
2. Most mental and emotional problems are manmade.
3. What we can cause, we can prevent.

GUIDELINES

Before we explore the changes and challenges of life, we need a few tips on how to read signs and signals.

The basic language of human behavior begins with that most precious of gifts, the human mind. The mind is the seat of our soul—an invisible, intangible, immeasurable essence of our being. The brain is not the mind. The brain is physical and measurable (and indispensable to the mind).

The brain is the mind's PC—its personal computer. It gathers information about the world around us, collates and files it away in memory banks, and acts in the service of the mind to express its intentions in words and actions. In other words, the brain drives the body, but the mind drives the brain. The brain collects vital information, and the mind sorts it out and decides what to do.

Introduction

Two basic elements contribute to this process: thoughts and feelings. These two dynamic forces provide the substance for the language we develop along the way.

There are those in the behavioral sciences who believe our thinking intellect is of prime importance in separating us from the animals and directing our lives. As a species, this may be true, but the more dominant influence in our individual personal journey through life is our feelings. Let us examine the two most constant and familiar feelings that accompany us along our trip from birth to death: anxiety and depression. Anxiety and depression are not simple one-dimensional emotions; each is made up of a cluster of components. The two act as sentinels along the pathway of change, one anticipating the inevitability of change and the other reacting to certain events. From these two major feelings flow dozens and even hundreds of emotional colorings that affect our daily lives.

ANXIETY

Simple fear is a healthy human response to a known danger. It allows us to recognize real threats to our well-being and avoid them. Fear leads us to jump out of the way of a speeding vehicle as we cross the street. Anxiety, on the other hand, prevents us from crossing the street even when there is no traffic.

Anxiety is a fear of the unknown. It usually arrives as a sudden sense that "something bad is going to happen to me and I can't prevent it." Derivatives of this experience include panic attacks, major breakdowns, and phobias. On the emotional level, we experience painful fear, apprehension, panic, confusion, and a sense of complete helplessness as well as an overwhelming sense of doom. Physical manifestations include rapid heart rate and breathing, sweating, dry mouth, weakness, dizziness, and an urge to run. The body, as we will learn to appreciate, is the mind's best friend. In this sense, it works desperately to drain off the unbearable emotions by absorbing the invisible pressures onto our "mortal coil."

DEPRESSION

Depression is the flip side of human emotions. Depression is the human response to loss, the feeling that something bad has already happened and it's too late to do anything about it. Loss of health, wealth, job, prestige, and self-esteem, the death of loved ones—these are but a few examples. The more familiar term in response to these common losses is grief.

The feelings that arise from depression include sadness, emptiness, helplessness, and hopelessness. Seldom recognized or discussed but always present are two significant emotional reactions: resentment of the loss and guilt feelings. Throughout the book, I will refer to the depression triad of *sadness*, *madness*, and *badness*. The more common physical manifestations of depression are linked together by a characteristic down quality, including fatigue, lack of energy, loss of appetite, insomnia, weight loss, and crying spells.

Because our human nature clings to what is safe and secure, each of the inevitable growth changes in our lives invites a potential depressive event. *Potential* is the key word. That is where the issue of trust enters in. Natural changes in our lives can be handled naturally given the right support and love early in our lives.

⸺

There is much more to learn about the role of anxiety and depression in our lives, but it becomes much clearer as we see it in action. Let us now begin at the very beginning: the day of birth.

Chapter One: The Early Years

CHANGE

Birth

Our first change of life begins with the process of squeezing from the safety of our mother's body out into our new home, Planet Earth. To understand the child's reaction to these events, the child will describe the experiences of birth for us, even though in reality it has no capacity for organized thought, let alone communicating same.

> *I'm moving and twisting. It hurts. My head's being crushed. What's happening? It was all so quiet and peaceful. Now I hear noises. Strange noises. Loud noises. Screaming. Crying. Pounding, pounding all around me. Something's squeezing my face and neck. Pulling and stretching. Stop! Please stop! It hurts. I'm scared.*
>
> *What happened? It stopped. No more hurt. Where am I? Now I'm cold. My eyes! It's so bright. It hurts my eyes. Oh, oh. I'm moving again. Something's holding my feet up. More funny noises.*
>
> *Where am I going? Don't hurt me anymore. Please! I want to go home. I don't like it here. Someone please help. Mommy, Mommy! Please take me back!*

Happy birthday, little one!

Birth is not a pleasant time for infant or mother, but is necessary to allow the baby to leave its underwater habitat for a new air-filled world. The squeezing and stretching force intrauterine fluid from the uninflated lungs so that air can move in.

Modern medical research has confirmed the fact that not only neonatal life, but also prenatal life, responds to direct stimuli. The response is measured by body movements and muscle contractions. The baby before birth and after birth can feel.

Even the first moments of life produce feelings such as warmth or chill, pain or pleasure, and hunger. Most importantly, the newborn will register loudly and clearly its dissatisfaction that it had to leave its first home, mother. Thus, even though the tiny brain cannot process the feelings, the body of our newest citizen of Planet Earth loudly proclaims its objection.

The infant screams lustily and cries loudly, accompanied by tears. This is not just a reflexive muscle contraction. This is a wondrous initial statement of personal protest against eviction from a very low-rent apartment, mother's womb. First, the baby is terrified and panicky, then sad. The terror is understandable. Strange creatures with green masks and rubbery claws are pawing and probing. Bright lights are overhead and weird sounds all around. Something bad is happening and can't be stopped. What was, is no longer. No warm dark fluid to comfort the skin. No quiet, no harmony. No peace.

First comes anxiety, the response to the unknown danger that is life. And then comes depression, the natural sadness and madness over the cruel and unfair loss of the good life.

Homecoming

The next experience is comforting. The care given by the nursing staff in the newborn nursery restores some sense of security after the birth ordeal. Mom gets a well-deserved rest while her baby is introduced to the gentle experience of feeding, bathing, diaper changes, and blessed sleep. An infant gets more than twenty-two hours a day of slumber to shut out a world that still makes no sense. Mother and child are reunited several times a day by the nurses: the first steps in the physical and emotional bonding.

The helpless infant reacts to biological needs. Feeding and stroking feel good, but once again the brain cannot yet recognize who is responsible for this service. And although mother has a natural affection to offer, it is tempered by a body that is still weak and bruised from the delivery.

Most mothers would agree that discharge day arrives much too soon. (Most insurance companies disagree.) The precious moments of recovery are short. For the infant, leaving the comfort and safety of the newborn nursery represents another change of environment and requires another adjustment. In a sense, leaving the security of the nursery world means giving up the most perfect equal-opportunity society it will ever experience. The tender, well-regulated care by the nurses is rendered to each baby regardless of race, creed, color, social position, or political preferences. Once outside the hospital, there are no guarantees. The helpless, innocent child will enter a family situation where the single most important factor in its health and security is the strength of the relationship between mother and father. Their love for each other will now be tested, for they must learn to share it with the product of that love—a squiggling, cuddly, wonderful, helpless, very much alive new visitor.

The Early Years

The courting, the romancing, the dancing, the wedding, the honeymoon have taken their turn. No one is quite prepared for the parenting. From the moment the infant leaves the hospital, the earliest minutes, hours and days in the company of its co-creators will set the course of the child's life. The trip home from the hospital is the start of a wonderful but challenging venture for all three. The eyes and ears of the infant absorb strange noises and shadows from the safety seat while mom and dad stare straight ahead—proud and grateful, but partially numbed by the sense of responsibility that they will never quite relinquish.

To make this point clearer, two brief polarized scenarios come to mind. Both begin with father stepping out of his car at the door of the hospital, greeting wife and nurse attendant, strapping the infant into the safety seat and assisting wife into her seat and ultimately driving off.

The Day of Homecoming

Scenario One

Husband: "Hi, Honey! How do you feel?"

Wife: "A little tired but okay. I'll be fine. How are you? Do you miss me at home?"

Husband: "You bet! Funny. It's just been a few days but I miss you so much. It feels like a part of me is gone. The house is like an empty cave. I love you, Hon! How's the little one? The nurse said she had a rash on her chest."

Wife: "It's fine. They gave me some cream. She is so beautiful. We are very lucky."

Husband: "Talk about lucky. I have some more good news. I got a promotion: $10,000 more a year."

Wife: "Darling, I am so happy for you. Now we can buy that gorgeous crib we were looking at—she'll be out of the bassinet before we know it!"

Husband: "I love the name you picked. Cute but classy."

Wife: "We picked. Remember! It's we all the way. It's we three now, my darling."

Scenario Two

Husband: "Hurry up! Let's go! I get nervous around hospitals. Besides, I've got things to do."

Wife: "Thanks a lot, buddy! A little consideration wouldn't hurt. You know I just had a baby. And I'm not ready to run a marathon."

Husband: "Hey, what do you want from me? Getting pregnant was your idea, not mine."

Wife: "For god's sake! Are you still on that kick? You really piss me off! This is your son as well as mine."

Husband: "It better be my son! 'Cause time is running out with you and me. I'm still not convinced that one of your faggot friends from that rock group didn't drop the seed."

Wife: "This is great! What a hell of a homecoming!"

Husband: "Speaking of coming home, I've got news for you. We got our eviction notice for nonpayment. You've got two weeks to catch up on the rent or you're out on the street."

Wife: "What do you mean catch up? I gave you the money every two weeks. What did you do with it?"

Husband: "I owed some money. They wouldn't wait. So shut up about it."

Wife: "You son of a bitch! You owed someone! The horses or the dope? Which one? Or was it both?"

Husband: "Get off my back! I mean it! Here we are. Take the kid in! Ive got to go somewhere. I'll be gone a couple of weeks."

Wife: "You walk out on me now, and you'd better keep going. I've had it. You are a lousy excuse for a husband and father. But if you take off, mister, you'd better look over your shoulder, because I'll get a lawyer and hunt you down for support money. You're not getting away with this."

Husband: "You send a shyster after me, you bitch, and I'll come back to kill you and the kid!"

The walk from the car to the front door may be short but it offers private, thoughtful moments for the mother. Despite her weakened condition, she holds her precious newborn close to her body, mindful of the awesome responsibility ahead. Their bodies are rejoined in a most natural and necessary way. The baby is totally dependent. To survive and grow healthy, it must absorb mother's message of love and safety flowing from her touch, voice, and smell.

With their relationship in mind, let us conclude the two scenarios.

The first one is simple. Guided her own sense of security and connection with her husband, mother passes good messages to her child.

But scenario two fails in this regard. Mother's residual fury as she lifts the frightened newborn from the car seat adds to the sense of tension and danger in her touch. Father slams the door behind her and issues his last warning.

The Early Years

This tale of two newborns concludes. One enters a home with a good chance for health because of the ample supply of love and devotion. The other has the misfortune to be caught up in a dysfunctional parental unit and will be deprived of the essential commodities of love and nurturance at a most critical time.

Let us move on now to look at the more significant events of the first year of life and how these different beginnings just described might play out.

Settling In

The infant's physical development during the early months depends mostly on a well-functioning gastrointestinal system. The ability of the child to ingest and digest food is critical. Similarly, the unformed elements of the infant's psyche require nourishment in the form of tangible messages of safety and security. The brain and the nerve fibers throughout the tiny body ingest and digest the sounds, sights, touches, tastes, and smells of its immediate environment. Gradually, the messages become more recognizable by repetition and by the development of a memory bank. The infant recognizes and responds to pleasurable sensory experiences and reacts negatively to the upsetting ones.

Mother continues to be the main supply of both. The good times revolve around the taste of warm milk and cereal, gentle hands caressing the skin, soothing bath water, sweet-smelling baby powder, rocking to sleep in the arms of someone who coos and sings.

Life isn't that bad after all!

The eyes soon learn to focus on the moving form that delivers these pleasures, and that form becomes a familiar face. The predictable presence of this face brings a sense of trust, and the bonding really begins. The face and the pleasure become joined and lead to an awareness that the other one out there is truly an extension of oneself. The infant's world during its waking moments gradually includes the Mom and the I as one.

In time, other sights, sounds, and faces intrude on the blissful daily routine. Assuming that dad, siblings, extended family, and friends are equally caring, the baby will respond as best it can with approving smiles and gurgles.

In these early encounters, we must also acknowledge the meaning of the child's existence to parents and family. The love that is lavished, the worry triggered by physical discomforts, and the pure joy of claiming responsibility for a precious human life create a drama of magnificent proportion.

With all of this happening, the central character remains ignorant of everything in these early days but its own comfort. During these early weeks, the infant's perspective of early life is shaped by some basic issues.

I feel. I need. I feel better after my needs are met. Someone out there services my needs. And I expect that service to continue.

About halfway through the first year of life the free lunch phase ends. Heaven and earth are about to collide. The imperious reign of infancy starts to tremble. The unconditional rights and privileges of infancy must yield to a give and take, a quid pro quo. Here we go again! Another change. Only this time, a challenge as well. Mommy's role in this is quite serious. For she must orchestrate not only the necessary challenge but preserve the early trust built so carefully from the moment of birth. Even though the imaginary dialogue that follows seems light hearted and casual, the determination by both parents to nurture and guide their precious offspring is vital. All parties are acting without a script in this singular event where for the first time parents explore the need to set simple limits.

All of this occurs within the confines of the baby's crib. The stage is set. The only prop is a rattle. Let the play begin!

The Day of the Rattle
Mommy: "Now, my little darling, it's time for a nap. It's been a long morning. Here you go! Nice clean blankey to keep you warm. And look what Mommy's got for you! A brand new rattle. Listen! Hear the funny noise? Okay? Sweet dreams! Here's a kiss for my precious one."

Baby: *What's with her? I'm not ready for a nap. I'm not even tired. I don't want to be here. I want to be with mommy. I'm gonna cry real loud now. She'll have to come back.*

Mommy: "My, my! What's the problem? My poor baby. Let me pick you up. That's okay. Don't cry now. Let me check your diaper. No, everything's okay. Are you sick? Oh, I hope not. You feel so hot. I'll walk you around for a little while."

Baby: *She still doesn't get it. Sure, I stopped crying when she picked me up. I want to be with her. I don't want a nap. Oh, no. She's putting me back down. What's that thing she's shoving in my hand? That foolish little toy with the weird noises.*

Mommy: "Bye-bye, honey! Be good now. Go to sleep. Mommy's got so much to do."

Baby: *She went away again. I'll show her who's boss. I'll really make a fuss. And I'll toss that foolish toy on the floor. Who needs it?*

Mommy: "Now, little dumpling, enough is enough. You really need to nap, and what did you do with that cute little rattle? Naughty! Let's try it again. Here we go! Nighty-night. Be good now. Don't throw it out again or mommy might get mad."

Baby: *What is she saying? What does naughty mean? What does mad mean? I've never heard those sounds before. Now she's gone again. It's dark. I'm scared. That wasn't like mommy. I've got to have her back. I'll really cry loud now. And here goes that rattle. I hate it!*

Mommy: "I'm really ticked, little one! You're really being bad. Mommy's got no time to play games. Too much to do. So down you go! And this time no rattle. I'm sorry, honey, but this time you have to cry yourself to sleep."

Baby: *Another new word. Bad! She said I'm bad. Her voice was loud. She's gone again. Will she come back? What did I do? This never happened before. I thought she loved me. I deserve to be loved. She has to love me. Now she's gone. She's upset with me. And she said I'm bad.*

⁌

The words are the author's, but the feelings attendant to this shocking event belong to all of us who have lived through the early weeks of life. A sense of vulnerability and insecurity lingers. Whereas those same feelings overwhelm the child at the moment of birth, there is now a terrifying new sense of having caused the bad things to happen.

Recall the definition of anxiety. The feeling is, "something bad is going to happen and I can't prevent it." Only now there is an extra twist. The possibility that I have caused it.

Following the mini–guilt trip that arrives with the Day of the Rattle, the notion that one can cause something bad to happen becomes planted in our souls forevermore. This type of anxiety is *conscience anxiety*, as opposed to the more predictable, change-of-life version.

From this awful experience, another awareness befuddles the baby—a sense of separateness. The blissful bubble of righteous entitlement is popped rudely. Up to this moment, the child's world was made up of an "I" and some moving form that erased all the physical and emotional discomforts. The rattle game, however, caused an irreparable split between the "I" and the servant. Slowly the baby sees itself not only as an "I" (subject) but as a "me" (object). This is in comparison to mommy, who is now not just a slave and who now expects something back for services rendered. *Mommy went away from ME. Mommy was mad at ME.* No more undiluted, indivisible oneness. And no more simply "I" as the center of the universe.

Forgive the starkness of the language and the air of tragedy. In truth, these moments are not tragic in the context of life's inevitable changes and challenges. They are necessary. But the little one at the time of this crisis would surely not agree.

The trauma of these experiences will heal gradually—walking, sleeping, bathing, eating, and cuddling soon restore the world's proper spin. A new kind of trust will grow out of the child's awareness that its behavior can affect mom's reactions and mom's response and availability. For mom, balancing her wish to love with establishing reasonable expectations of her little child is at first awkward. There are likely to be reruns of the rattle experience, but they will be less upsetting to both parties as time goes on.

The Day of the Potty

The second major challenge to mom and child occurs many months later, usually starting around the "terrible twos." The Day of the Potty represents a sequence of events. At issue is mom's urging to give up the diaper and begin using the toilet. Whereas the infant is physically incapable of meeting this challenge early on, the advanced toddler is not. But being able to and wanting to is not the same thing.

This event is so important, not because it triggers another parent-child struggle, but because it invites the child to accomplish something, to succeed. This is in contradistinction to the first struggle over going to sleep, where the child resisted giving up its autonomy—now there is the potential for gaining some pride in an accomplishment. Potty training also moves the bond between child and parents up to a different level based on cooperation.

Hundreds of articles and books in the field of mental health have cited this struggle as pivotal in the early development of the child. Sociologists, behaviorists and psychoanalysts emphasize different facets. But they all agree that the issue of control is at the core.

On the Day of the Rattle, the child surrendered a piece of its autonomy because it had no choice. Without the love of the giving mother, it would cease to be. The emotional bartering began with a quid pro quo: "You be a good baby and I'll give you a cookie." Not so bad!

But lingering in the heart of the infant are the memories of paradise lost, and as the toilet training days approach, there is a growing confidence that round two could be different.

Whereas the infant had no control of its anal and urethral sphincters, the two year old does. The site of the struggle is thus a forgone conclusion. The parents logic is clear. Just as the leg muscles grew to allow walking and vocal cords produced talking, it's now time to control bowel and bladder.

Most parents wait until they know such voluntary control is in place before they seriously embark on the training efforts.

It is at this point that the little tike senses that it can exert another kind of control. It can willfully affect the parents wishes and reactions. It can please them or annoy them. An exciting power struggle looms. But in the end, the need for love and approval from the parents determines the outcome no matter how long it takes.

There is no one blueprint for success. Whether it be coaxing, scheduled trips to the toilet, training pants, bribes and rewards, the success of the process usually rests with the strength of the bond that has already developed between parent and child. At the center of this bond is the child's trust of the parents. If the parents don't trust each other or if the family structure is completely chaotic, the process of toilet training will be affected.

The process usually begins around the second birthday. Mom's agenda is simple: fewer diapers = less work. The child does not start out with an agenda. Only when it realizes that some changes are on the horizon does it react. For change means something of its comfortable lifestyle will be disrupted and lost. Precious to that lifestyle is mom's indentured obligation to obediently clean up the daily mess down below. The agenda for the toddler initially takes the path of resistance. The haunting memories of the rattle episode return. A righteous entitlement to mom's service ended that day and now she wants more time off. *It's just not right*, thinks the little one.

Enter the issue of trust. To fully understand how important this is, we must look at the damage control efforts by mom after the monarchy collapsed over the rattle. Ideally, mom puts the events in perspective. That means accepting the little one's frustration over her act of civil disobedience and getting on with the work of loving and nurturing her truly helpless baby who could not survive without her.

Up to this point, I have emphasized the role between child and mother. A loving dad is never out of the picture. But in our society, his presence in the earliest years is unpredictable. While generations of men have welcomed the role of actively parenting a baby, millions of children grow up in fatherless families. The one constant is the baby's natural need for mothering. If there is a caring father to join mother in the loving and teaching roles, then the issues of toilet training become simpler for child and parents. For even though the inevitable struggle may last weeks or months, the child gradually accepts the change knowing that the bond between itself and the parents is even stronger.

Part of the parents' care now involves teaching: about the realities of life, about how to deal with frustration, about how to delay gratification. This is not best accomplished by pulling a disappearing act when a child throws another temper tantrum. Such punishment is felt by the child as harsh and is too strong a response to what is just a misdemeanor.

There is another way now—a way to create something, something good out of a bad situation, a way to secure the natural bond of love. *Building trust.* It takes time and effort (mostly by mom). It isn't easy.

Consistency and predictability are two important factors in trust building. As the infant leaves the crib stage and advances through the highchair and playpen weeks into the crawling and toddler months, it needs to know that mom is there for the good times as well as the bad. She is there for the bumps and bruises, the teething and the scratches, and she is there to help blow out the birthday candles and to giggle and to cuddle. The reliability of mom helps to advance her other role as teacher. When she cautions a crawling infant about eating things off the floor or pulling out electric cords from the wall sockets, it allows the child to process the insult to its tender pride more quickly: *Mom isn't being nice but I know she still loves me.*

Indignation gradually yields to trust. Although the indelible imprint of mom's stomping out over the silly rattle still remains, the toddler now senses that life with mom and dad is much more than a power struggle. *They are there for me. They really do care about me.*

Whereas the infant was initially horrified to realize that it had the power to drive mommy away over the rattle issue, it now realizes that it has the power to please mom and dad and thus control the flow of love. This is one of the most significant moments in life. Three magnificent events occur at this point in the life of the child—all around the potty issue. (God really does have a sense of humor.)

First, the heretofore entitled and self-centered child accepts some responsibility for its behavior. Second, despite the fears of loss and giving up its rights to be served unconditionally, the child agrees to please mom and dad and gain more love and approval because of it. Third, the germinal seeds of self-esteem are planted. The child senses that by doing something good the child itself is good.

The details of potty training are etched in the memories of every parent. Coaxing, pleading, promising, laughing, crying, celebrating, and hopefully, a minimum of threats go into the process. The success of this struggle helps the child, the parents, and the family. Not all struggles end up successfully, however. In scenario number two of the child's trip home from the hospital, the parents themselves were struggling and their bitterness did not bode well for the child's future.

As we approach the third important early childhood challenge, it is worth noting that failure to help the child master these necessary changes will build up a considerable uncertainty about life itself. Each opportunity to develop confidence, trust in others, and a sense of worth may be thwarted by a fear of loss and hurt.

We have to grow older, but we don't have to grow up. As trivial as the rattle and potty issues may seem, they represent important milestones. Without loving and sensitive parents, children will not learn to trust their parents, themselves, or the world in which they live. If the earliest years of growth and development are thwarted by inadequate loving and teaching, the child will suffer. The body must grow but the mind, heart, and soul of the child will not keep pace and that child will begin its journey through life playing catch-up. We will appreciate this more as we look at the challenges of adolescence and adulthood.

But now to the third and final hurdle of early childhood.

The Day of the School Bus

Several years ago on television, a life insurance company ran a commercial with the warning that "the future is now." It depicted a timid young boy and his mother walking slowly through the rain toward a school bus. Both wore bright yellow slickers and held hands tightly. With grim determination she lifted him up the large steps. He glanced back over his shoulder for what was, to him, possibly the last time he would ever see his mommy. How could she do this to him? Turning down the aisle, he cringed at the din of screaming and crying that roared through the dungeon on wheels. Since no one offered him a seat, he stumbled his way to the back of the bus as the pneumatic doors hissed shut. No escape now. The commercial faded with the portrait of the little boy's nose pressed against the watery rear window, while his watery eyes pleaded with the woman on the sidewalk to rescue him. She gallantly wiped her watery eyes and despite a ton of guilt and anguish, smiled and waved good-bye.

Another change, another challenge. Another loss, another potential gain. Another risk, another possible reward.

> *Where has mommy gone? Will I ever see her again? I don't like this bus. These kids are big and mean. They might hurt me! I miss mom so much. I need her. And dad too. He would protect me. But he's not here!*

> *Why did they leave me? I'm mad! I don't deserve this! I have been good. Or have I? I didn't eat my supper last night and I skipped brushing my teeth. Am I that bad? Is that why she left me?*

As with the previous two crises of early childhood, the forced separation via the school bus has special meaning. The apprehension and fear that slowed the little feet en route to the ominous yellow bus are obvious components of natural anxiety. And the tears from inside the rain-soaked rear window are ample signs of the horrible sense of loss and instant depression. There are two parts of this event worth noting.

One is the child's realization that, like it or not, the world outside of the family must be faced. Even mom and dad cannot protect the child from society's demands to leave home and participate. The second is gathered from the hijacked student's mournful musings. In a simple and uncomplicated way, the three feelings common to human depression are expressed: *sadness, madness, badness*. Throughout this book, we will appreciate the importance of recognizing and dealing with these three responses to change and loss.

Before leaving the preschool years, a final word on that vital ingredient to growth and emotional development: trust. No child can handle the changes and challenges of the preschool years without consistent love and guidance from caring parents. No parents can provide this perfectly. What is vitally important for the child is that the parents are trying to do their best. The child then feels valued and wants to maintain that value by doing its best to please them. Out of this comes perhaps the most important achievement from the emotional standpoint of the early years of life: a mutual trust.

The following story illustrates the vulnerability of the child regarding the trust issue at this time of life.

Jimmy

I met Jimmy in my role as Medical Director of a Child Guidance Clinic. Jimmy was five years old when he was brought to the Nazareth Child Care Center in the Jamaica Plain section of Boston. This was a modern, well-run home for neglected children staffed by an order of nuns called the Daughters of Charity. Anticipating the emotional plight of their children, they had developed a caring mental health program on campus.

By court order, Jimmy had been removed from a single-parent home in Dorchester. Over a period of months, he had been physically abused by mother's live-in boyfriend. He finally was admitted to Boston City Hospital, where he stayed a month recovering from a cerebral hemorrhage that caused him to lapse into a coma for the first four days. In addition to the skull fracture, the boyfriend had fractured his left arm and leg.

I first met Jimmy in the Rosary Clinic at the request of Sister Frances, who cared for the children in this cottage. I was to evaluate his readiness to receive a visit from his mother.

He was small for his age but walked with a firm gait which ended several feet from the two chairs I had arranged by a window. He stood still in the middle of the room surveying me. My "Hi, Jimmy" was ignored, as was my effort to shake his thin little hand.

He turned his head to the side and stared at the wall avoiding my gaze. It was then I saw the crescent shaped scar arching across his scalp over the left ear. His thick brown curly hair had grown back but could not take root on the site of the surgical incision. For this distinctive physical aberration, he'd already acquired the nickname "Moonbeam" from some of the older kids.

From the standpoint of communication, the first meeting was a bust. Jimmy refused to talk. It took two more encounters to establish a monosyllabic response to my offer to mediate between himself and his mother. He preferred to stay at a distance as we walked around the beautiful autumn-tinted grounds of the campus. Body language came first. He would shrug his shoulders to acknowledge some of my efforts. It was a beginning.

A few weeks later, I tried again, this time with an invitation to play catch with a mini-football just outside the walls of his cottage. It worked. He was impressed that the "witch doctor" could throw a perfect spiral. He agreed that it was okay for me to speak with his mother regarding her request to visit. An appointment was arranged for two weeks hence.

The administrator of the clinic filled me in on the mother from her brief contact the week after Jimmy had arrived. She had married and divorced three times. She was now thirty-eight years old and had given birth to four other children, the oldest of which was sixteen and confined to a youth detention center for armed robbery. She had two daughters and another son two years older than Jimmy. None of them lived at home. She was living on General Relief funds, having lost her right to Aid to Dependent Children funds when Jimmy was removed by the state authorities.

Sister Martha, the psychologist, described her as a woman of average intelligence, controlled manners, and a seductive charm in the form of a plastic smile and engaging humor. Direct eye contact was impossible. The smell of her breath from across the room suggested a significant blood alcohol level at the time of their meeting. What made the biggest impression on Sister Martha was her attitude toward Jimmy's placement at Nazareth. Having labored through hundreds of similar interviews, she was accustomed to themes of blamelessness and injustice from legally branded "unfit mothers." Jimmy's mother was different, however. She thought that it was wonderful. Nazareth was just the right spot for her boy. She seemed relieved and curiously proud to have a child at that institution.

Jimmy's mother was on time for our meeting. She was somewhat startled when I entered the sparse, dimly lit alcove off the front hall. She immediately stood up and crushed out a half finished cigarette into the Styrofoam coffee cup. I invited her to the more comfortable surroundings of a family visiting room down the hall. Her high heels clicked mockingly at the silent stares of the saints and angels held captive along the walls by wooden frames.

Sister Martha was right. She did have a certain presence and charm. She slid into an upholstered chair, crossed her legs, and asked if I wished to join her in a cigarette. I declined but found myself awkwardly fishing for an ashtray to accommodate her. She laughed at my clumsiness and reminded me that she had her own, the empty cup.

"How's my Jimmy, Doctor? I hope he's being a good boy now."

"Jimmy's fine. He's coming along very well," I replied.

"I hope he's eating better. He lost so much weight in the hospital. He almost died, you know."

I asked her how life was going. No complaints other than the size of her monthly General Relief check—not enough to make ends meet. Without some occasional help from certain friends, she couldn't survive. I had some questions about her friends in the light of Jimmy's beating, but she quickly took the initiative, starting with a dramatic profession of love for her son.

"Jimmy is very special to me, Doctor. He's my youngest, my baby. God, he was so cute when he was little. Always smiling and giggling. I could just eat him up."

I asked about the other kids.

"Well now, let me see. Jimmy is five years old, then Tommy is the next oldest by a couple of years. Poor Tommy! He was a lot like Jimmy, sweet and gentle when he was little. Then he got to running off. Gone for days at a time, even before he was ready for kindergarten. I think he resented me having Jimmy. Anyway, the state took him and placed him in a couple of foster homes for a while. They were no good for him. The judge said he was sexually abused in both places. They should put people like that in jail, don't you think? Anyway, the state figured he'd be safer in what they call a more structured environment run by some nuns up in Lowell. Something like Nazareth but not as nice. It's hard for me to get there."

She stopped momentarily to catch her breath.

"Rita's a little older than Tommy. I'm not sure how many years. I get mixed up on ages. She's adopted now. Nice family in South Boston. He works for Gillette. Good job! The agency won't let me contact her. I gave her up when Tommy was born. I couldn't cope with two at a time. She was a sick one. Colicky. I never had a night's sleep. She wore me out. And speaking of problems, let me tell you about the oldest one, Bruddy. His real name is Brendon. Trouble from the day he was born. Things weren't good at the time. I was living with his father in a secondhand trailer in my grandfather's backyard. My guy got jailed on a drug bust when Bruddy was only a year old. I didn't know what to do.

"The nuns said he was the wildest kid the school ever had. Drove them all crazy. Last I heard, he had gotten arrested again out in Holliston. They put him in a youth detention center or something."

The Early Years

Before she talked about her fifth child, she felt the need to compare her own childhood experiences with those of her children.

"You see, doctor, I know what it means to be in different homes as a kid. I never knew my own mother and father. They took me away when I was a little baby."

"Who took you away?" I asked.

"The state! It's always the state. I don't know who it was but they were working for the state. Don't get me wrong, now. I'm not complaining. The state's just doing its job. When a mother or a father isn't doing right by a kid, they're supposed to step in and take charge. That's how I was brought up and that's how my kids are doing it."

The note of inevitability startled me.

"Did you actually expect the state to take charge of Jimmy's life at some point?"

"Sure, doctor. That's the way it is. Poor people like me can't do it. I came from nothing and I've got nothing. I can't bring up a kid on a measly check I get from welfare. No way!"

Her logic was fixed, impenetrable, and numbing. I decided to complete the inquiry about the other children.

"You have one other child, a daughter?"

"Oh, yeah! Sorry, doc, not much to tell. She's about thirteen or fourteen now. No one knows where she is. Ran away from every place that they could find. The police in Canton think she's dead. Terry was her name. Poor kid!"

"Any other children?" I asked. Once again I was completely unprepared for her response.

"No! None that's alive anyway. It's funny the way it happened. Kinda weird really. I had a total of nine pregnancies and only five kids made it through. No abortions. You aren't gonna believe it but the four that never got born were all by three different husbands and the five that came out alive were by guys I wasn't married to. How do you figure it, huh?"

She laughed and shook her head. I asked if she had an explanation.

"Well, I'm no doctor like you, but I often wondered if something went on between my head and my body. What I mean is, maybe it was a repeat of me and my mother. She wasn't married to my father, from what I heard. Maybe down deep, I didn't want a baby with a legitimate father. Like I told you, the state's finally responsible."

After the meeting, I recommended to Sister Martha that a supervised visit was probably okay as long as the mother was advised to stick to here-and-now issues and avoid any promises of early return of Jimmy to her custody. Two such meetings were held, one in mid-November and another a month later. It was then that the mother asked if she could take him home on Christmas Day. Jimmy himself was cautiously enthusiastic, especially when she described the tree and the toys that awaited him. Sister Martha and I discussed the pros and cons and decided to go along with the idea, providing we could prepare both parties as to reasonable expectations. Sister Martha was to call the mother and I would work with Jimmy.

A few days before Christmas, I arrived at the clinic for our appointment and found a message from Jimmy's cottage mother, Sister Frances, that he was sick in bed and could not attend. I decided to go to him.

He was lying in bed with his head turned to the wall when I entered. He did not answer my greeting for several seconds. Then his whole body started to tremble, and I could hear muffled cries building slowly in intensity. I knelt down beside the bed and put my hand gently on his shoulder.

"Jimmy, it's okay! Don't worry! We don't have to do anything you don't want. Nobody is going to hurt you. I promise."

The sobbing continued for another five minutes. I felt helpless. He couldn't be reached. I stood up and again tried to reassure him that he was safe. I headed for the door promising that I would return the next day. I caught his voice before the door closed.

"Don't go! Don't go! I'm okay."

I reentered and again knelt down beside the tear-soaked face. It took a few minutes for him to compose himself. The theme repeated itself several times.

"Mama wants me to go home for Christmas. I'll go, but I just don't want to be hurt."

Christmas morning arrived. It was bitterly cold outside, but the predicted snowstorm had blown out to sea. Mom was due at nine o'clock. Jimmy arrived in the visiting room fifteen minutes early in the company of Sister Frances. He was dressed in warm woolen secondhand brown trousers with a bright red shirt. Both had been carefully laundered by the nuns. Sister carried with her the outerwear, a slightly worn plaid mackinaw and a bright new white scarf and ski cap, gifts from Santa Claus.

For the first hour, Jimmy sat stiffly and quietly. Sister Frances called the mother's number. No answer. For the next two hours, he sat alone. Sister Frances told him to have his mother call her at the cottage when she arrived, then returned at noon to walk him back to his room. He threw himself on the bed and began a long cry. His mother never arrived or called.

The Latency Phase

Child psychiatrists call the next half dozen years the Latency Period. It is a time not so much of dramatic change and more of consolidation. Individual roles within the family structure become much clearer.

The Early Years

The world outside the family revolves around school and after-school activities. For the child it is a fairly disciplined, orderly lifestyle, programmed by teachers and parents who rely on the hours and days of the week for cues as to where the child should be and what the child should be doing. It is a learning time. Not only does the child's intellectual growth advance, but social exploration is inevitable, particularly in school situations. Interaction with other kids is unavoidable. Learning to give and take, to win and lose, to express feelings of fondness and friendship are wonderful new experiences.

Perhaps the key word in describing the latency years between first grade and adolescence is *gradual*. The cadence of growth and development flows with the calendar of events, the school months, vacation time, family birthdays, holidays. It is a time for parents to grow also. There is no script for parenting, and this is the time mom and dad must shift gears from providing total nurturance to sharing responsibility with teachers and even the child itself. The child still craves love and attention but likes to be with other kids. All the while the child is absorbing adult values, particularly from the parents.

Kids also compare parents at this stage. They are basically interested in what other parents let their kids do or not do. But that is not all. The inquisitiveness is much more than gathering ammunition for stretching evening TV time or buying a shinier bike. It is a genuine effort by the child to build a sense of confidence and security in themselves, their family, and the world around them.

Latency-age kids are more aware of the world around them than people realize. They gradually become aware of that taboo thing called sex, as well as drug abuse, alcohol abuse, crime, and cruelty. Much of this awareness comes from the media. These issues can be threatening and confusing. The latency child needs parents who can help them deal conceptually with the problems of an imperfect world outside the family. They need parents whose own behavior is the most reassuring element in terms of building a value system of rights and wrongs for themselves.

Latency-age kids are not too young to begin forming a personal reason for living. Other than those who go to religiously oriented schools where issues concerning life's meaning are openly discussed, there may be more wonderment and confusion. Ultimately, it is the constant exposure to the parents' beliefs that guide the child. Once again, a solid trust between parents and child is the key to progressing through these years to the next major challenge, Adolescence.

If the foundation of this trust is faulty in the preschool years, the child must drag some unfinished emotional business into latency, making the task of mastering normal challenges and changes more difficult. Sometimes the early foundation is solid, but events during the child's latency years can cause setbacks—uncontrollable losses, such as sickness, injury, or death within the family, are a few. Economic reversals or natural disasters will take their toll also.

Perhaps most devastating is a disruption in the marital relationship of the parents. Sociologists tell us that most marriages are at the highest peak of disruption during the first year. The second highest peak appears to be around the "seven-year itch." If the marital union starts to dissolve, the child senses danger within the family. Anxiety over what they cannot control and depression over pending or actual loss interfere with their daily life. The normal changes and challenges of the preadolescent years become magnified, and trust in parents, other adults, and themselves becomes shaky. If a marriage fails, often the child is influenced more by one parent than the other. In the legal awarding of child custody, the child is powerless to choose.

Two common reactions are thus forced on the child who cannot by itself emotionally divorce the divorcing parents. One is a reflexive sense of guilt or betrayal regarding the noncustodial parent. As artificial as it may be, it cuts deeply into the child's delicate sense of self-worth. The second response may be an exaggerated dependence on the custodial parent, with the hope that that person can repair and sustain a sense of security in an unstable world.

It is this situation that leads me to explore another major pathway to emotional instability. Up to now, I have emphasized the tragic consequences of too little parental love and loyalty. The scenarios outside the birthplace and Jimmy's story are examples. However, "too much" love can seriously stunt the child's emotional growth. Too much love by a parent takes the form of overprotection, over-affection, and a subtle message that the outside world cannot be trusted.

It usually begins in the preschool years, as a result of one parent's need to supplement an inadequate supply of love and emotional nourishment from the spouse. Mostly, but not always, it is the wife who is caught in this dilemma.

As we shall see later in the book when we examine the challenge of marriage, the problems may reside less in the other spouse's ability to give sustenance than in premarital emotional malnutrition that leads to unrealistic expectations in the marriage.

Nevertheless, the child may become the natural choice to supplement the love of a disappointing spouse. This may not be planned or designed, and there is no script. But it may be an insidious and serious pattern of parent–child relationship that truly will interfere or cripple growth.

The Early Years

For the emotionally hungry but immature child, the seductive process is irresistible. The message from the parent is one of extra time, extra love, extra closeness. *The two of us are special. I will take special care of you. We belong together. Other people cannot be trusted to be part of this.*

What the child and often the parent do not realize is the price tag on this relationship. The parent needs the child so much that growth, independence, and separation become unacceptable threats to this unhealthy union.

This concludes the description of the changes that affect the earliest years of our lives. What should be apparent is the helplessness of the child to deal with these events without love and guidance from the parents. What an awesome responsibility this is! No parent deliberately sets out to hurt the flesh of their flesh. However, the whirl of pressures, whether marital, family, work, or financial, can lead to unintended patterns of neglect.

A picture is worth a thousand words. Thus, this book follows the lives of two infants who leave the newborn nursery the same day. Their experiences and those of their families and extended families illustrate the changes, challenges, and choices that face us all.

These stories are not copied or borrowed from actual case histories. They are fictitious but are meant to describe the real-life challenges that confront all of us.

CHALLENGE

Billy Smith

The brakes squealed. The baby squirmed. The mother screamed. The father swore. Welcome to the world, William Thomas Smith III.

Bull Smith pressed the brakes with a vengeance. The traffic light turned red and so did he. How dare that bitch insult him. So he was hungover. So what! It wasn't the first or the last time. Melanie had barely placed her newborn baby in the car seat when she tore into him for his stagger and his smell.

This wasn't going to work at all. He was fed up. If she had aborted the kid, like he insisted, the marriage would be history by now. Sayonara! Miami, or the West Coast maybe. Friends there and elsewhere. Mostly on the lam from the DEA or the FBI.

His infant son, William Thomas Smith III, let out a pathetic wail. From the back seat, Melanie screamed, "What the hell are you doing? We've got a brand new baby here. Jesus Christ, Bull, will you grow up?"

The car jerked forward from the hospital exit onto Highland Avenue, and from there made a series of jarring lefts and rights to the third-floor apartment in a troubled section of town known as the Point.

His mind was not on the driving. He had been fired from the school bus company yesterday. No way was he going to tell her that now. He refused to take the baby upstairs after they arrived. She should have kept her mouth shut. He needed a drink to clear his head.

Time was running out on their marriage. It really started to come apart when she broke the news about the pregnancy eight months ago, when he stormed out of the drab three-room apartment, muttering and swearing. He was gone for about a week, claiming the needed to get some space to clear his head. She gathered from her waitress friends that he had help with his thinking from a lonely, young widow in Peabody.

He finally returned only to demand that she get an immediate abortion. Melanie was hurt and angry. Realizing that the marriage was a bust, she began thinking seriously about abortion. Her mother informed her that she would have aborted all her children if she had it to do over. Over the years Melanie harbored a deep resentment over mother's casual dismissal of the worth of her offspring. Partly in defiance of that attitude and partly because of her identification with the helplessness of her baby-to-be, she decided to continue on.

The pregnancy passed slowly. Ernie, her boss at the Clam Shed, turned out to be her only support. Quite often, after closing they would sit, have a drink, and talk. Many nights he drove her home when it was apparent that Bull was busy elsewhere. She hated to go into an empty apartment, so they would sit outside and talk some more.

But now there was the baby, little Billy. A beautiful, squirming, cuddling, innocent, and totally helpless child. And she had all the responsibility. Bull would not help; Bull could not help.

She laid him on the bed and gazed down into his face, his eyes. His eyes searched her own face with a startled, frightened quality. He was already affected by an unsettled world. She picked up her son, held him close to her face, and burst into tears.

Bull had been the talk of the town then. He was captain for the football team in his senior year, and Melanie was a cheerleader. He acquired his nickname as a bruising fullback who converted on seventy percent of short yardage downs. A school record.

He was a local hero. He loved it. And he never let go of it. He accepted an athletic scholarship to the University of New Hampshire and tore a ligament in his right knee during the first month of practice. He left the school before Christmas, an academic failure.

He and Melanie rented a small house at Salem Willows during the winter with little heat and little furniture. When summer arrived, the rent tripled and they had to leave. From there on it was a series of rooming houses, cheap flats, and seasonal jobs.

Bull worked briefly as a ticket taker at Salem Willows, ran an ice cream truck for a few months, and worked for a year in the city park department. Melanie was forced to waitress full time, a job that she maintained until just before the birth of her first son.

Ruth Malone

Exactly one hour after the Smith family drove away from the hospital, another car pulled up. A smiling new father greeted his wife and brand new baby girl, Ruth Angelina Malone. In his excitement, he shook hands with strangers at the door, snapped photographs, kissed the maternity nurse, and gently put his daughter into the car seat.

He had trouble keeping his eyes on the road. Through his rearview mirror, he glanced frequently at the two most important people in his life. And what a life it was! So very good! True, it was not an easy pregnancy for Rita, but it was over. She had gone through the ordeal of a miscarriage a year ago. Despite that, she had insisted on working as an O.R. nurse at the hospital until one month ago. Quite a woman!

Eddie Malone was bursting with pride. He couldn't wait to tell her his surprise. He had planned on holding the good news until they arrived home. But, to hell with it!

"Honey, I've got some great news. I'm about to become a junior partner in the firm. Big raise, new office, the works."

"Eddie, that's great! You deserve it. Congratulations, honey."

She leaned over and cooed softly to her precious newborn. "Did you hear that, darling? Your daddy's a big-time lawyer."

Eddie Malone's background was middle class Irish and first class Catholic, deeply rooted in the proud corner of Boston called Charlestown. He was Wednesday's child, the third of five boys born to big Mike and Mildred. He wasn't the brightest, best looking or most athletic of the brood. But he was the most determined.

Eddie's father was a longshoreman and was steward at the local union hall. He was known as a peacemaker but could not successfully arbitrate a dispute between rival factions. He was gunned down on his way to work at the height of one bitter union dispute.

The Malone family was devastated. Eddie was ten years old at the time. No one felt the loss as deeply. Had he let his father down? He had never been the best at anything. His oldest brother Paul became the man of the house. Eddie was unimportant as usual. He did not know his role amidst the devastation of the family loss.

By the time he reached high school, his star began to rise. The Malone tradition helped. Boston University offered him a hockey scholarship. In his senior year, he was a first string defenseman on a championship team. His degree in education landed him a job as a math teacher at Jamaica Plain High School.

Rita Malone came from Malden. She was the only child of Angelo and Francesca Caruso, both second-generation Italians with common roots in the northern town of Pisa. Francesca hemorrhaged badly at the time of delivery, and an emergency hysterectomy was necessary. Thus Rita became a "princessa," a title given to only girls in the multi-children Italian families of her generation. As a young child she enjoyed the pampering and protection that went with the title. By the time she went to Boston College, she had grown to be an independent soul and wanted to break some of the ties. She insisted on living in Chestnut Hill and not commuting. Her parents were hurt when she told them it was time to "let go of the love leash."

Music and art were her first choices, but then again they were the choices of her parents. They encouraged her to continue the tradition of her Tuscan forebears. Once again she bolted from her expected role and switched her major to nursing in her junior year. Rita loved the academic challenge and the excitement of campus life. A year after meeting Eddie Malone, she received her degree in nursing.

Their courtship and engagement were long by peer standards at the time—three years. There were actually three reasons. The first was money. The second was Rita's wish to use her degree before starting a family, and save some money. The third was the natural reluctance by all parties in the Caruso family to separate.

Eddie's income went from modest to borderline poverty after he left teaching for law school. Through family connections he worked an occasional shift as a longshoreman. Rita got a job within a month of graduation and commuted to the Salem Hospital from Malden. She loved working in the operating room and felt that this was where she belonged for the rest of her life. She knew she had a lot to learn but truly loved her work. What she didn't have was any emotional and physical distance from her doting parents, and eventually she moved to a small apartment in the Salem area.

Eddie and Rita announced their engagement on Christmas Eve in the kitchen of the Caruso home. Eddie had saved enough money to buy a substantial diamond ring. The Carusos predictably went through several emotional stages that included crying, laughing, yelling, hugging, and finally dancing in the kitchen. They were happy, they were sad, they were grateful, they were suspicious, but all in all they were so proud of their baby for all she had accomplished. Until the wee hours of the morning, they drank wine and planned the biggest wedding reception ever.

Billy Smith

Little Billy Smith was a tense, fussy infant. For good reason. The real world away from the hospital nursery was an unpleasant, uncomfortable place to be. He was surrounded by angry voices, strange sounds, nervous hugs. His reaction was to cry himself to sleep several times a day, which indeed was the only shut-off switch he had to blot out his unpleasant surroundings. His cries were actually a series of weak spasmodic shrieks. Melanie was beside herself. Bull was no help at all. The pediatrician became annoyed with her phone calls and visits on a more-than-average basis during the first two months. Not knowing all the details of the home life, the doctor blamed it on infant colic and prescribed a mild antispasmodic sedative.

Melanie was exhausted, emotionally and physically. Bull was out of work, so she had to return to her old waitressing job. A few dollars a week were spent on neighborhood kids to watch over the infant baby, because Bull refused to stay home at night. The work of parenting a screaming kid belonged to the woman of the house, he believed, and she was screwing it up royally.

Bull's rejection of wife and baby continued over the first several months. Excessive drinking led to cocaine, a little heroin, and then a lot of heroin. He wanted to avoid all responsibilities and could shut out the nagging guilt only with drugs. Melanie resented it when he came home at night smelling like a garbage truck, bumping into the walls and furniture. Some nights he would stand and pound on the door and swear and scream until he dropped. Little Billy would respond to the noise by whimpering and occasionally breaking into harsh shrieks. After several minutes, there would be blessed silence for Melanie.

Melanie renewed her constant plea to have him return to the family and have him take responsibility. His response was, "Screw the family. I didn't want one anyway." She sought out his best friend, who told her it was too late. Bull was set for a court hearing within a week to answer charges of cocaine possession. As far as he knew, Bull was planning on skipping town before the court appearance and heading out to the West Coast.

In desperation, Melanie turned to her mother, who also lived in Salem. Melanie, the second of three daughters, was born just after Gertrude Foley left her first husband. Gertrude resented the timing of that pregnancy but decided not to abort, although she often reminded Melanie that it would have been better for her, for both of them. Gertrude was now on her third marriage. Judd was no better than the other two—couldn't hold a job, drank too much, and had a foul mouth.

Melanie was in the way from the start, thought Gertrude, and now she was asking for help with a child who would be nothing but problems. "Damn," she shouted as she slammed down the phone. "I told her to get rid of that kid right from the beginning." Judd overheard her comments and outdid her in his own profane response. Oddly enough, it stirred up enough resentment against the foul-mouthed husband to prompt a return call to her desperate daughter. She told her to grab a taxi and come over and stay with her for a few days. By the end of the week, she laid out the terms of a longer stay. Melanie was expected to keep her nighttime job and pay thirty dollars a week toward the running of the apartment. In addition, she would be responsible for buying food for herself and the baby, do her own laundry and the baby's, and clean the entire apartment once a month.

If the first year of Billy's life was the year of crying and doctor visits, then the second year was the year of retaliation. Despite his small size, he exhibited a strong and powerful scream that heralded his temper tantrums. Most frustrating was what Melanie felt was a malicious refusal to be toilet trained. To her it was personal. With all of her problems, Billy's stubbornness was an obvious attempt to show who was boss. His will against hers. The angrier she got, the more diapers and training pants he filled. The third year ushered in what his grandmother considered an intolerable show of impulse and destructive ability. He would move so quickly that they could not salvage ashtrays, lamps, or dishes. Grandma issued an ultimatum to Melanie that she either discipline her son or move out. Melanie's insistence that it was Gertrude who was spoiling the child fell on deaf, angry ears. Despite that, they remained guests in the apartment up until the time Billy was five years old.

It was on his fifth birthday that he finally heard from his father. The card was postmarked from Folsom Prison in California. He was sorry for being gone so long, but would make it up to his son when he came home. There was no message for Melanie. She was hurt and confused but relieved at the same time. At least she knew where he was. She lay awake many nights wondering what she would do if and when he came back. Would he be changed? What was he in prison for?

By the time Billy was ready for kindergarten, Melanie had saved up enough money to rent an apartment in south Salem. Gertrude, as expected, offered no support but managed to confuse her daughter with a mixed message: "It's about time you moved out."

Billy and Gertrude had grown close to each other, and it was a difficult scene when he finally left. Billy had no great fondness for Judd, who was rude and crude with him from the beginning. But he could not bear to separate from the woman who had given him so much even if it was to excess. This was his first major change, away from a person that he loved and into a situation of new surroundings to be followed by his first exposure to a gathering of other kids.

Ruth Malone

Rita and Eddie reflected on the events of the day. They moved into their bedroom, sat on the edge of their bed, and stared silently at the little miracle in the bassinet. Rita leaned over, put her head on Eddie's shoulder, and cried softly. She said that she never felt so tired and so happy at the same time.

Using her mothering instincts as well as her nursing skills, Rita offered little Ruth a safe and loving environment during the first year of life. Appointments with the pediatrician were scheduled and were not crisis driven. At the end of the second year, she returned to nursing part-time on the surgical ward rather than in the operating room. Ruth had some initial tantrums over mommy leaving her with the high school neighbor until daddy arrived home. Some of that aggravation may have led to a bumpy toilet-training period. At annual checkups with the pediatrician, Rita and Eddie received good marks as parents during the preschool years.

Alan Peter Malone entered the world a few months shy of Ruth's fifth birthday. Rita once again worked right up to the time of delivery and then stayed home with her two children for the next couple of years. The arrival of baby Alan gave his father particular joy. He dreamed great dreams for his son and promised himself that Alan would not be ignored or suffer the unintended anonymity of his own childhood. Things were going well in Eddie's career. He was now a full partner in the law firm, and his income kept up with the promotions.

Ruth experienced a brief period of unrest when the new baby came home but quickly adapted, basically because of a close bond with her mother. The next test was kindergarten, and Ruth entered that world in a natural and accepting way. Mom and dad were always there. They could be trusted and did not lie.

Eddie and Rita picked out a lot in Topsfield and built a spacious ten-room home. The housewarming—which doubled as Alan Malone's first birthday party—was a gala affair with the Malones and the Carusos enjoying the party immensely.

There was a downside to all of Eddie's success. Busy, busy, busy! Not only was he unable to be home for supper most weeknights, but the firm was grooming him for their foreign accounts. He and Rita talked about it and decided he should continue with the job as long as he could. Within a year, he was averaging one trip a month away from home with an average duration of about a week.

Billy Smith

The most reliable witnesses to early childhood development are doctors and teachers. Pediatricians measure height and weight, muscular coordination, speech patterns, and—last but not least—behavior. They have the unenviable task of calling it like it is, hoping to sustain and support parents rather than alienate them. By the time the child is in kindergarten they pass on the job of assessing emotional growth to the teaching profession.

William Thomas Smith III, also known as "Billy the Kid" by the pediatric associates, had pretty much worn out his welcome by the time they relinquished oversight of his behavior to the unsuspecting kindergarten staff. The frequent calls to the emergency room, the bumps and bruises, the head colds and the ear infections—those were worrisome. But it was the disruptive temper tantrums, reckless damage to the waiting room furniture, and occasional punches aimed at other kids that distressed them most.

When Billy was three years old, he was referred to the Children's Hospital mental health clinic for a psychiatric and neurologic evaluation. He could not sit still for any length of time and had developed a rhythmic rocking movement of the upper body. The neurological workup was essentially negative. Melanie cried when the recommendation for psychiatric intervention was made. She was not a bad mother, dammit! She refused help once again two years later after a most disruptive kindergarten experience. Billy's teacher recommended repeating that year, and once again suggested professional help. This time Melanie was ready, as much for herself as for her son. At the Children's Hospital that summer, they explained that dealing with her stresses was important and wanted her to be involved in the therapy. She was determined to keep her son on the right track and insisted that he at least be given the chance to start the first grade with his peers rather than repeat kindergarten. It was a disaster from day one.

The first day of school was a complete disaster. Billy had to be dragged into the building with the teacher's help. No amount of coaxing could keep him from ear piercing screams or efforts to leap out the door. The principal advised that he be taken home. She phoned later in the day to discuss different strategies with Melanie.

He missed most of the first week but managed to attend morning hours a few of the days. His behavior was very disruptive to the class and the teacher throughout the first half of the school year, but Melanie's pleading allowed him to stay.

The Early Years

A special conference concerning Billy's behavior was held a week before Christmas. In addition to the school authorities, a consulting psychologist agreed that Billy was not ready to advance into a second term. He had major problems with his attention span, frustration tolerance, memory scores, and social interaction.

Melanie had other problems. By this time, she was three months pregnant by Ernie her boss. She refused to have an abortion, despite the advice of her mother and sisters.

As with her first pregnancy, she was driven to have the baby almost in defiance of her mother's reminders that she should have aborted her. Ernie promised financial support during the pregnancy but nothing else. He announced that he was moving to Florida within a few months to open a new restaurant.

She continued to work until a couple of weeks before the delivery. It was a difficult delivery, with labor lasting more than twelve hours, and a cesarean section was required. While in the hospital, she acquired an infection that did not respond to antibiotics. Thus her mother, Gertrude, came to the rescue again with the usual amount of whining. She kept Billy at her house and took the infant Sarah Jane out of the overcrowded newborn nursery while Melanie remained in the hospital recovering from what was now bilateral pneumonia.

Billy resented the arrival of his baby sister. He did not know how to handle it. In the first few days in his grandma's apartment, he would sneak into the bedroom and throw toys on top of her blankets. Gertrude heard him one day screaming with his face right up next to the baby's bassinet, "You sent my mommy away. I'm going to kill you." It took both her and Judd to calm him down and lead him out of the bedroom.

Whereas Billy's first days on earth were filled with the unintelligible loud sounds of arguing and shouting, his sister was greeted with long hours of silence. Gertrude was a good substitute mother. Her difficulty in communicating with her own adult children did not prevent her from assuming a natural mothering role while Melanie was recovering. However, when Melanie joined her new baby at Gertrude's apartment, the tension between all adult parties, coupled with Billy's episodic forays into her bedroom, caused a significant disturbance. The result of this was a repeat of the colicky episodes that Melanie had endured with her son. Sarah Jane was actually hospitalized for IV fluid replacement by the time she was three months old.

Melanie moved back to her apartment a few weeks before school was to start. She had tried hard to convince Billy that the second try in school was going to be different. She focused on the fun times, highlighting recreational programs, holiday projects, and birthday parties.

Billy insisted on a system of reward for any special effort he might make to stay in school. Without any other recourse or knowing any other tricks, Melanie agreed with him that she would provide some goodies if he would only comply with the need to attend school five days a week and do the best he could. These rewards included ice cream, store visits, video games, and an extra thirty minutes of TV time at night. Melanie's social worker at the clinic gave up on trying to coach her on some more reasonable approaches and agreed that whatever worked was in order at this point in time.

By Christmas the results were not great but were more acceptable than those of the year before. Another school meeting was held with Melanie, the teacher, and the psychologist, and they agreed that Billy's behavior and level of maturity were slightly better; they would recommend that he continue through the second semester. Special attention from one of the teacher's assistants plus continued family counseling at the mental health clinic were recommended. Melanie came to look forward to her sessions with the social worker at the clinic. She finally found someone who was not judgmental, listened well, and offered sensible suggestions. School ended in late June. Melanie threw a party for Billy with some of the neighborhood kids to celebrate the success of the school year.

Her joy over Billy's accomplishments was short-lived. On one bright sunny July morning, she answered the front door bell to find the haggard form of her long-lost husband. Bull Smith let out a loud whoop, rushed through the door, lifted her up, smothered her with kisses, and said "I'm home, honey."

She was paralyzed by a rush of conflicting emotions. Shock and revulsion headed the list. He was disheveled and very thin and wore long matted hair and a scraggly beard down to his chest. He rushed through the apartment, laughing and joking. He proudly proclaimed that he had successfully hitchhiked all the way from California and was a better man for it. He took out his wallet and showed her five dollars and said that he had made the trip spending only $195 from the allotment given by the prison warden.

She was in a state of shock and did not know what to do. Little Billy was outside playing with a neighborhood child. She sat down at the kitchen table, and she continued to ponder the meaning of it all. Bull was not part of her life and she wanted it that way, and yet there was something in her that physically and emotionally yearned for a mate—and he was the only mate she had. She was still legally married to him. But she knew she did not want him to be her husband. Bull got up after drinking half a cup of coffee and again searched the apartment to get his bearings. He took a peek at Sarah Jane still sleeping in her crib and came back to his wife, who by this time was crying silently.

"No one told me about another kid, Melanie. What the hell is the story? Boy or girl? And who's the lucky father?"

He was angry but he did not lose it. Something was different. Whether it was the experience of jail or a genuine growing up, Bull kept a low profile during that day and during the next few weeks. He seemed eager to fit in. Melanie insisted that he not sleep in her room, but rather in the parlor on the sofa. She told him she need time to adjust, and oddly enough he agreed without a lot of noise.

Billy was quite fearful and shy at first. Who was this stranger? Who was this bearded loud-mouthed guy coming into his home? He was afraid of most men as the result of his crude treatment by Judd. Bull, however, reached out to his son with laughter and genuine affection. In a few weeks, the guys were doing guy things. Bull yearned for the smell of the ocean and would take his son to the beach at Salem Willows. The two of them became lost in the simple pleasure of skipping stones over the water, playing tag, climbing rocks, and then finally returning home by way of a downtown diner for soft drinks and cookies. Bull was making up for lost time and seemed to enjoy it.

Sarah Jane was not included. She was still a toddler and clung to her mommy, especially when this stranger was in the room. She was fearful of the voice and roughness of his touch. And to Bull, Sarah was evidence that his woman had given herself to another man. That was forever unacceptable to his male ego.

Melanie's doubts were realized by the end of the summer. Bull tried a succession of jobs around the Salem Willows Amusement park. The selfish, entitled attitude reappeared and the smell of alcohol on his breath bode poorly for his self-styled reformation. The final scene was ugly. Bull insisted that he have sex with her for the second time. She refused. The police plowed through the broken dishes and furniture and subdued Bull with mace after a bruising struggle. Billy and Sarah cowered in their rooms.

To make matters worse, she discovered within a week after Bull's arrest that she was pregnant again. It was too much for her to bear. She came home from the obstetrician's office, went to the bathroom and swallowed half a bottle of aspirin. Then she quietly lay down on her bed. Within fifteen minutes she was unconscious, and Sarah Jane began crying when she could not arouse her mother by tugging on her arm. It wasn't until Billy arrived home from school and found her that she was brought to the hospital by ambulance.

Melanie spent three days in the intensive care unit and was released from the psychiatric ward two weeks after the overdose. The fetus did not survive. Tranquilizers and antidepressant medications were prescribed, and appointments were set up in the adult mental health clinic to help support her recovery. But there was something missing. Her mood and affect continued to be flat and lifeless, and there was an air of helplessness and futility about her.

Her recent suicide attempt in the company of her children caused the hospital to comply with a mandate to report the case to the Department of Social Services. Their investigation only served to further confuse and aggravate Melanie's tentative recovery. Within a couple of weeks of her return home, Social Services through a court order insisted that her children be awarded to her mother for safekeeping; the alternative was a foster home.

The stage was now reset for more stress and more depression on Melanie's part. With her children in her mother's home, she was separated from them and became more and more depressed as she had more time to contemplate her sense of helplessness and hopelessness. She was legally declared an unfit mother, and that was difficult to take. Bull had always convinced her of her low worth, and now his words seemed to be vindicated. Gertrude, who had custody of the kids, continued to put Melanie down and consider her a disappointing daughter. Only the psychiatric counseling in the clinic helped Melanie keep her head above water.

Gertrude now had to deal with Billy's problems at school and found herself traveling more than once a week to talk with school officials and, on other occasions, to bring him home after a particularly outrageous classroom scene. Sarah was confused, although she did take to the limited stability of Gertrude's home. By Christmas, the Social Services worker believed that Melanie was ready to resume the care of one child only, and Gertrude insisted that it be Billy. She was completely worn out taking care of him, and she found herself to be comfortable with Sarah; they had a mutual affection. Gertrude also wondered if there was something strange between Judd and Billy—she feared that there may be an unhealthy situation brewing. Billy had told her of seeing Judd walking around the house naked when they were alone. She did not reveal any of these thoughts to the social worker or her daughter.

Billy was awkward when he returned home to his mother. Resenting the fact that she had gone to the hospital, he was not immediately affectionate or trusting. It took him several weeks to offer any spontaneous hugs or kisses. In his own mind, mom had abandoned him again. Deep down, he felt that his bad behavior had caused her to go away from him. Although he could not talk about it, this feeling increased his sense of badness and unworthiness. So often mother had shrieked at him in a state of total frustration, "If you keep this up, I don't know what I'll do, but I might have to just go away and not come back."

The Early Years

Billy continued to struggle in school, but over the next few years with special attention and special education, plus the use of Ritalin for his attention deficit problem, he was able to work his way up through the sixth grade. He was two calendar years older than his classmates and his very size protected him from the taunts and abuse by the other kids.

If Billy managed to get pushed through school, his after school hours were not as successful. He was a loner, no close friends. He just couldn't join in with the other kids. They saw him as weird and made fun of him.

He did not fit in with other children, and he did not fit in with adults. Billy took to his room most of the time when he was home and developed different patterns of amusing himself. His imagination seemed to take over and blended in well with the exciting and somewhat bizarre movies and video games. Quite often Melanie would see the light on in his room late at night, and when she entered, he would be shooting down aliens on the screen and smiling and laughing. On occasion he seemed to erupt and be caught up in a fit of anger and frustration, at which point he would break toys and even write on the walls with crayons.

There was no male model in his life. Bull's abandonment left him at the mercy of only imagined male adults, not real ones. Gradually, his behavior became such a worry to Melanie that she talked about it to her counselor and also to her mother. No one had a real answer. For his eleventh birthday, Melanie bought him two goldfish, hoping it would give him a sense of responsibility. He was expected to clean the bowl weekly and feed them regularly.

One day in the spring, she noticed that the fish were missing and the bowl was empty of water. He claimed that Sarah had thrown them out because she was jealous. His sister denied it. Not long after, while searching his dresser drawers, Melanie smelled a hideous odor behind the furniture. She saw the dried, pale fish lying side by side on the floor, each of them squeezed tightly by a large paper clip.

Ruth and Alan Malone

Eddie Malone's law career drifted slowly onto a collision course with his marriage. Promotions were commensurate with his energy and ambition. He needed to be noticed, to be appreciated. He was driven to get the attention that he never seemed to get as middle child in the Malone family.

The price of his success was high. He hardly ever made weeknight suppers, and Saturdays were spent on the golf course during good weather. "Corporate networking," he called it. Rita turned to her family for support. Despite the distance, either she would drive to Malden or the Caruso parents would come to Topsfield on weekends. At the hospital she cut her hours down to two nights a week. Working required an outside neighborhood babysitter, because her husband was just not available—nor in retrospect had he been for several months.

Tension between them was kept in the house, except for what was noticed by the family at gatherings. Eddie's brother, Paul, made an overture on the golf course one day, regarding some possible problems at home. Eddie refused to discuss it. On one of Eddie's two-week trips to Japan, the same brother called Rita, who broke down and cried. They decided to meet in Boston the following week to talk. Rita told him that it didn't look good. They had already been to a marriage counselor for six months with joint sessions and independent appointments. Eddie refused to let go of his "professional responsibilities." Eventually, he dropped out of the marriage counseling altogether.

Rita's parents were furious with his behavior, and this only added to the marital rift when their reactions were communicated to Eddie. Rita told him that she would give it until Christmas, and if his neglect of her and the kids continued, she would ask for a trial separation. By this time, she had lost fifteen pounds in six months and was averaging only four hours of sleep a night.

An awkward holiday family gathering led to an ugly confrontation between the two of them after the company had left. The children were standing at the head of the stairs crying. Both Eddie and Rita sheepishly walked up the stairs and put the kids back to bed, offering them consolation and promises that things would be okay. They then walked downstairs without speaking to each other and took separate seats in the parlor. Eddie told her that he was leaving the house because he had been seeing another woman for over a year. She was not surprised but was numbed by the simplicity of it and by the lack of any remorse. When he was finished talking, she rose from the sofa, climbed the stairs, and closed the door of her bedroom. She cried herself to sleep but actually had the longest, most peaceful sleep she had had in a long time.

After breakfast the next day, the kids went upstairs to dress. Eddie quietly moved a couple of suitcases down the stairs into his car. He glanced at Rita, who stood at the kitchen window, avoiding him. He went upstairs to say his goodbyes. It was then that he was struck by the enormity of his decision, and paused at the head of the stairs to shake off a brief wave of nausea. A sickening thought raced through his mind. No matter what his father and mother had done, no matter what their sins of omission had been, no one in the Malone family had ever abandoned the others.

Ruth had finished dressing and was pulling on her snow boots. An early morning dusting of snow had started, and it looked like it was going to be a day of troubled weather. She sensed something was wrong as her father moved slowly to her bedside, quite silent and quite sad. Her eyes widened and her mouth dropped expectantly.

"What's wrong, Daddy? You don't look right. You should be at work by now." Eddie knelt down in front of her and started to fit on the other snow boot.

"Pumpkin, I've got some bad news to tell you. Mommy and I have decided to separate for a little while to think things over. You heard what happened last night. We both need some space. And we don't want you kids to get caught in the middle of our problems." Ruth started to cry and reached out to hug her father, who was still kneeling on the floor.

"But why can't you stay? I don't want you to go away. Mommy needs you. I need you. Alan needs you. Don't go!"

She suddenly flipped herself on the bed and buried her face in the pillow. She began crying convulsively, catching her breath with difficulty. Eddie stood up feeling totally helpless.

"Honey, it may only be for a little while. I'll come back to see you. I'll be there this weekend for the Christmas holidays. It's just that we can't stay together right now."

She turned her head away from him.

"No, you won't. I know you won't. You don't love us anymore. Go away! I don't want to see you anymore."

Her father leaned over and kissed the back of her head. She let out a mournful wail. Just then, the tiny form of little Alan appeared in the doorway. Eddie took him up in his arms and carried him back to his bedroom, closed the door, and once again knelt down to be at eye level with his confused son.

"What's wrong with Ruthie, Daddy? Why she crying?"

"She'll be okay, son. Daddy just had a little talk with her."

"Did she do something bad? Did you scold her?"

Eddie caught his breath. The innocence before him was overpowering. He felt tears welling up.

"Alan, your sister did not do anything wrong. She is a very good girl and a very good sister. You must take care of each other now." The frail little body twisted from his grasp.

"Why should we take care of each other? You and Mommy take care of us."

"Alan, Mommy and Daddy have decided to stop fighting. We are not going to live together for a while, sort of a time-out."

The child's body froze. He turned and ran quickly into the arms of his crouching father. "No! No! Don't do that. Don't go away. I'll be a good boy. You can't do that. I want my mommy and my daddy." Eddie could feel the warm tears rolling down his neck. He picked him up, went over to the bed and sat his son on his lap on the edge of the bed. He rocked until the crying had subsided.

He then helped him put on his warm sweater over his shirt and carried him downstairs where Rita and Ruth sat huddled on the sofa in the living room. He placed Alan on the other side of Rita, got his parka out of the closet, and turned to take a mental snapshot of the family that he was leaving. He repeated that he would return over the holiday weekend and instructed Rita about the extra car keys on the kitchen counter. He said he would be in touch regarding his clothes and his computer.

She told the kids to remain on the sofa and walked to the door behind him.

"Did you tell them why? "

"No, I didn't."

"You bastard." He turned and walked out into the swirling snow.

Billy Smith

Before his twelfth birthday, Billy Smith was removed from his mother's home and placed by Social Services into a foster home in Medford. It was the last time mother and son would ever live together. Immediately after the court hearing, Melanie went home by herself and lacerated her right wrist almost beyond repair.

The circumstances leading to the court action were not entirely clear but were indeed serious in terms of a continued scarring inflicted on the fragile soul of a confused and tormented boy.

It started a year before when Melanie slowly descended into a depressed mood following her third abusive relationship. Each of the guys she had picked up at the bar took their turn tossing and tumbling with her and then abandoning her crudely.

There had never been any intimacy and no tenderness, the very thing she craved. Gertrude held tightly to her care of Sarah Jane and took every opportunity to flaunt her success and her daughter's failure. Billy, meanwhile, continued to develop disturbed behavior patterns. He had been suspended from school twice that year for unacceptable conduct. Melanie felt alone, abandoned, and unloved. What started as a single nightcap after work every night turned into a six-ounce glass of vodka on very few rocks. She developed a habit of falling into bed after having one or two of these glasses.

Perhaps out of guilt, perhaps out of a feeling of wanting some knowledge that she was not alone, she started dropping into Billy's room to see that he was sleeping quietly and covered with his bedclothes.

On one cold winter night after a hellish shift at the bar and a double dip of her vodka supply, she turned down the bedclothes and gently slid in next to him. He was half asleep and turned away from her. She put her arm around his chest and hugged him, gathering to her body the warmth of his listless form. Both mother and son slept peacefully as the wind and snow beat against the window. Billy woke the early morning and without a word turned and snuggled close to his only friend in the world.

It was the beginning of a ritual that neither one of them wanted to stop. Eventually Melanie inadvertently discovered some of her lingerie in one of his clothes drawers. There were panties and pantyhose thrown in with bras and a slip. She confronted Billy, who admitted the intrusion into her privacy. She scolded him and said that her dresser was her own private domain and he must never do this again.

She felt it wise to return to her own bedroom even though he begged her not to. She did not relent until one night when he crawled in next to her just before daybreak crying over a terrible nightmare. She had neither the heart nor the energy to refuse, as she was awakening from a monstrous hangover.

Melanie continued to retreat from the outside world. Her drinking increased over the months to the point where she could not leave the house day or night and ultimately lost her job. Gertrude threatened to report her again to Social Services. Her righteousness stopped just short of taking Billy back to her own apartment where she was taking care of Sarah. She really didn't want Billy back. Once a week, she brought in a meager supply of groceries and left the apartment echoing with a stream of threats and insults. The school authorities called but Melanie did not respond.

Billy's erratic attendance at school became alarming. He wore the same clothes for days on end and was unwashed and smelly. His pants bore the stains of spilled food. When asked how things were going at home, he said, "okay." His homework deteriorated into unintelligible words and incomplete answers. Before the school authorities decided to intervene, a call to Social Services was made by Gertrude. The day before they were expected to arrive at Melanie's apartment, Gertrude herself went to find a shocking scene. She arrived at four o'clock in the afternoon alone and looked in the bedroom of Melanie's apartment. She found her daughter totally intoxicated, lying naked on her bed cuddling with her son, who was also stark naked. Amid yelling and screaming, Gertrude moved to the telephone and Melanie, in a fit of shock and despondency, ran to the kitchen, pulled out a carving knife and cut her right wrist. She was taken to the emergency room, and Billy once again stayed for a week with his grandmother while legal procedures took place. Charges of sexual assault on a minor were entered at the district court, but action was postponed pending Melanie's release from her latest hospitalization. This time her diagnosis was more complicated.

Major depression recurrent with suicide attempt by skin laceration. Added to it was *alcohol abuse.* And finally, *sexual deviation, incestuous type.*

Within two weeks, she was safe to return home, but was required to attend the psychiatrist daycare program for another two weeks. She also began attending AA meetings.

The Social Services workers wanted a substantial geographical separation of Billy from his Salem relatives. They found a home in Medford. Both foster parents had been born in the Dominican Republic, had been married and divorced and had a total of four children. The father's name was Aurelio and the mother Carmilla. He worked as a night baker in a local supermarket, and she stayed at home but had a side job as a seamstress. Their oldest son, Felix, was a tall, thin, pimply-faced adolescent with a surly manner and a mean streak. He immediately resented giving up his privacy and insisted that Billy's cot be placed at the foot of his bed so that he didn't have to see him. The three other children were girls. One of them, Marissa, was a foster child like Billy. She was a year older and wore a look of anger and disgust. She stood about two inches taller than he and was extremely nimble and athletic. She told him the first week that she had beaten up boys who were bigger than he. Billy discovered later that she had been physically and sexually abused by her stepfather and brother before being placed in the home. Rosalie and Anna were Carmilla's daughters. Rosalie was Billy's age and little Anna was in the second grade. She was the only one was pleasant to this strange new kid the day he arrived.

Billy felt lost and desolate. For the first few weeks, he cried constantly. He missed his mother terribly. The social worker who came every two weeks told him that his mother was alive and coming home soon. "When the judge decides" was her pat answer to his plea for a reunion.

The Medford school system was not impressed with Billy's performance in Salem and declined to promote him. His first semester in that system was not a great success but sufficient to allow him to continue on. Incentive for getting passing grades was the promise by his social worker of a possible reunion and return to his Salem home. Billy's intent to lie low and not cause problems was interrupted during the winter and spring months.

Shortly after the winter holidays, his mother was allowed a visit in the company of a Social Services worker. It was quite apparent to Billy that she was drunk the minute she came up and lathered wet kisses on his face and lips. They then sat on a sofa in the parlor and she inappropriately began hugging him and fondling him. The meeting was cut short when the foster mother entered and called Billy a born troublemaker. Melanie took a swing at her and fell on the floor.

The Early Years

A second problem was of longer duration and was much more serious. One late winter afternoon, his teacher decided to peek in on the boys' lavatory to see if anyone was still there. She found him huddled on the floor crying in a partially kneeling position up against the wall. She brought Billy back to the classroom and asked him to explain what had happened. She was alarmed when he told her that he could not sit down because it hurt too much. She then learned about the terrible events that had been going on in his foster home since the Christmas holidays. Both she and the principal spoke with the foster parents. The school department was notified as was the Medford Police Department and the Department of Social Services. The complaint by the school was ongoing sexual and physical abuse of William J. Smith III in the foster home.

Billy described two separate types of abuse, the first of which began around the holidays. It involved two of the girls in the home, Marissa and Rosalie. The second series of events involved Felix.

At first the two girls in question set out to taunt him about his morbid fear of the dark. They knew of Billy's habit of keeping a penlight on under his bed because of his panic of the strange, darkened room. They demanded he give it up, and when he refused, they began to take advantage of this terrible fear.

One night when the foster parents were out, Marissa and Rosalie dragged him upstairs and pushed him into their bedroom closet where he pleaded for release before he suffocated. Only after an hour did they let him out, forcing him to promise that he would be nice to them. He complied with their wish. He staggered out of the closet and ran into the bathroom where he vomited. They followed him into his room laughing and threatening to do it again if he told anyone.

A week later, they decided to have more fun. It was midafternoon and Billy's school bus pulled up to the home. Marissa let Billy in, taunting him again about how the stupid one had done at school. Carmilla had gone out briefly to the shopping center with Anna. Felix, as usual, was with his new gang. Billy rushed up to his room with his school bag. They followed him, giggling and laughing about how smelly and stupid he was.

They headed him off before he could reach the safety of the locked bathroom. With much pushing and shoving they crammed him into their bedroom closet once again. After a half-hour of screaming and crying they let him out. This time he didn't run. He was paralyzed with fear. They brought him over to one of the beds where he remained lifeless and whimpering. Neither of the girls showed any pity on the crybaby from Salem. Instead they took turns laying next to him or on top of him offering mock affection for his torment.

The games continued episodically throughout the winter. Only little Anna had any real notion that something was going on. On one occasion when she heard all three of them in the upstairs bathroom behind a locked door, she was told to stay downstairs. She wondered why the girls were laughing so hard, and Billy was so silent behind the door. She told her mother about her concerns but in a vague way. Anna said that she did not want to remain alone with the other children at night, when she and her foster father went out. Carmilla's response to this was you must stay at home because we need our time off, away from you kids. The net result was that neither parent inquired as to what was of concern to Anna. Throughout the remaining weeks, the erotic schemes arranged by the girls were changed but the roles did not. Clearly, Billy was a victim and not a perpetrator. Both girls were in the early phases of pubescence and neither understood nor were ready for full sexual intercourse.

Billy's subservient role had a strange effect on him. Added to the experience with his mother, he began to think that sexual relationships were not a give-and-take phenomenon but a contest. The bigger, stronger person ultimately took pleasure from the other.

Up till now, women and girls were the winners. He had to bide his time, wait it out. There would come a day. His day. As dirty and ashamed as he felt, he knew two things. In a perverse way, he felt that he had some control over his tormentors. They wanted something that he had. That something, which was a service, could be bartered. In a sense, he was negotiating, certainly from a weak position, but he was avoiding punishment as a result of his compliance. The other thing that he became aware of was his size. He realized that slowly but surely his body was getting taller and heavier. He dreamed of the day that he would be bigger and stronger than any woman, and then it would be his turn.

He was also aware that his placement in the home was limited to one year, subject to review. He desperately waited for that one year to end. His mother did visit during the February holidays, and he was surprised and grateful that she was sober and more controlled. There was some hope after all that he could return home. He deliberately kept quiet about the abuse he was taking from his foster sisters, hoping to avoid any notoriety that could weaken his chance to leave the foster home.

Unfortunately, there was another problem of abuse developing. His roommate Felix quit school during the midwinter months and temporarily vacated the house. His parents were frustrated and had no way to handle him at the time. He challenged them by admitting that he was smoking marijuana and insisted on his right to do so. They demanded that he get a job and pay board, and then he disappeared for a month.

One night he slipped in the front door without them knowing it and tiptoed up to his room to sleep in his own bed. He found Billy sound asleep in that bed. His first impulse was to toss the smelly little intruder on to the floor, but that would have awakened his parents who had banished him from their home. Instead, he crawled in next to him. By daybreak, he found himself both pleading and threatening the sobbing object of his act of sodomy.

Billy was angry, hurt, and confused. Felix had actually apologized. No one had ever apologized for hurting him. He could not sort out the conflicting emotions. Out of a sense of fear, loneliness and a need to be protected, he drifted into a sexual liaison with the older boy who offered both intimacy and strength.

One early morning around daybreak, the foster father Aurelio burst into their bedroom enraged by the broken glass in the hallway caused by Felix's late night entry. He found the two boys with the covers thrown off performing a sexual act. Aurelio was shocked and totally enraged and immediately ordered Felix to leave the house.

The enraged foster parents closed the bedroom door and preceded to slap and shout at the cowering form. They ordered him to speak no word of the despicable behavior to anyone, less they lose their foster care certificate. To teach him a lesson, they beat him on the exposed buttocks with a frying pan until their fury had abated.

He lay motionless on the mattress for about an hour sobbing over the event and the terrible pain that was now shooting down his right leg. He thought he was damaged permanently and wondered if he would ever walk or sit again.

Two days later, his teacher realized that he could not sit without excruciating pain and took the matter into her own hands.

Sarah Smith

Physical and sexual abuse were not part of Sarah Jane Smith's life—quite the opposite. Her grandmother Gertrude had all but adopted her legally. Her life since she was a baby was spent under the sheltering wing of her protective grandma. She never knew a genuine father. Once in Florida, Ernie never bothered to contact Melanie or his daughter. When Bull returned briefly to the home of Melanie, he showed deep resentment toward the child sired by another man. Billy never quite accepted his sister other than as an intrusive biological event. When Sarah was asked about her brother's whereabouts after the foster home placement, her answer was, "He's gone to live with some relatives in Medford."

Her mother, Melanie, actually moved back again into Gertrude's home after another overdose, which seemed to coincide with the news from Medford about Billy's abuse. Once again, Gertrude set strict limits on her daughter. Soon after Melanie moved back in, Gertrude insisted that her entire welfare check be turned over to her for the cost of her own care in the house as well as her daughter's.

Sarah was aware that something was wrong in Billy's life from conversations in the home and around the supper table. She neither sought any further information nor asked in any way to be in touch with him.

Sarah was indeed comfortable in the world that centered on her grandma. She had one friend in school whom she never invited to the apartment and only communicated with on school property.

Sarah Jane was not a brilliant student but she got by. The teachers complimented her on her good conduct. She knew how to comply and please adults. She could have won a medal for being unnoticed in the latter years of her grammar school education. As she approached puberty, Gertrude noticed that she became more sullen and more testy. She oddly avoided and even contested casual comments about how tall she was. More than once, she outright told her grandma that she didn't want to be tall and did not want to be noticed as somebody who was growing up. When Gertrude asked her why, she said that growing up meant you were closer to dying.

She confided to her grandmother that some of her classmates were gossiping and giggling about body changes and their first period. She also said that she was not interested in participating in the talk or asking about details. Gertrude told her that if she wanted accurate information to go to the school nurse. Gertrude did not offer her a sit down discussion about what lay ahead.

Sarah not only spent more time in her room but began leaving the lights on both day and night. All in the household realized something was wrong but did not know what. Inevitably, she showed signs of her terrible confusion and fear of her menarche. She began to lose weight. Both mother and Gertrude coaxed her to eat more food, but the more they coaxed her the more she seemed to adopt a pattern of eating morsels at supper and avoiding breakfast altogether. Her weight dropped significantly and her general health deteriorated. Head colds and headaches were common. Gertrude took her to a pediatrician who told her that her frailness and dehydration could lead her into a hospitalization where fluid replenishment would be necessary. This information drove her into crying fits and even more withdrawal and anorexia.

Two days after her first period, she was inconsolable. It took all three adults to force her into the car for the trip to the hospital. The level of malnourishment and dehydration required hospitalization for about a week. A psychiatric consultation was requested.

Rita Malone

Rita Malone survived the initial shock of separation and divorce with the help of her parents, neighbors, and friends at the hospital. For the better part of a year, she felt that her life had lost its purpose other than caring for her children. During the next three or four years, she stuck to her routines of transporting the kids to school and games and going to work every day. There was a dull ache inside her and a deep sense of loss and helplessness. On occasion she would fall into a funk and obsess about her role in the divorce.

> *Was it my fault? Did I do enough? Life seemed too good then. Was I naive? Sure, I was a spoiled girl. I was the only child. But this! This isn't right. I never cheated on him. Dammit. I've got to stop thinking like this. I've got a life to live.*

Rita was forced to refocus her attention on her mother when Francesca told her at Ruth's First Communion that she had been diagnosed with breast cancer. Rita did not react well to the news. She couldn't collect herself for days. As a nurse, Rita knew what was ahead and agonized over the course of testing and treatment that was in store for her mother. Francesca seemed to take it better than her husband or her daughter.

But she pulled herself together, offering to move down to Malden with the kids if it would help. When that suggestion was rejected, she insisted that her parents sell their house and move to Topsfield with her, but the suggestion went nowhere.

Radiation therapy began and Rita made sure that she drove her mother to each session. To make time for her mother and the kids, she cut down on her hours at the hospital and occasionally had babysitters to help with the kids.

She was bothered by new thoughts and sensations regarding her ex-husband, Eddie. Faced with the sad news about her mother's illness and what she anticipated would be an early death, she began to think longingly on the better days in her life when she had companionship. She caught herself thinking at times of the comfort that her husband did offer her in the early years. The familiar touch, the whisper. His common sense, his ability to get practical things accomplished. She needed a man, and yet she scolded herself for even thinking about it.

Before the start of the school year, Francesca had completed her course of treatment. The doctors were very satisfied with the results and recommended no further treatment at the time. All family members seemed exhausted by this time. Rita decided to give herself and the kids a break and rented a condo on Cape Cod so that they could change their family pressures and unwind. Just what the doctor ordered. Sunshine, swimming, shopping and showtime at the local cinema.

Refreshed, the kids returned to school and Rita to her hospital job. Francesca and Angelo Caruso were quite thankful for the love and support received during the trying months of therapy. They themselves became much more involved in the life of the Topsfield Malones.

Angelo reordered his daily and weekly routines to find more time to spend with his grandson Alan. He decided that the Malone family was more important than golf, bocci, and twice-a-week card games. Over the next few years, the families did a lot together. Little Alan himself benefited enormously from his grandfather's attention. Angelo drove him to his sporting events and taught him how to fish.

Meanwhile, Eddie Malone was withdrawing slowly but surely from his son and family. He followed his star at the law firm and explained that he simply did not have the time for the visits that meant so much to his son. His oldest brother Paul called Rita around Christmastime and in the conversation revealed that Eddie had divorced his second wife and was going with another woman who lived in Providence, Rhode Island.

Ruth fared better—she had Rita. Ruth was a bright, intuitive, and affectionate child. The two women needed each other and filled a void in each other's life right up to the time Ruth entered puberty. Rita felt a real vulnerability during the scary times of her mother's treatment for cancer. She altogether stopped what was an already infrequent pattern of dating. As her mother recovered, she began to listen to friends and neighbors about the possibility of finding the "right man." Rita in her mid-thirties was an attractive woman, with dark wavy hair, high cheekbones, and light olive skin. Years had added a few pounds, but she wore well her generous hips and breasts. Although she paid attention to diet and exercise, she did not wish to assume the skinny frame of fashion models. Rita in her mid-thirties was mature, sensual, and sensitive—her time had come.

Her friends in the hospital eventually produced a possible match that she was interested in. His name was Dr. Joseph Reardon, a middle-aged cardiologist working at Salem Hospital. In his mid-forties, he was a widower with two children and was considered to be a solid, generous person.

The first impression on both sides was good. She was quite taken by his quick but gentle wit—he was genuinely funny, but not at the expense of others. The good doctor was also down to earth. He drank beer, not wine, loved TV sports, and did the daily crossword puzzle when he had time. He belonged to both the country club and the yacht club but made sure that he spent a good amount of time with his two children. He was attached to his home in Marblehead, did his own landscaping, and went to Mass every

The Early Years

Sunday; he was just beginning to forgive God for taking his beloved Rachel from him.

He had never met a woman like Rita. He was taken early by this beautiful woman with the full, sensual body accompanied by a warmth and honesty of personality. On their first date, a dinner in downtown Salem, she pointed out a patch of salad dressing on his cheek, and when he helplessly fumbled with his napkin, she leaned over, wiped it off, and kissed the spot gently. She told him it was an Italian custom.

They dated for almost a year, more for the kids' sake than theirs. Their initial fascination turned quickly into a deep respect and trust. Joe Reardon and Rita Caruso were from two different cultures, but they had one thing in common. They had both lost their spouses. They were survivors whose grief and bitterness had waned. They were ready to try again. They were capable of hoping and capable of giving. And they both wanted to share what was good inside them with someone else.

During the months before the wedding, they learned a lot about each other. Rita was fascinated with Joe's life before and after he met Rachel. She compared it to one of her favorite movies, "Love Story." The only real difference was the reversal of social standing when boy met girl. Rachel had come from an influential family in Larchmont, New York, and Joe was not to the manor born. Joe was the oldest child in a large family located in Pennsylvania coal country. His father lived and died the life of a miner; black lung disease was the cause of death. Local tradition demanded that the eldest son step up and become a fill in for a deceased coal miner. Joe's mother had other plans. She encouraged him to reject the miner's life after high school and take the athletic scholarship to Penn State.

Although not a gifted student, he did quite well, ending up in the top ten percent of his class. Athletically, he had enough baseball talent to play first-string varsity in his senior year. A minor league baseball contract was offered, and he turned it down to attend the University of Pennsylvania Medical School. From there he completed a residency at Johns Hopkins Hospital and a fellowship in cardiology at Massachusetts General Hospital.

At the end of his first year in Boston, he vacationed at a little cottage on Martha's Vineyard with two of his medical colleagues. He literally bumped into his wife-to-be while jogging along the beach on a warm, foggy morning.

Rachel Bromfield was bright, beautiful and bred for the good life of the east coast aristocracy. On a foggy morning in Nantucket, the two ran into each other while jogging on the beach. Their verbal encounter was spontaneous and witty enough to draw them together a few nights later at a trendy disco. They were married a year later at the Episcopal Church in

Larchmont, New York. The Bromfields and their starchy friends were properly polite but terribly disappointed over the social mismatch.

The in-love phase moved into a genuine love and respect relationship as Rachel and Joe settled into a modest house in Marblehead, Massachusetts and began raising a family. Joe became a member of a very popular cardiology group practice close to Salem Hospital. There as an eight year gap between their first born Michael and baby Jessica.

In the fifteenth year of their marriage, Rachel was diagnosed with a malignant brain tumor. The family was jolted, the in-laws devastated. Michael turned to Joe for support. Jessica, on the other hand, became strangely remote with all in the family and showed less affection. Her mother was very worried about this drastic change.

The cancer was inoperable. Palliative chemotherapy was used. Although Rachel bore up well during the winter months, her weight and her will seemed to shrink.

Her parents insisted that she return to Bromfield Manor where they would pay for twenty-four hour nursing care and thus relieve the pressure on Joe and the kids during the summer months. Joe reluctantly yielded when her realized it was a way to reestablish some semblance of normalcy within the Marblehead family. His kids were no longer talking to each other.

His decision seemed to backfire as it affected Jessica's behavior even more negatively. She would sit for hours in her room day and night watching cartoons on T.V. while clutching her toy dog "Missy." She refused to get in the car for shopping trips and gradually declined her dad's invitation for walks along the beach.

By August, Rachel required intravenous therapy at a Larchmont Hospital as her appetite continued to wane. She was dying and no one could stop it. At that time the doctors gave her a month at the most. They also recommended that she stay with her parents, mainly because of the generous supply of nursing attention that was available.

Joe was confused, angry, and very tired. How could this be happening? His beautiful wife was shrinking before his eyes. Her parents had reclaimed her. His son was in torment, and his daughter was deeply scarred emotionally.

Feeling very helpless, he consented to the plan as long as they would keep Jessica close to her dying mother and help her with her grief. He planned to drive down from Marblehead during the weekdays and stay there all weekend.

Rachel died at Bromfield Manor in her own bed, away from her husband but in the company of her parents and her daughter Jessica. Joe was upset at Jessica's condition upon her return home from the agony of the

The Early Years

final few days. He immediately sought professional help from a child psychiatrist, but deep down inside, he felt that both women in his life were lost.

It seemed that the spirit and warmth of his young daughter had been drained.

Three years after Rachel's death, Joe took Rita Caruso Malone to the Justice of the Peace and they became married. Rita had refused in principle to seek nullification of her eight-year marriage to Eddie Malone, so according to the rules of the Catholic Church, they were denied a nuptial mass. The kids joined her in taking on the Reardon surname. They had discovered that Dr. Joe was a popular guy around town and well known on the North Shore. There was some hesitancy on the part of young Alan Malone in the beginning, but he finally agreed.

Joe Reardon had been a widower for three years. His son Michael was finishing up high school and was looking forward to life at Syracuse University. Jessica managed to attend school, but there was a definite pall on her previously vibrant personality. Rita and Joe talked about it often and agreed that it would take time for the complete grief of her mother's death to wane and more time to accept a substitute mother.

Rita's kids openly complained about leaving their friends in Topsfield, but they soon adapted to their first summer in Marblehead. Joe reached out to include them in all the fun and activities. Ruth took to him sooner than Alan did. She realized that he was not taking her mother from her as much as giving her mother something that she couldn't. She warmed to his humor and his gentleness and knew that it was better to share her mommy then to struggle for complete ownership.

Alan, on the other hand, never quite got over what he felt was abandonment by his friend and father. He missed the laughter and the hugs. He yearned for the noise of the raucous FleetCenter fans, the hot dogs, and the popcorn. He was scarred in terms of trusting other men and sought comfort with his peers and fellow athletes in Marblehead.

It became apparent at an early age that Alan was a gifted athlete. He turned to athletics to gain the companionship and the approval he once had from his father. Dr. Joe was a good guy, but he simply could not let him get close. He did not want to be betrayed again.

CHOICE

Change, challenge, choice. For the child, the first twelve years of life offer enormous changes and challenges, but few meaningful choices—most of the significant choices are made by adults. And the young folks are compelled to respond to their parents' choices. The infant may choose to throw the rattle out of the crib. Later on, the little tyke may choose to soil diapers as an angry protest against adult dictators. Further on in the schoolroom, the child is offered the choice of compliance, avoidance, or protest. But these responses are reactions to everyday pressures. What is not available are the well-measured, deliberate selections that will affect the child's life and the direction of it. These personal choices come later.

The adult choices made within the Smith and the Malone families had a decided impact on the lives of their children. In different ways, the two fathers of these families abandoned their spouses and their children, setting the stage for enormous difficulty (for both adults and children) in meeting the changes and challenges that came their way. Even though these men did not calculate to hurt their families, the impact was devastating. What complicates the decisions made by adults, particularly when their children are small, is the fact that their choices are not meant in an anticipatory way to hurt; rather, they are the result of their own faulty adaptation to their responsibilities. This also may be a product of a dysfunctional upbringing or inequities in their own childhood.

Despite the fact that the adults who came in touch with these children would not have intended to disrupt or harm them, it is apparent that the interaction in some instances was extremely helpful and in others devastating.

Billy Smith

From the moment he left the warm, quiet confines of the newborn nursery, Billy experienced a world of harsh, angry voices, trembling hands, hurried hugs, erratic feedings, and the smell of fear wafting from his mother's body. The incomplete circuitry of his little brain was flooded with sensations of sound, smell, touch, taste, and blurred sights, all sending a message of uncertainty.

Melanie did her best while fending off her husband's barbs and threats. But in truth, Melanie was not a well-nurtured child herself and simply could not cope well. Billy's response to the overload, as with all infants, was sleep, the blissful return to that womb-like existence, where foreign sounds and sights are shut out. As the months wore on, sleep was not enough to control his helpless anxiety. The little mind did not have the resources to sort out what was going on around him. The day-to-day tensions would build to a point where he would either cry or scream. Gradually, only one part of him could absorb the signals of danger and react to them—his body.

In Billy's case, he developed gastrointestinal symptoms. Gas, pain, and esophageal reflux became commonplace. In essence, his body manifested the painful messages coming from two dysfunctional parents. The body problems also earned him trips to the doctor or the emergency room. As scary as the needles were, he welcomed the interruption, as brief as it was, from the chaos at home.

When his father left home, there was relative calm and quiet. His mother's anxiety decreased. However, Billy's anxieties were just beginning. The route he took to control this anxiety became entwined in the changes and challenges of his young life. He found that he could actually control his mother through his reluctant and frustrating toilet-training period.

Each episode of avoidance produced a victory that was not without consequence. In essence, he wore his mother out with the burden of single parenthood, as she tried to cope with an obstinate young child. Added to these pressures was the loneliness of a single parent, the need to work, the inadequate income, and a rejection from her own mother. Melanie was already on the path to her first emotional breakdown.

The loss of his mother threw Billy into a tailspin. It was one thing to react to the chaotic early life crises perpetrated by two quarreling parents. It was another thing to have his mother missing from his life. His dependence had been complete. He was unable to function without a reference point and the reference point was gone.

Little Billy went through a major depression where his emotions touched all three major bases. He was indeed sad. He was also enraged that she could leave him. Perhaps what he found most difficult was the sense that he himself might have caused her demise because of his own badness. The concept of badness at the earliest stages is not well formed, but the germ is there. The feelings that carried over at her return were anger and resentment. He was cool to Melanie for many days, sending a message that by leaving him, she had done wrong by him.

The event of his mother's hospitalization was a forerunner of another change: entering the ranks of his young peers in the school system. His failure to meet the expectations of the kindergarten and first-grade teachers resulted in more lost time, more sense of failure, and more pressure on Melanie. The efforts by the mental health clinic staff were only marginally successful but did offer his mother some respite. The earliest diagnoses that were pinned on his record by both teachers and mental health counselors mentioned adjustment problems of early childhood with avoidant and impulsive behavior. As Billy headed for the preadolescent phase of his life, his behavior was marginal in terms of school accomplishment and behavior modification. His mother became more and more adrift and eventually turned to the insidious anesthesia of alcohol. Following this, in the twilight days of her alcohol addiction, the devastating level of depression and sense of futility led her into the unimaginable behavior of seducing her own son. Her actions gave Billy a skewed and unrealistic appreciation of child/adult relationships.

Billy found himself living on another planet when he was displaced into the foster home away from any semblance of recognizable and supportive family. Once again the depression brought him to the deep sense of sadness, accompanied by a rage against those who had abandoned him. And this occasion led him into a serious confrontation with what he believed was his empty and worthless self.

His self-esteem was at rock bottom, and the poor estimate of himself was validated by the coarse and cruel treatment he received from the foster children. There was simply no sense of affection or love when he needed it most. He then turned to a device that, later on in his adolescence, would turn against him, and that was an attitude of survival where he simply could not trust people but would have to take the abuse until he was old enough to retaliate. Billy lived the life of a helpless, hapless boy to be played with and discarded by others. But inside of him was stirring a volcano of rage and vengeance that was all that kept him from breaking down his own mental apparatus. By the time he was taken from the foster home for another change and challenge, he had experienced inevitable pubescent masturbatory behavior. It was almost at the same time that he realized that his body was getting stronger and that his twisted sexual fantasies would someday allow him to hurt back. Billy had never truly been in control of his life. He realized that someday he could control it and the one emotion that was the key to this was anger.

Sarah Smith

Sarah belonged to her grandmother, Gertrude, and Gertrude belonged to Sarah. Sarah's mother was too battered and bruised early on to accept the role of caregiver. Sarah escaped the uncertainty of mom's mood swings by her extended stays in the home of Gertrude and Judd. She was not unhappy with that situation. She had, after all, been the object of Billy's pranks and, for a brief time, Bull Smith's obvious resentment. But having Judd as a surrogate father was the price to pay for joining her beloved grandmother. Judd was nasty and demanding of Gertrude but for the most part stayed to himself. Sarah never felt comfortable in his presence, however. She was an unwelcome intruder.

Gertrude was steady and had routines that offered Sarah some stability. As a result, Sarah mastered some of the earliest confrontations with change and challenge. Her tantrums were more elongated whining episodes, unlike her brother Billy's explosions. Grandma's firm but loving hand guided her through a fairly uneventful phase of toilet training.

Sarah learned quite early in life that by pleasing her surrogate mother she would be loved and protected. She had all but given up any hope that her own mother would re-emerge in her life by the time she started school. She did not miss Billy; there had never been any intimacy with him. Rather there was the memory of his taunting, his tantrums, and his awful body smell.

In school she was bright but not brilliant. The teachers agreed that Sarah would get by and not cause problems. Her shyness in the classroom was accepted, and she was challenged by neither teachers nor classmates. At the end of the school day, her eyes would light up and she would smile in anticipation of returning home to her beloved grandma who always had milk and cookies.

So it went for the first seven or eight years of her life. She was jolted when she heard about Billy's placement in the foster home. No one told her why.

It was the other major change in the family that shocked her. Gertrude suffered the first of two strokes a week after Sarah's tenth birthday. For the first time in her life, Sarah had to cope with the possibility that Gertrude might not be in her life. Death for her was an unacceptable abstraction and caused her to retreat into her fantasy world behind the closed bedroom door. She felt that such a possibility was unfair and could not happen. This mentality extended to the whole concept of growing up. To grow meant to come closer to death, and death simply could not happen.

Sarah wanted the world to stop, but she could not make it. Instead she took on the job of controlling her own life and her own world. Perhaps if she stopped growing, things would be okay. She was obsessed with the uncertainty of body changes that the other kids talked about. She didn't want to develop breasts or have monthly periods. If she made herself small, she thought, it would all go away. The choice to avoid the changes and challenges of adolescence was translated into an eating disorder. Without really thinking it out, she instinctively began cutting down her food supplies, and soon gained another satisfaction—attention.

Ruth Malone

Right from the beginning it was good. Rita and Ruth were not only mother and daughter but they were friends. She was a good baby. She posed no problems during the preschool years. It was as if Rita had given birth to a piece of herself. Ruth reacted to her father's abandonment with a healthy grief, highlighted by sadness and some anger. But at no point did she suffer guilt over the event. She had done nothing to alienate him. She loved him very much, and his affectionate response to her was the hardest thing to forgo.

Her school marks were more than adequate and were pleasing to her teachers and her mother. She particularly liked to perform for her grandparents, the Carusos, but in a joyous way rather than pretentious. She seemed to have a natural, solid self-esteem. It was neither inflated nor at any time in doubt by her. As adolescence approached, she confided in her mother and trusted in the explanations she received.

Rita's remarriage to Joe brought some moments of anxiety and doubt regarding the path of the family life. It was difficult for her to consider her mother's affection being shared with a stranger. She wondered about the living arrangements—they would now have two other kids in the family—once Michael Reardon went to college, the family had three children.

She did not understand her stepsister, Jessica, and was somewhat offended when Jessica rejected her overtures to develop a sisterlike relationship. She spoke with both her mother and her stepfather, who were at a loss to explain. Nevertheless, within a few years, Ruth became quite adjusted to living in the new house in Marblehead, having a generous and kind stepfather, and still having the comfort of her mother and her brother.

Alan Malone
The initial stability and serenity of the Malone family was shattered when Alan's father divorced his mother for another woman. Alan was his father's little alley cat. The relationship was easy and genuine. Rita did all the important things in mothering him through the first few years of his life, but his father was the one associated with fun and games.

At no point did Rita resent this. She felt it was normal and enjoyed their relationship as much as they did. After Eddie left, both Rita and Ruth seemed to take some umbrage by the exclusive attention Eddie gave Alan. When he returned from the weekend visits, Alan sensed that they were upset.

Try as he might, he simply could not trust the genuine offer of Dr. Joe Reardon to be his father. The original wound still hurt. Alan lived in the Reardon household, but his choice at that point in terms of a more comfortable environment was definitely on the athletic field with his teammates and coach.

Jessica Reardon
The death of her mother was a pivotal event in Jessica's early childhood development. To the rest of the family, her role in that event was a mystery. Jessica was unable to describe what happened at Bromfield Manor, and it left a huge ache in the heart of her father. Her behavior both in school and at home was worrisome. No amount of comfort and reassurance seemed

to penetrate the flat, blank facial expression and dull emotional response. Jessica offered no indication of her feelings about her father's remarriage. She moved through her life the same way she moved through her house and through the school system. She preferred to be unnoticed and undisturbed. Rita made special efforts to include her stepdaughter in the world of the Reardon women. Ruth was disappointed that she could not get closer to her stepsister. She confided to Rita on more than one occasion that she believed that Jessica was disturbed. Jessica was not ready to face the changes and challenges of adolescence. It would prove more than she could handle. Her family, friends, teachers, and doctors were frustrated and saddened.

The diagnostic impression by the child psychiatrist was ominous: adjustment disorder, early adolescence, with unresolved grief over her mother's death and with avoidant and psychotic features.

Chapter Two: Adolescence

CHANGE

The terrible, terrific, testing, torturous, tempting, tender, and sometimes tragic teens. Above all, temporary! Six or seven years of unavoidable growth and development; ready or not. The transition time from childhood to adulthood. No two kids start at exactly the same time. And no child is really ready.

Changes in the body come first. By the earliest teen years the body's endocrine system begins to secrete hormones that announce the beginning of a journey away from the innocence of childhood. Pubic hair and changing distribution of body fat and muscle are early objects of curiosity, but ejaculation by boys and menstrual bleeding by girls are more memorable events. Each is accompanied by different emotional stirrings.

Let's take the boys first. Lacking any firsthand experience, most preadolescent boys develop a natural interest in the mysterious body activity of adults. Aside from the alarming annual rise in the number of fatherless families in this country, the sit-down one-to-one discussion between dad and son regarding pubescent rites of passage is rare. Too embarrassing for both sides. Pamphlets issued by school nurses or pediatricians may help. Gradually, a personal fantasy life develops, joining one's naughty, sensual ambition with an innate sense of both impotence and guilt. Before puberty, all of this is still an exercise of thought and feeling. Then it changes forever.

For boys, the magic moment of pubescence arrives at the height of some warm and wonderful sexual fantasy. Suddenly, something feels different down below. An unaccountable and indescribable sensation courses through a stiffening penis. It ends in a matter of seconds with the emission of a strange, foreign, milky gray fluid.

My God! What just happened? What did I do? Yuk! It's messy! Got to clean up.

> *I'm scared. It happened so quickly. Nobody warned me. I just couldn't stop it. Gosh, it felt good. Like nothing before. So why do I feel bad? I know why. Because I had dirty thoughts before it happened. And now I feel kind of dirty.*
>
> *Who can I tell? No one! No one would understand. Does this mean I'm a man now? My God, I feel so alone. I'm scared!*

For girls, the onset of puberty is also a shocker, but without any compensatory rush of orgasmic pleasure. The official name for the event is *menarche*. The unofficial response to it all is similar. Panic, confusion, and even disgust. For good reason. For no matter how well prepared by well-intentioned elders or peers, when bleeding occurs uncontrollably from any part of our body, it simply does not seem normal.

> *My God, I'm bleeding! What's happening? Where is it coming from? I may need a doctor. I could die. Mama, I need you! Make it stop! What's happening? Did I do something wrong? I'm scared!*

Despite the gender-determined differences, the two experiences have some similarities. One is the sense of helplessness and vulnerability, and the reflexive yearning for parents and/or God. Another is feeling dirty or bad. The naughty pre-ejaculation fantasies add to the feelings of guilt that come with the new found thrill of orgasm. Not so for girls. However distorted or irrational the sense of badness is more connected with a wonderment of physical defectiveness. Bleeding is not natural. Something's wrong! Soon we will explore how these issues affect the continuous journey toward adulthood.

On the Day of the Rattle, the infant was forced to descend from Mount Olympus and begin the give-and-take relationship with Mom and Dad as a fellow mortal.

On the Day of the Potty, another bond was fashioned by the knowledge that a self-controlled act pleasing to the parents would yield a return of love and affection.

On the Day of the School Bus, the child's first bold venture into the cold, cruel world was rewarded by Mom and Dad's reassuring presence and support.

But what about the rites of puberty and the first change of life experience that lies ahead?

The child silently yearns for help and guidance but at the same time realizes that the feelings are too jumbled, the questions yet unformed, the urges too embarrassing to share. Even though Mom and Dad are around, they simply can't solve the problem. To a certain extent, every child must go it alone—never quite sure what to say or when to say it and never quite sure how to act or not to act.

The burden of unsureness is indeed the central theme of the adolescent struggle. But before we explore it, let us reflect on that one indispensable element for healthy growth and development: the availability of two parents to offer love and limits. Adolescence introduces to the family a brand new ballgame, and neither team is sure of the rules.

Unsureness

The malaise of unsureness is a day-to-day, year-to-year burden during the teen years. Unsure of one's appearance. Unsure of one's emotions. Unsure of one's abilities. Unsure of one's worth. Unsure of one's values. Unsure of one's ambitions. Unsure of parent's values. Unsure of one's sexual stirrings. Unsure of the rewards of adulthood, the responsibilities of adulthood, the necessity of leaving the safety and entitlements of childhood, one's readiness to face the future. Unsure of the very meaning of life and death.

In this uncertain world of adolescence, kids instinctively seek some standard, some reference point by which to measure themselves.

It used to be so easy! Parents and teachers served as mirrors of one's worth, based on what the child did to please them. Compliments or criticism provided a tangible measure of one's worth. In the highly charged emotional turmoil of adolescence, the bewildered child cannot trust the old system of compliance and compliment. If the parent knew what was really on the child's mind, they would be horrified, thinks the teen.

Thus, a new system replaces the old: peer approval. This system is far from perfect, but it offers the child some creatures to identify with. On a practical level, teens can blend into the crowd, hiding all their imagined physical and emotional imperfections. Membership in a group of adolescents is vital to shore up the sense of isolation and to develop a sense of worth. The type of group, of course, is of great importance—some minglings help, and some hurt.

The child of ambitious parents is often denied the comfort of peer interaction. The exceptionally talented child may be slotted for special tutoring or training to perfect a skill that becomes the total measure of their worth in the eyes of their parents, but ignores the more necessary process of "doing one's best" instead of "being the best."

Identifying with other kids is one part of the growth process of adolescence. As the journey continues, the need to maintain safe anonymity within one's peer group gives way to the certain knowledge that adulthood awaits, and sooner or later one must stand alone and not just be like others but "be somebody." At the end of all this, life demands that each adult has a unique identity.

Thus the process of identifying with other unsure teenagers gradually slows down and shifts to the process of identifying with older folks in preparation for being an adult. This process is vital but not without its hazards.

The Identification Process

It is a mental process, primarily. It occurs quietly and discreetly in the recesses of the subconscious mind. Few adolescents would acknowledge that it even exists, for fear of seeming needy or weak.

This process is basically one of copying admirable traits in other people. To someday "be somebody," one must first yearn to "be like somebody." With the ever-changing physical characteristics of adolescent growth, the teenager becomes obsessed with appearance. Thus, the earliest signs of the identification process appear as cosmetic alterations. Radical changes of hairstyle by both girls and boys seem to be the most common indicator. Vocal intonations and body posturing reflect an allegiance to an admired rock star or athlete. Because the unsure child can only do so much with its unreliable, awkward torso, the surest way of accurately copying an idealized adult is to drape the body with an unmistakable stamp of admiration and loyalty. Names, numbers, and logos are the ticket. It is hard to imagine a single teenager in this country, at this time, who does not proudly display a T-shirt, sweatshirt, parka, headgear, or footwear advertising its search for somebody to be like, to resemble.

Media models may satisfy the teenager's craving for success and status in these early years of transition, but as the time approaches to move on and graduate to the next stage of life, another set of models gets the nod. The identification process takes a serious and necessary turn.

Teachers, coaches, older relatives, neighbors, and parents become more acceptable in the eyes of the adolescent. The child realizes that the job of acquiring a distinct personality and a value unto itself goes way beyond just appearances. One needs to develop something deeper, something stronger, something lasting from within. The focus of identifying with others shifts to measuring adult values, not just appearances, and absorbing those values that are appealing and important. In opposition to this gradual process are the still deeply rooted teenage maxims that all adults are simply not hip, not cool.

Of all the adult models, the most important are the parents. And the parent of the same gender is definitely the most necessary. Neither that parent nor the child is usually aware that this silent dynamic scenario is occurring. Mother Nature mandates this ultimate choice of models. The body disturbances at puberty lead to an instinctive need to accept one's given gender and develop an identity that is consistent with that gender. Who, then, but the parent of the same gender can offer not only the sexual characteristics, but the emotional, social, and spiritual values to help one grow up and be somebody?

The responsibility of the parents at this stage of their child's life is awesome. No script or training program is adequate to prepare them. Mom and Dad's energies are already stretched pretty thin with the demands of working, paying bills, making time for each other, dealing with family-of-origin and in-laws, maintaining adult friendships, and parenting other offspring.

While all this is going on within the family, the parents themselves are moving toward their own change of life. Traces of one's own unresolved adolescent turmoil have a way of resurfacing. This complicates the parents' ability to respond to the child's need to idealize them one day and to scapegoat them the next.

Parents, unfortunately, are the perfect foil for the volatile mood swings of the adolescent. Armed with the knowledge that *no matter how annoying my behavior is, my parents will not disown me,* the teenager becomes free to silently admire Mom and Dad and then openly defy them. *Who else would put up with me?*

The dark and troubled side of the child's emotions cry out for relief. The constant feelings of unsureness, insecurity, guilt and impotence can be internalized for just so long. The pressure is most commonly transferred to the unsuspecting parents in the form of rebelliousness, confrontative behavior. How the parents respond is vitally important. Burdened by their own pressures, some parents unwittingly release their frustrations on to the child. In this scenario, the child may lose a certain amount of respect for the parents/model it subconsciously yearns to imitate.

It is necessary for parents, amid the onslaught of protest and criticism, to keep their cool and to stick to some commonsense values even if the angry, brittle child acts out in defiance. Sooner or later, the child will return to the love and loyalty it cherishes after all the adolescent turmoil has ended.

The identification process, en route to gaining an adult identity, continues beyond the teen years. Appearances become less and less important, however. And as already mentioned, values to live by and the character of the admired elder are silently grafted onto the developing young adult personality. Subconsciously, a selection and rejection mechanism allows this person to become the elusive "somebody."

With some understanding of the dynamics of the identification process, let us now examine at least three pathways for growth that a teenager travels from the moment of puberty.

Pathways for Growth

Intellectual Growth

The brain of the teenager is alive and popping. It is hungry. It gobbles up bits and pieces of information, oftentimes faster than it can digest them. So much going on! So many things to learn!

The learning process is interrupted only by sleep. The confused, anxious, unsure adolescent can't afford to miss any and all morsels of information to guide it through the uncharted rapids of the first "change-of-life" experience.

One is constantly measuring oneself against the norms presented by other kids, in school, out of school, on television, and in the movies. The manners and mores of adults are less important.

The more formal learning takes place in school. The rigidity and discipline attendant to schoolwork are generally resented by the restless voyager, but the fringe benefits, including athletics, non-athletic activities, social events, and boy-meets-girl opportunities, more than make up for that.

If the brain of the adolescent is running in high gear because of the thirst for knowledge, then paradoxically the ability to absorb and retain that knowledge may be compromised by the same process. The ability to concentrate suffers while the emotions are running wild. Most kids find a way to handle it. But for some suffering from an overload of home grown anxiety and depression the capacity to absorb and retain information may be seriously compromised.

The four-year high school course ultimately proves to be a wonderful invention. It formalizes the effort-and-reward system. At the beginning, high school seems an insurmountable mountain. But by senior year, most kids realize what they've accomplished and the recognition and reward that await on graduation day.

What each child absorbs from the high school curriculum is officially measured by report card grades. For some, this is a carefully constructed springboard to honors and even scholarships. For most, it is a fair reflection of capabilities and effort. For a few, it is a reminder of intellectual limitations, and for a few others, it is a sad commentary about an attitude problem or emotional disarray.

Whatever else it represents, high school is an experience that begins on a certain day and ends on a certain day. For most, but not all, it takes four years.

Before finishing this chapter, we will review in more detail some of the experiences of high school leading up to commencement day.

Physical Growth

At about age thirteen through nineteen, the body gets taller and gains weight. Genetic determinants dictate shapes and ultimate size. Depending on gender, all teenagers attempt to assist Mother Nature by adding muscle and make-up. Appearance is indeed everything in the earliest years of adolescence (and almost everything toward the end).

Size and strength appeal to many boys to allow them to stand apart from the crowd via athletics. The body serves as a vehicle for recognition, as well as an acceptable instrument to release aggression. The less well-endowed little guys must find other solutions.

Similarly, the physically attractive girl is likely to use her natural beauty to satisfy the need to be somebody special. All too often, however, the jocks and the prom queens lose their perspective and abandon themselves to the glow of popularity. They give up the work of acquiring an adult identity at this most vulnerable time. They peak too soon, and they stop growing emotionally.

Like the tides, physical growth cannot be held back at this busy time of life. But there is one behavior of adolescence, mostly in girls, that comes close to stunting and even reversing physical growth. It is the problem of teenage eating disorders. Much more detail will be given about this problem in the story section.

Sexual Growth

Recall the onset of adolescence—that unforgettable moment when the body said, *It's over little girl, little boy. You will never be the same again!*

The indelible stamp of male or female gender is pressed firmly into the psyche of the frightened child at this moment. The anatomical site is the genital area. The tangible proof is the flow of fluids: semen and blood.

The initial shock leads to questions already recorded by us. *Why is this happening? What is it all for? Why can't I control it? Did I do something wrong? Who can help me?*

The whole event is so fraught with guilt and uncertainty that the child rejects the option of discussing it with Mom and Dad. The safer choice is to pick up some pieces of information from the other kids. Locker rooms and slumber parties reverberate with jokes, insults and boasts. They offer the confused adolescent some comfort. Relax! Everyone's in the same boat. No one has all the answers.

What lies ahead? Among all the changes and challenges of the next half dozen years, the frightened child must cope with the private issue of sexual maturation.

In other times and in other cultures with much shorter life spans, this might not have been such a problem. Boys and girls of centuries ago upon reaching pubescent age may have copulated, had babies, and died of old age in their thirties. But life expectancy projections for the next century are approaching the eighties, and our cultural norms insist on the child getting beyond the teens before taking on family responsibility.

Thus, the main dilemma of adolescent sexual development. On the one hand, there is the urge to express natural sexual desires and, on the other hand, cultural and moral prohibitions. What at times seems grossly unfair to the fantasy-ridden teen desperately trying to cool their glandular engines may in fact be a wise warning from the elders. Go slow! The body may be ready and willing, but the mind and heart aren't always in synch. Sex produces babies, but adolescence doesn't necessarily produce capable parents.

Of sexual issues in adolescence, masturbation is a natural but misunderstood concept. For centuries, at least in Western culture, it has been a source of great controversy. Some moral theologians consider it sinful. Generations of parents who have forgotten their own torment consider it dirty and disgusting. Sociologists are prone to ignoring it. Psychologists cannot agree on what role it plays. And the unsure, guilt-ridden kids who are presently struggling with it delight in the pleasure and abhor the sense of weakness and lack of control.

There are two basic ingredients in the phenomenon of masturbation: thought and action. Of these two, thought plays the major role. Mental health professionals disagree as to the nature and significance of masturbatory fantasies. This phenomenon deserves closer attention as we add to our conceptual alphabet en route to understanding mental illness.

Masturbatory Fantasies

One dictionary definition of fantasy is, "A play of the mind; imagination. A picture only existing in the mind; queer illusion." Shakespeare put it differently: "Fantasies seem real to a delirious person. A daydream is a fantasy. I talk of dreams, which are the children of an idle brain, begot of nothing but vain fantasy."

As we might expect, the Bard says an awful lot in an entertaining way: First, he touches on the phenomenon of wild imaginations perceived as real by some people. This we will explore later, specifically on the topic of delusions. Most importantly, Shakespeare equates the term *daydream* with *fantasy*. He then embellishes it with the curious use of the word *vain*. By reorganizing these ideas it seems fair to say that "a fantasy is a vain daydream."

But what is a dream, anyway, daydream or night dream? How do dreams fit in to our normal, everyday life?

Put most simply dreams are stories that we tell to ourselves. Awake or asleep we cannot live without stories. There are two kinds of stories most essential to our life on this planet: those that are to[...] those we create for ourselves.

The first category may be divided into two parts: where we are in the evolution of the human race ar[...] who we are in the here and now.

We rely on dates and calendars to establish how w[...] forbears. Essential to our search for roots are history bo[...] lore, and religious traditions. Then there are the stories that relate to who we are now. As to our constant quest to shape our identity and personality, we are in no short supply of stories in the written, visual or audio media. We are constantly at work reinforcing our values by accepting or rejecting the messages that we absorb daily from other persons or through the media.

Now let us look at the necessity of dreams in our daily life, the stories we tell ourselves.

In the latter part of this century, sleep research has become an important part of the behavioral sciences. One of the most important discoveries is the intimate relationship between the mind and the body in the dream state. After careful research, it was found that for every eight-hour sleep period per night approximately ninety minutes is spent dreaming. This hour and a half is divided into two or three discrete events. Most importantly, the researchers found that while the person is dreaming, the brain, as measured by electroencephalogram findings, produces a seizure or epileptic kind of pattern accurately matching the exact time of the dream state. Unlike the disease of grand mal epilepsy, the arms and legs of the subject are unaffected by this seizure of low energy. But evidence of the existence of a seizure is found by lifting the eyelids and observing an involuntary rapid eye movement (REM).

As part of the research, volunteer patients have been awakened to validate the presence of the dream state as well as to explore its contents. Of less importance to the dream researchers but of much importance to us is another phenomenon. If the research subject was intentionally wakened at the beginning of the dream state and deprived of the nightly allotment of beneficial dream time, they tended to be irritable and restless on the following day. They also tended to produce more dream minutes the following night to compensate. If the dream deprivation experiment continued, there was a definite craving to make up for all the lost time, at least until the fourth day of sleep deprivation. Following this, the normal ninety-minute pattern resumed.

Before moving on to the issue of dream content, we may assume from the above findings that human dreaming is essential to our natural daily cycle. Of great significance for this particular part of the chapter is the

...nal finding that during the dream state there is both a mental and ...ysical component. The mental component is obviously the fantasy life that makes up the dream, and the physical component is a mini-seizure. This seizure-like activity is in fact natural and necessary.

What about the mental part? Again, volumes of published theories abound, especially since Freud offered his psychoanalytic interpretation a hundred years ago. My intent is not to interpret dream content but to compare the combined mental and physiological components of night dreams with daydreams, particularly those daydreams that are identified as sexual fantasies. For these fantasies, and the coloring and the meaning of them, will ultimately shape our adult sexual habits.

Instead of theories, let us borrow from our common experience. The basic features of our dreaming have to do with three things. First, dreams take the form of drama or acted-out stories. Second, they are quite personal and private in that we alone are the producer, director, and central character of the drama. Third, regardless of the psychological meaning of the story in the dream, the material that is created and blended together is made up of at least two kinds of experiences in our lives. One is a distorted and often fragmented recall of events that occurred the day preceding the dream. The other—and this is most significant—is the equally distorted replay of emotional unfinished business from our memory bank.

The combination of the psychic energy needed to generate the dream drama and the physiologic energy that is dissipated during the dream state suggests something akin to the household garbage-disposal unit. Our human brains cannot absorb and retain all the data and experiences that pile up each day of our lives. Dreams are a necessary way of relieving the congestion and pile-up that occurs in the brain. Recall the irritability of the research subject whose dreams were interrupted.

Now back to daydreams and specifically those fantasies that are sexual in nature. As with night dreams, there is a drama that takes place and on many occasions, depending on the desires of the adolescent child, a physical manipulation of the genitals that can lead to an orgasmic release, which, like the seizure phenomenon of sleep dreams, cannot be stopped until it is completed. Once it starts, it resembles the involuntary flow of physiologic energy that resembles the seizure of the dream state. The fantasy part of the masturbatory act ends abruptly with the completed orgasm. This is followed by a clear sense of physical and emotional release.

Thus, both the nighttime dream process and the masturbatory process bear similarities of combined mental and physical activity, but most importantly, they are also expressions in a necessary way of our human nature. Despite this, adolescent masturbatory activity is wrapped in mystery, ignorance, and taboos. The perpetrators, in their confused and unsure state of mind, instinctively feel shame.

Given the constant burden of unsureness that the adolescent must bear, coping with masturbatory fantasies and physical drives, it is difficult to reconcile all of these features. Waiting to become an adult when the natural urges lead to healthy give-and-take lovemaking offers small consolation to the immature adolescent during these everyday battles.

We are well aware in our society that more and more teenagers refuse to wait and instead exchange masturbation for the real thing. Kids from dysfunctional, chaotic families or no families at all are particularly vulnerable to the uncertainty of their sexual drives. Their need to be held, touched, and nurtured drives them into sexual relations with other kids of similar needs where the outcome is too often a disappointing break-up and rejection, a possible sexually transmitted disease, or an unwanted child.

Before leaving the subject of masturbatory fantasies and adolescence, it is important to draw attention to one major difference from the themes of sleep-induced dreams. That difference lies in the role that the central character plays. The broad range of dramatic material available in night dreams leads to incredible variation in the plot, outcome, casting of characters and continuity of themes.

The composition of some dreams seems chaotic and disconnected; others blissfully rewarding. The difference between sweet dreams and nightmares! And even though we are the central player in night dreams, it is rare to feel in total control of the outcome. On occasion, we are filled with relief when we wake up from a bad dream.

The pre-orgasmic masturbatory fantasy is different. The entire theme is built around our own personal pleasure. And the material used to build up the plot is a reflection of the outer and inner recesses of our being; our yearnings, our fears, our doubts, our anger and, most importantly, our incredible search to retrieve that lost paradise of infancy when we were number one, deserving total love, affection, and attention immediately. En route to the moment of orgasm there is a "me" and others outside of "me" who must bring pleasure. At the moment of orgasm only an "I" exists in the drama. Mental health workers call this event the sexual expression of primary narcissism.

To summarize the importance of these natural and necessary experiences during the time of adolescent growth:

Adolescent sexual development, as with other adolescent experiences, is a preparation for life as an adult. As we saw in the section on the identification process, the most important task is developing a mature identity, becoming one's own person.

En route to this goal, our sexual experiences reflect the progress being made toward that end. The themes of the masturbatory fantasies are a measure, not only of healthy progress, but also of some potentially crippling hang-ups. The adolescent who fantasizes love-making with an idealized movie star is on a different path from the angry, bitter soul who masturbates while torturing small animals.

Adolescence is the birthplace of healthy sexual adjustment in adulthood or the spawning ground for unnatural and perverted maladjustment. The course becomes set regarding our ability to ultimately integrate sexual intercourse with intellectual, emotional, and social intercourse.

Commencement

The term *Commencement* is borrowed from the word most often printed in the high school graduation program: "Commencement Exercises." Those in attendance come to watch the end of something. Four hard years of labor in that wonderful, wacky crucible of learning. Congratulations flow to those precious souls who have made it and to the proud parents who have endured it.

So, if it's a glorious ending, why the title "Commencement"? The answer is that many years ago some wise Headmaster or Principal understood the true meaning of the event and chose the correct name. Life goes on, and at the moment one phase ends, another begins. Such is the central theme of this book.

But unlike the change and challenge of the Rattle, Potty, and School Bus, commencement day portends the end of childhood and the beginning of adulthood.

The events that lead up to commencement day are worth pondering. For they represent an unofficial measure of the teenager's growth and development beyond the "three Rs." For most kids these experiences are oriented around their central activity: School.

I call these events "The Senior Year Syndrome." In medical school we were taught that a syndrome was a collection of symptoms and signs all pointing to a specific illness or disease. Indeed, the challenges of leaving one's formative years and venturing forth in uncharted territory produces some dramatic and even tragic responses. At the beginning, I describe two opposite scenarios at the door of the hospital as the infant and mother enter the car and drive home. Those vignettes were meant to show the plight of the newborn child placed in the care of parents who were either together or troubled.

Somewhere between idyllic parenting and a totally dysfunctional or absent family upbringing is where most of us live our earliest years. Thus, we ourselves have experienced early on the limitations of parents to do a perfect job. Parents try their best usually. They offer their child seven days a week, twelve months a year for eighteen years as much as they can in terms of love and limits. Few parents deliberately set out to cheat or hurt their own flesh and blood.

But, in varying degrees, kids are hurt. Commencement time is the time of inventory to tote up how far the child has come in this imperfect world of family life. And what does each child now have in terms of the proper tools to keep growing? The unloved child will arrive at this juncture emotionally malnourished. The battered or abused child will arrive bitter and mistrustful.

The graduation ceremony is set for a certain day and a certain time. Tradition demands it. The school authorities are in lock-step with Mother Nature. But for many kids something is scary about the expectations. *You've gotta grow older, but you don't gotta grow up.*

The Senior Year Syndrome may begin within a few months of school opening in September. One of the first hints that a child is having difficulty is absence from class. Physical ailments predominate. Most are presumed to be viral in nature and hard for the pediatrician to document. Flu-like symptoms. For many years I treated the victims of a strange autumn epidemic that produced the mysterious variation of a disease called mononucleosis. But regardless of the diagnosis, these children begin to lose precious time in class.

At home other signs of emotional unrest begin to appear. Irritability, seclusion, apathy, tearfulness. A generalized slowing down of activity and a growing fear of going places may develop right under the parent's eyes.

Parents and doctors are baffled. School teachers commiserate but are helpless to make up for the lost days and weeks that follow. By Christmas, the school principal arranges a meeting and dares to suggest that the child may need professional counseling. He or she also announces to the parents that unless there is a dramatic recovery the child may not be qualified to graduate in June.

If the child refuses to go to school and refuses help, parental empathy is likely to cool, and anger, born of frustration, sets in. The child's response is more withdrawal and more resistance.

At this point in time two scenarios are likely to occur. One involves burrowing deeper into the illusory safety of the home despite the tension within the family. The other is to spend more time out of the home, protesting the ignorance and intolerance of adults with other kindred spirits. But the safety of huddling inside the gang is short-lived. The bottom line is that the child is about to drop out of high school and drop out of growing up.

Either way the ongoing struggle between child and parents is likely to continue well beyond commencement day. All the parental plans and hopes for college or job are scuttled. The child may exact some degree of satisfaction from dropping out of the process of growing up and continuing on with their life at this point in time. But the parents are left to ponder the long-range consequences of their child's refusal to face the challenge of entering the next phase of life.

Two other behavioral patterns fit into the broad spectrum of the Senior Year Syndrome. Both are in response to the terrible fear of being unprepared to leave one's childhood and leave one's home. Both of these unfortunate events are accompanied by potentially self-destructive reactions. One pattern is hidden behind the glitter of what appears to be a successful senior year experience. The second scenario is a major mental breakdown.

First, let's look at the problem of being a super-jock or prom queen.

I once was asked to offer an opinion as a consultant on an orthopedic ward at our hospital. In the opinion of the surgeon who had successfully operated on a well-known high school athlete, the patient was behaving, post-surgically, in a bizarre way. He was playful, garrulous, and almost giddy despite the fact that the basketball team that he captained had to play a semifinal tournament game without him. He thoroughly enjoyed his teammates' visits and showed no sadness about his crippling injury.

Before seeing the patient I spoke with his parents who shared the doctor's concern about his uncharacteristic euphoria. They were more concerned about the outcome of his recovery, however. His upper leg fracture, the result of a drinking-and-driving spree, was likely to permanently hamper his athletic future. This was all despite the fact that he had been accepted at three colleges and had been given scholarship awards that had not yet been finalized.

I found the young man propped up in bed in a jumble of white sheets, white ropes and pulleys, and sporting a grotesque white plaster cast, extending from his toes as high up as his abdomen. He was giggling at the morning cartoons on television and seemed casual sipping a cola from a plastic cup.

He reluctantly gave up his amusement and finally turned the volume down rather than off. He did then grant me an audience. He wore a childish grin and said he had been warned that a "shrink" was coming to "fool around with his head." I told him that my purpose in coming was not to fool around with his head but to offer him any help that I might regarding the emotional shock of his car accident and the hospitalization.

"Doc, that's great, but let me tell you I'm fine. I'm having a ball here! The nurses are terrific, the food's not bad, and the other patients and I get along fine."

We talked for several minutes about his life up until the accident and he presented a much more serious tone. He spoke of enormous pressure to perform as a three-sport star in high school. He lamented that he had had no time for himself since Christmas. When the team wasn't playing, he was traveling to colleges to be interviewed by coaches. His phone was busy nights and weekends with calls from media, alumni, and well-wishers. He was sick of it!

I reported that his family and friends were concerned about his apparent lack of concern regarding his medical problems. His reply said it all.

"Doc, sure I care. There are times I think I'm going crazy lying in this bed. I miss being home. I miss my friends. But I don't miss the sports. Always having to win.

"I lost track of who I was. I felt people were using me. Even my parents were on that bandwagon. I need a time out. Man, I'm just not ready for college. I'm scared!"

The analogy to this dilemma of being burned out, of being scared of growing up on the female side is the dilemma of the prom queen. The young girl who is cursed with beauty and good looks may be prone to ignore all the growing-up pathways that we have listed so far in deference to being popular and to feeling good because of it. By the end of the high school years when the diplomas are being handed out, this person again may reach a conclusion that she is simply not prepared to go on with her life without all of the adulation and superficial praise that has buoyed her during the four years of high school.

The problem may not be an accident that requires hospitalization to slow this trip down, but it may be a sense of grave depression and anxiety that may literally stifle her ability to go beyond the high school years.

The second scenario, the breakdown, is a most serious event. The name given to this breakdown is schizophrenia. Because this constitutes the number one major mental illness that human beings can suffer I will devote much more attention to it at the end of this chapter in the last section. Schizophrenia is like no other emotional disturbance. Although rare, it is the one true mental illness.

The few words that will be offered at this point serve only to point out the timing of the onset of this illness. They in no way match the dominant impact of this illness, which is singular in the field of mental illness.

One hundred years ago the term *dementia precox* was used to describe what we now call schizophrenia. As with so many diagnostic labels of that era, the Latin language predominated throughout Europe as the common root of expression in the field of medicine. A rough translation would be "precocious dementia." Early dementia! Dementia before its time.

What is dementia? Today, psychiatrists limit the term to organic or physical brain damage. Aging is the biggest culprit. The natural erosion of cortical brain cells claims the greatest number of victims. Alzheimer's disease is a form of dementia where the damage is not natural or age related. It usually occurs much before the aging process would dictate brain erosion.

Over the past century, we have learned that most mental disorders are not caused by physical brain damage. Instead, the lack of sufficient emotional nourishment in our childhood and the inability to cope with change and challenge in the adult years are the major contributing factors. By the end of the senior year of high school, these two factors combine in the lives of some teenagers to produce either a slowing down or a stoppage of emotional growth.

A severe mental breakdown complete with a crippling thought disorder is indeed a rare event now. Thirty years ago, when I started my psychiatric practice, it was much more common. As mentioned, we will explore this unique illness called schizophrenia soon. But for now what is important to note is that even a hundred years ago in different countries with different cultures the pressures of leaving childhood and commencing an adult life could produce such a devastating blow.

For whatever reason, there has been a decline in incidence of late teenage schizophrenia in the latter part of the twentieth century. Oddly enough, with the decline of this most malignant illness there have been replacements in terms of behavioral abnormalities that serve as an alternative to psychosis, but also serve as an alternative to commencement and continued emotional growth. One in particular stands out: the so-called eating disorders. The two most common forms are anorexia nervosa and bulimia.

Also at the end of his chapter, more detail will be included to offer explanations why these problems occur before commencement time. But for now it is important to note two parts to the eating disorder problem that are consistent with the theme of the chapter. The first is that eating disorders almost always begin in adolescence, and the second is that the essence of these disorders is an anti-nourishment, anti-growth behavior.

CHALLENGE

Billy Smith

Joe and Jeannette Miculski were Lawrence natives. They were considered by their friends to be a salt-of-the-earth, pillars-of-the-church couple. Hard work and faith in God were their guiding principles. They were proud of themselves, their children, and their Polish American heritage. Jeannette gave birth to three children within the first five years of marriage—two boys and a girl. Tragedy struck when Karen, at the age of nine, was hit on her way to school by an out-of-control motorcycle. The Miculskis arrived at the emergency room too late to say goodbye to their daughter.

That was many years ago. Now their son Richie was about to enter the senior year in high school, and they envisioned an empty nest within a year. Their eldest son Paul was away at law school in Philadelphia.

It was with some interest that they listened to the speaker at Sunday mass. She was a social worker from Catholic Charities Association in the greater Lawrence area. Her theme was the need for homes to help displaced and abandoned children in the Commonwealth of Massachusetts who were really quite desperate.

They dismissed the idea as soon as mass was over, but that evening over supper they briefly discussed her appeal. Within a week, they sat in the office of the same social worker for a preliminary discussion about the possibility of taking in a foster child. Placing Billy Smith was no easy task for the agency. The turmoil of his previous placement left him emotionally bruised and left the Department of Social Services with an uneasy sense that trouble would follow this child and thus follow their agency.

The Miculskis left the first meeting feeling somewhat deceived and disappointed. They did not realize that the child in question was really part of another system and did not belong exclusively to the Catholic agency. The social worker reassured them that each child was evaluated and screened and that they would take great pains to scrutinize the record, meet with the child, and if agreed only have that child live with them on a temporary basis until all parties were comfortable. The next step was to meet Billy in their own home, an event that was marked by a certain uneasiness, particularly by Billy. An agreement was made for a summer placement to be reviewed before Labor Day. What made it work was the trip to Hampton Beach for two weeks. It was an annual affair for the Miculskis, and quite coincidentally it was exactly what Billy needed to shake loose from the trauma of the Medford experience.

The water, the waves, the sun, the sand, and the breeze were heaven sent. He felt free and he felt clean. Richie and his friends actually included him during the daytime with the games and the horseplay while on the beach. At night, because of his age, they did exclude him while they strolled along the boardwalk in search of "chicks."

While enjoying himself at this summer playground, Billy quietly tried to size up the Miculski parents. He took an instant like to Joe, who was a giant of a man but who had a soft voice and giving manner. He was not quite sure of Jeannette, and the feeling was mutual. She told Joe one night that she could not be sure of this little boy who seemed so tense and so frightened. When Joe pursued the subject, she said it was his eyes. They were sad and angry.

Their house rules were fair and simple. Billy realized that he must comply to avoid another placement. Clean up your room once a week, put your laundry in the bathroom hamper, make your bed each morning, turn the TV down at night, be at the supper table at 6:00, say grace before meals, go to Sunday mass, and no foul language.

Billy did his best to blend in to his new environment, keeping to the rules as best he could. It was all so orderly and all so simple. But his own private world was not. There were no rules for his thoughts, feelings and fantasies. Following the chaos and cruelty experienced in Medford, he was developing anything but well-ordered fantasies.

His nightly masturbatory fantasies were highlighted by jumbled images of naked adults and children engaged in primitive sexual rituals. Sadism and masochism were the themes. As the weeks and months rolled on, Billy took comfort in the small but steady growth of his arm and leg muscles, as well as his penis. He would stand for minutes, both in the morning and the evening, posing before the mirror to admire the growth of his body. He imagined himself becoming closer to the goal of becoming the hurter, and not the hurt one.

By the end of the summer, the adults in his life felt that Billy had passed the initial test. There were no major disruptions, and the next problem was to consider what grade he should enter and in what type of school. The DSS worker made a pitch for the mainstream of the Lawrence school system but was outvoted by the school board. He was set up for a special education program in the inner city. Within a week of being bused to the select classroom, Billy and the Miculskis encountered their first crisis.

Billy found himself in a class of twelve pupils. He told his foster parents about his nervousness on the first day, but by the end of the week he came home crying and said that he had not been able to sleep for the past few days. He pleaded with them to take him out of that class because he felt unsafe. He said that the experience in the Medford foster home was still with him and he could not concentrate.

Another meeting was held with the school authorities with the focus on Billy's posttraumatic stress disorder. Despite the recommendations by parents and social worker, the authorities felt he should continue but with some extra counseling and support in the form of a special teacher meeting with him every day.

Billy enjoyed this special attention. She was a young woman, fresh out of college, who made a lot of him and made him even more comfortable by taking him out of the school building for trips downtown for ice cream. For the first time in his life, Billy felt that he had someone who understood him and was on his side.

His mother, Melanie, showed up with the DSS worker on the Friday after Thanksgiving. Their meeting was supposed to be chaperoned but the social worker did allow them some time by themselves. She drove them to a park along the river where they walked along the river bank for a few hours all alone.

Melanie kept the conversation going with endless chatting about familiar people and events in Salem. Billy was not really interested to hear about her job, nor was he interested to hear about his sister and grandmother Gertrude. What was on his mind was the termination of this foster home placement and the eventual return to his mother in Salem. As they returned to the car, Billy found it necessary to ask the question of both women. The social worker answered directly. The courts had ruled on the matter, and had said quite clearly that Billy would need to stay at least one more year in the foster home before consideration for return home could be brought forward to the courts.

He refused to talk to the two women in the car on the way back to the Miculskis and jumped out the back door and ran into the house wiping the tears from his eyes.

Christmas at the Miculskis was a happening—a curious blend of religious traditions and secular displays for joy and merriment with an overabundant supply of lights and wreaths. Friends and neighbors popped in during the weeks before and after the holiday. There was a constant coming and going of adults and children of all sizes. Amid the merriment, there was substantial food and junk food in the form of candies, cookies, and cakes. Conversation was on the light side, but Billy could simply not get into it.

Billy received only two Christmas cards, one from his mother and one from his grandmother. Gertrude sent a message that she wasn't feeling well and asked for him to pray for her. His mother called around suppertime on Christmas day and said that she could not make it out to see him. He assumed that she was intoxicated from the sound of her slurred voice.

Despite the generosity of the Miculski family who went out of their way to supply him with practical gifts, he spent most of the day in his room. He did not fit in with the celebration and it caused him a few moments of doubt. He asked himself why he could not enjoy what other people could enjoy. Amid the gaiety, he felt down and depressed, wondering, what is wrong with me?

Later that evening he found himself watching TV and being disappointed in the meager selection of kids' shows. He tuned in to an old version of "A Christmas Carol" and fell asleep before it ended. His own sleep was as disrupted as that of Ebenezer Scrooge, and he found himself waking more than once to ponder the meaning of the ghosts of Christmas past, present, and future. His mind would not shut off. It was riveted on the cadaverous figure in chains who represented the ghost of Christmas future. He feared that this was a vision of his own self. Had a piece of him died already? Was he one step away from the ghastly figure in his dreams?

He was alone, totally alone. No mother, no father, no friends, and no God. He did not believe in anyone or anything. He pressed his mouth into his pillow to muffle the sounds of his agonizing screams.

Enough of this Christmas crap. The next day he called a friend from school, a boisterous kid by the name of Ramon Hidalgo. He was stir crazy and he needed to get out the house. Ramon was the youngest of four kids whose parents had emigrated from Haiti. He was the only child born in the United States. For whatever reason, the two of them got along well. Perhaps part of it was that they were the tallest kids in class, the result of being two years behind their expected grade.

They hung out at the mall and seemed to enjoy the anonymity of the crowded postseason shopping center. On a few occasions they met up with other kids from the school and did the usual gawking and swearing that went with the age.

During the spring break, Ramon invited Billy to sleep over. His brother Jose, with whom he shared some space in the apartment, was away for the weekend. Joe and Jeannette were initially skeptical but approved after gaining Billy's promise to be home first thing in the morning.

Ramon lived in a cramped third-floor apartment close to Government Center. His brothers shared a room with his two older sisters. Ramon's older brother Jose shared space no bigger than an oversized closet. Two old army cots were wedged in tightly and that was their bedroom space.

Ramon's mother was a serious, small, pinched woman who scurried around the apartment, constantly complaining and constantly moving. Her husband was serving a life sentence for the murder of another drug dealer.

Adolescence

After introductions, Billy and Ramon took off for a walk downtown. Ramon told Billy that he had something special to show him. They ran full tilt a few blocks, breathing in the new spring air. They made a few right and left turns and found themselves at the river edge about to cross a bridge. Billy asked where they were going, and Ramon said it was a surprise but he would like it. They moved between the cavernous walls of long-abandoned woolen mills until they came to a structure that looked about to cave in. Ramon took Billy around the rear and moved slowly up the darkened stairs. There wasn't a sound other than the squeak of the rotting boards on the stairs and the landings. Suddenly, Billy smelled a sweet aroma and yelled at his friend to come back down the stairs before the building went up in flames. Ramon laughed and encouraged him to keep following him. The building was not burning. He knew where the smoke was coming from.

They reached the third floor and made their way through the darkened corridor to a door with a light showing behind it. The odor was much more pronounced now. Ramon knocked gently and entered a room that he obviously had visited before. Jose was startled. Both he and a naked young woman were puffing away at their marijuana joints, angry at the intrusion. He screamed at his little brother.

"What are you doing here? I told you never to come back here, you little bastard. And who's that with you?"

On the far side of the room, two entwined bodies continued their rhythmic movements despite the shouting. Jose slapped his younger brother hard on the cheek and shoved both boys toward the door. Before the door closed behind him, Billy caught the glance of the red headed girl who took a break from her lovemaking. She flashed a playful wink and then laughed.

School ended in mid-June and there was happiness and harmony in the Miculski home. The family rejoiced over Billy's marks being higher than expected. There was additional joy in their anticipation of another trip to Hampton Beach. Richie would not be with them this summer. He was going to work on the Cape at a restaurant owned by the family of a high school friend.

Billy was excited. The memories of the open space, the warm sun, the beach and the water gave him much joy. It had been a long, cold winter. He yearned to walk and run and swim and stare at the half-naked women. He would miss Richie, who in retrospect was a fairly good guy who gave him more attention than he was used to. Before leaving, Richie gave him the names of some of his beach buddies and told him that all he needed to do was follow the frisbee to find them.

There was one hitch. Jeannette's sister, Marie Brennan, asked if they could make room for her daughter. Billy had met Jim and Marie Brennan at the Christmas parties, but he had not met their daughter. There seemed to be some secret and something mysterious about her and about the request for her inclusion in their summer venture. He overheard fragments of a conversation between the adults one night and was sent up to bed so he could not discover the details.

He left his door ajar and sat close to the opening so that he could hear what was going on. From what he could gather, their daughter Terry was not in current favor. The Brennans wanted the Miculskis to take her off their hands. He heard pieces of sentences and words, but the occasional use of such words as probation, cocaine, and abortion were mixed in with the scramble. Joe and Jeannette did not have the heart to refuse family. They would do what they could to cool off the Brennan family crisis.

Before they parted, they paused in the hallway, and at that point, Billy knew that he was the subject of discussion. Joe reassured the Brennans that Billy would be no problem. He was a good kid. He kept to himself, did his chores, minded his own business. Jim Brennan was not completely reassured and commented that they were both teenagers. They all discussed the fact that there was a gap in their age, with Terry being on the young adult side of the curve. They all laughed and chuckled over the mystery and mire of adolescence.

Before Richie left for the Cape, he visited Billy in his room. He offered him the names of his buddies and a few telephone numbers. He asked Billy if he had ever met his cousin Terry, and when he shook his head, he sat down on a bedroom chair for a more lengthy conversation.

Richie smiled, shook his head, and proceeded to discuss "Terry the Terrible." She was basically a good kid, who unfortunately had a chip on her shoulder. Halfway through high school she had hooked up with a really bad crowd and had been one step away from doing some prison time. Terry was a whopping disappointment to Jim and Marie. They had adopted her after Marie found out that she could not have any more kids of her own. Terry's biggest sin was dropping out of her senior year in high school one month before graduation. Their own children had gone on to be valedictorians in high school and phi beta kappas in college.

The Brennans brought their wayward daughter to Hampton Beach twenty-four hours after the Miculskis began settling in. She remained in the back seat of the car while the adults offered each other hopeful hugs and kisses. Her delayed entrance was casual but dramatic. She slid out of the car lazily, offering the viewers a full glance at her voluptuous figure. The face was frozen in a composite mask of petulance and boredom. The short and neatly trimmed crown of auburn hair was a giveaway to Billy. She offered her aunt and uncle a polite peck on the cheek and then came over to Billy for a more intimate handshake. Her head tilted slightly and her lips widened to smile and say how happy she was to be at the beach. She gazed into Billy's frozen face and continued. "Hi, Billy. I'm your cousin Terry. Nice to meet you. I've been looking forward to this. I know we'll have a good time."

Her voice was soft but crisp. He could not bear to look at her face any longer. Instead he watched the full sensuous lips move as if in slow motion. He was forced to focus on the deep cleavage of her v-neck white cotton T-shirt.

The grown-ups took it all in, and all four of them were relieved to have the introductions over.

The Miculskis promised the Brennans that they would call on Friday for an end-of-the-week report. By Friday they had little to report. The weather had been good, the temperature was in the high seventies and the kids were getting along just fine.

The Miculskis were not a complicated pair. Although they did not announce the menus for the week, the suppers seemed to revolve around pastas, chickens, aand the inevitable hamburgers and hot dogs. The meal was set out at six o'clock, and grace before meals was predictable. Occasionally, Terry and Billy would look at each other in subdued amusement. The older and the younger teenager did not hang out together. Terry had her routines, which was to do her morning chores and spend the morning completely on the beach either swimming or tanning. Billy would sit on the wall and watch her, whenever he wasn't joining in a frisbee game or taking a swim himself. She was well aware that his eyes were on her and she managed to give him an eyeful of movements and gestures whenever she could.

The first week was indeed a pleasant one, with the adults doing their thing and the young ones going in separate ways while out of the house. The second week was different.

The mind of the adolescent is a fast-moving kaleidoscope of brightly colored thoughts, feelings, and fantasies. No one else, especially the adults, is allowed to share the drama. Thus, the much appreciated good news offered by the Miculskis after the first week failed to capture the intriguing by-play between their obedient charges. Billy was intensely aware of Terry's presence, despite his nonchalance. His eyes were the lens of a camera recording everything about her. He took note of her clothing, hairdo, makeup, whether she wore sandals or sneakers or nothing on her feet. Her movements gave him a stir even at a distance on the beach. At home, if she twisted slightly, bent over, sat up, or rose from a chair, he captured the moment for his nightly review. The scent of her soap, shampoo, and perfume penetrated his nostrils and was the cause of many an erotic fantasy. Her voice, laughter and giggles, added to a composite that was put together slowly and carefully in his mind. Even at night, while they all watched television, the antennae inside his ears recorded the soft scratch of her slacks shifting position on the sofa. To him she was some sort of supernatural creature and he was obsessed by her. To be living in the same house, eating at the same table, using the same toilet nearly drove him crazy. He loved the way she cluttered up the bathroom with her hair and body lotions. Each day he peeked over the porch railing to see the careless way that she draped her bikinis in the sun to dry. He made sure that he was close by when she left the bathroom from her shower, clutching her robe while fluffing her hair. She provided more material for his fantasies and dreams than he could fit in.

Terry welcomed the time out from the Brennan home. She was emotionally drained from the horrible experience of the abortion three months before. The father of the child insisted on the termination of the pregnancy and arranged it with a female cousin who had done it for other relatives. She hemorrhaged badly and after a 911 call from a motel room was rushed to the hospital. The senior Brennans were shocked and extremely disappointed.

Now she could relax and think out her next move. She quit school within a month of getting her diploma and the thought of going back passed through her mind. She had no job. She was in with a bad crowd. She did like the excitement and she truly loved the feeling that went with the marijuana and the coke. But she had been drugged and raped too many times to count and perhaps now was the time to turn her life around.

Lying on the beach all alone, she had plenty of time to weigh the choices of her life. Perhaps there was no way out. She had never truly had a friend she could trust and the adults in her life had always put her down. She thought of the pattern of her life since she had become a teenager. She recalled the shock at hearing about her adoption and she remembered vividly her determination never to be abandoned again. But the fact was she had just been abandoned and left to die. One memory kept recurring. It was the night that the Brennans in a fit of anger had told her that she wasn't their child. She couldn't be their child; she was too bad.

It was a crushing blow. She spent weeks and months crying herself to sleep. Why was she rejected? She didn't do anything wrong. Soon her grades began to slip in school. Her behavior became more conspicuous. Her temper became prominent in the school corridors and in the locker room.

She wanted to die, and in fact, she tried to kill herself several months after the Brennan's revelation regarding her adoption. She spent a week in the Holy Family Hospital psychiatric ward following the wrist laceration. It was here that she met Tomas. He understood her. He had been through the same thing. His parents had been gunned down on the street chasing a thief who had left their variety store. He vowed that he would find the killer and destroy him. A family member adopted him and felt he was outside the family structure like some sort of alien. Terry felt a kinship with Tomas. The common denominator was their rage.

Why was she thinking of all this now while basking in the warm sun on a beach in New Hampshire? She knew why. Last night, she talked too much. She couldn't help herself. Just before sunset, she invited her young admirer to stroll along the beach. Billy reminded her of Tomas. That haunted, hungry look. It wasn't quite the same, though. His parents were still alive. But like her own, they really didn't give a damn.

As she recalled last evening, she regretted some of the things she told about herself. He in return told little, other than his dismay over being abandoned. He was okay. He was her friend. When asked directly, he admitted to being the other kid in the room at the woolen mill. Neither wished to discuss the scene, but she obtained a promise from Billy that he would tell no one about their meeting.

Nothing really happened during the brief walk down the beach, but she sensed her power over him. He was five years younger than she, and at a stage where every moment in the company of a girl produced sparks and waves of delicious, sensual provocation. She admitted to herself that she had enjoyed teasing him and delighted in flaunting her bikinis. Seducing and provoking provided her with a warm feeling, which had led her into some tight situations over the past few years. Now it seemed kind of fun. The young guy was almost hooked, and she was feeling more and more horny as she led him on. She decided that it had been too long since she had had a really good screw.

Billy had his own set of feelings about the walk with Terry the night before. He recalled being drenched in the misty air of this real-life wonder woman. He had no will of his own. He felt helpless and loved it. She ran ahead of him and then she waited. She held his hand and let it go. She gave him seashells to hold and took them back. She was in complete control and he cherished it. At one point, at her request, he gently scratched an itch on her back. And when they sat on the seawall at the end of the walk, he obediently fetched her sandals and brushed the sand from between her toes.

The sound of her voice and laughter was intoxicating, but the words she spoke that evening confused him and worried him. She drew him into her life, a life that was troubled like his own. She spoke of being adopted and compared his lot with the Miculskis as similar. She recalled for him the crushing statements by the Brennans followed by their rejection and emotional banishment. Her eyes glistened with tears, soft and sad.

The "we" part was the most troublesome. At one point, she held him around his shoulders and hugged him tightly. Before letting go, she whispered in his ear. "Billy, we are so much alike. Both rejects. Both hurting so much. Some day it will be different."

At breakfast on Wednesday, Joe and Jeanette announced that they were joining their friends from up the beach for an evening at the local theater. Wednesday nights were half price, so why not. They suggested that Terry and Billy rent a video. They left plenty of chips and popcorn and soft drinks. Their only request was to not invite any other kids into their cottage while they were gone. If all went well, they promised a trip to the local restaurant on Friday to celebrate the end of their vacation.

Despite Jeanette's suggestion that the choice of the video be mutual, they returned a few minutes before the adults went out with the top hit "Pretty Woman." Joe asked Billy if that was his choice and mumbled something about the fact that there were no other good shows. In truth, Billy had chosen two Terminator movies that were totally unacceptable to his partner.

Alone with Terry. He had dreamed of it, and now he dreaded it. He felt so small, so awkward, so clumsy. After the Miculskis had gone out the door, Terry walked into her bedroom for a few seconds. She emerged smiling and standing on her toes, announcing that she had slipped into "something comfy" for the movie. It was cream-colored babydoll nightie with skin-tight shorts and a low-cut frilly blouse. The room suddenly closed in on him and he felt that he was in a closet again, although brightly lit. A wave of panic swept over him. It was Billy's turn to head for the bedroom, and it was not to slip into something comfortable. Against all of his urges and desires, he wanted to run away, hide behind the door and lock it. He simply was not ready. She followed him halfway to his room and pleaded with him to come back. She said she did not want to be alone, and that he really would enjoy the movie more than he thought.

Terry was oblivious to her nervous companion throughout the first half of the movie. She suddenly put it on pause, leaped up off the couch, and said that she was going to the kitchen to fill the popcorn bowl again. She asked him if he wanted another coke and he mumbled in the affirmative. The next thing he knew she was standing in front of him with the glass held tightly in her hand. She smiled and coyly stated that she had a condition before she gave him the glass. He looked up from the rocker and asked what it was, and she responded that it was a hug. She completely blocked his view of the TV set as she moved closer for him to comply. She set the glass on the floor, waiting for her reward. He started to rise out of the chair but she moved closer to him and her body disallowed any movement at that point.

Billy's recollection of the events of the next hour would be forever blurred by the ecstasy of an out-of-consciousness experience that fused uncontrollable yearnings with complete reward.

The Brennans arrived early on Saturday for the moving-out ceremonies. They brought gifts for the Miculski family. For Joe and Jeanette, a gift certificate to a local Lawrence restaurant. And for Billy, a video. He unwrapped it slowly, and smiled awkwardly. It was "Pretty Woman." They all laughed and explained that Terry had told them that it was really his favorite.

He spent the rest of the summer mooning about his separation from the girl he loved. Joe Miculski arranged a part-time job for him in a neighborhood variety store for a few hours a week. He could hardly concentrate on stocking the shelves and washing the floors. Her face kept coming before him, as well as the exquisite presence of her body.

There wasn't a day, perhaps even an hour, that he didn't think of Terry. Where was she? What was she doing? Was she thinking of him? Why didn't she call or come over? He knew she loved him; she said she did. And they were alike. They had a bond. They were rejects, but not to each other. They belonged together, and they would come together again. So often, he thought to himself, "God, I love you Terry. Please come back to me."

School opened in September but Billy did not return to the special needs schooling. The Miculskis were notified in August that he was to be bused to the West Lawrence Vocational School. The school board apologized for the late notification but stated emphatically that they had been under the impression that Billy's continued stay in the Miculski home was indefinite.

The choice of the vocational school was the result of tests Billy had taken in the spring. It revealed a definite proficiency in the workings of small objects and machinery. Billy hated the idea of being bused somewhere else, especially when he realized that he would lose touch with his friend Ramon. He was disappointed with the new routine and again fell into a moderately depressed state over the new change, something he had no control of.

All of this heightened his hunger to be with Terry. The night before school started, he called the Brennan home and left a message for his beloved partner. Two days later, Marie called back to say that Terry had left their home a month ago, and her whereabouts were unknown. Billy was absolutely morose. How could she do this without telling him? He retreated even more into a sulky, noncommunicative mood that worried the Miculskis. They knew nothing of his blissful affair with Terry and attributed it to the new school experience. The life seemed to have been drained out of him and nothing they could say or do pepped him up.

His longing for this one woman persisted, and nothing could spur him on to reorganize his life, such as new goals and new visions. However, a few weeks before Thanksgiving in the recreational area of the vocational school, Billy came home one day with his shirt torn and with a bruise below his left eye. No sooner had he arrived than the school principal called to congratulate the Miculskis on having a person like Billy living with them. He had become an instant hero during a major fight that had occurred on the lunch break. Both of the combatants were bigger than Billy and one had a knife. But Billy was on the scene and did not back away. Apparently when he asked them to stop fighting, the one with the knife attacked him and made a lunge toward his chest. The two of them tumbled on the floor and Billy managed to squeeze the knife out of his hand and throw it down the corridor.

The Miculskis warmed to Billy's modesty about the incident. Billy, on the other hand, was slow to accept the admiration that was growing within his peer ranks. He spent more time in front of the mirror, flexing his muscles, and began to imagine himself as all-powerful and at the same time, popular.

Billy knew it would happen some day, and some day was now. He simply couldn't be ignored anymore. No more being pushed around. He could push back and everyone knew it. He felt the strength in his bones and muscles, and liked the way he looked. Tall, gangly, skinny, but certainly the muscles and the strength were there. The growth of a few facial pimples was an annoyance, but he realized that they were a sign of his newfound virility. For Christmas, he asked the Miculskis for weightlifting equipment.

Along with this new sense of strength and power, he knew that his sex drive was in overdrive. Some of his classmates boasted of their prowess. He listened and he laughed, but inside he agonized for a return to the moments of rapture with Terry. No one could possibly take her place.

The second Christmas at the Miculski home brought a return to the down mood. No one from Salem came to see him, and he had no news about his beloved Terry. The Brennans dropped in for a drink on Christmas Day, and he listened intently to the conversation from upstairs. The last that they had heard about her was a month ago, when she had been brought to a Boston hospital with a fractured wrist. The details were fuzzy. All present agreed that the Brennans were well rid of her. She was not their flesh and blood. She had come from bad stock. No good would come of her.

As he had done the previous winter, Billy drifted into a crowd of kids at school that was on the fringe of the law. Tito Belvoir was the toughest one of the bunch. He had beaten up all who came to challenge him and welcomed any newcomers. He led a mixture of angry Anglos and Hispanics. His family claimed more relatives in prison than out. He did cocaine and ran errands for the town's heroin distributors.

Billy's exploits in the schoolyard before Christmas had earned him a nod and a handshake from the "big man." Billy really liked him. He bragged a lot but he could back it up. Billy was not about to challenge him. Quite the contrary. He felt safe as a member of "Tito's family." The other kids now looked up to him. He was somebody.

Billy got into the smoking and into the marijuana, but hesitated with the cocaine. Tito brought him along on a few errands. It was exciting. It was great. Breaking the law was no problem for him. It deserved to be broken. What had the law done for him, except take his mother away and stick him with families that didn't really want him.

The Miculskis confronted Billy in the early spring after a series of late arrivals for supper. He had explained it as extra projects at school. The call by Joe Miculski disproved this excuse and a major scene took place one night after supper. They insisted on knowing what he was doing. For the first time in over a year and a half, Billy yelled back. They were startled. He claimed that he was just hanging out with some friends, and he had a right to do this. Joe, on the other hand, insisted that he resume his regular schedule at school and at home and threatened that they would be forced to have a meeting with the DSS worker if he refused.

Billy erupted in a scary manner. He offered curses and complaints. He had a long list of bitches that he had been stomaching for too long. He didn't like all their rules and he didn't like being spied on. He took his rage to another level when he talked about being yanked away from his own family. Joe Miculski finally brought some calm to the out-of-control discussion and asked that all parties back off and think about the main issues. He said that they should meet again in a couple of days to discuss it.

While eating supper two nights later, Billy apologized and started crying. Jeannette sat quietly while Joe got up and put his arm around him. The two went into the parlor and sat side by side for about an hour talking in a much more civilized tone. As bad as he felt about being in the Miculski home, Billy knew that things could be much worse.

All went well for several weeks until a routine heroin delivery with Tito caused him a major trauma. He made a delivery to a notorious pimp known throughout town for ruling his harem with an iron fist. Rumor had it that the penalty for trying to steal a freebee from one of his beauties cost a broken leg or a broken arm. The price tag for any of the girls in his stable who tried to cheat him of his rightful income was higher. Small amounts of money withheld resulted in multiple bruises and larger amounts were likely to cause disfigurement of the body and face.

When they entered the abandoned gas station on the edge of town, Billy and Tito had interrupted a midafternoon nap shared by three people. The pimp was one and on either side were two women. One of them was Terry Brennan.

They quickly untangled from their knot of close body postures and all three sat on the floor to confront the intruders. Abdul quickly snapped a menacing pistol from underneath the mattress.

He ordered Tito to hand over the powder and tasted it quickly. He got up, pulled on his trousers, and turned around to see Billy and Terry staring at each other intently. He screamed at Terry, "You know this little shit?" Billy remained motionless and quiet. Terry looked away abruptly and then responded. "Of course, I don't. I don't know any little boys."

She was gone from his life as suddenly as she had entered it. Another betrayal. Another abandonment. He had allowed himself to fall in love. He trusted her, and she was playing with him now. She had used him and now she was dumping him. At the beach he truly believed that sex and love went together, two parts of one wonderful experience. Each one gave and took gently, freely, generously. Their bodies were the instrument of their souls. Simple, honest, innocent.

But it was a mirage, a hoax. The sexual abuse that he had suffered was now coupled by a different kind of sexual abuse, namely betrayal. Sex was really for the bigger, stronger person. She took pleasure with him, and she ultimately used him and hurt him. She dominated him, and she controlled him. He vowed that if these were the rules he would now play by them.

On a warm, humid June evening, the new roles and the new games began.

It was a good night for a walk through the park. It had been a busy week with Tito and the delivery business. Tito brought another guy who joined him at the edge of the park and offered him a beer. As they strolled along the pathway around 10 o'clock at night, they laughed and swapped war stories. The police busts and the close calls. The park usually emptied out around 9 o'clock and at this time they had the area pretty much to themselves.

They rested on a park bench while continuing to talk about the week's exploits. A young couple passed by their bench holding hands and smiling.

Tito threw an empty beer can in front of them and ordered them to return it to him. They shuffled off hurriedly, sensing trouble. He looked at his two buddies, grinned and said, "Let's have some fun, guys."

They caught up with the nervous couple within seconds. Tito barred their progress and rudely reminded them that they had disobeyed his orders regarding the tossed beer can. He then shoved the guy into Billy's arms with the command to hold him while he had some fun with the quivering girlfriend. Billy was the last of the three to rape her. The others were surprised with his brutality and his final message which he shouted out loudly. "You deserve it, you little slut."

The incident made the police blotter, the local headlines, and the six o'clock news. An extensive investigation followed. Miraculously no formal charges were made for lack of positive identification, even though Billy and the other two were suspects. The only clue the district attorney had was the girl's recollection of the rapists calling out a name that sounded like Tito, but it was not enough. Despite these findings, Joe and Jeannette Miculski were beside themselves. They had warned Billy months before about his new friends. They felt shamed and embarrassed by the repeated visits to their home by uniformed police.

Billy maintained his innocence throughout the whole sordid affair. For weeks he avoided contact with Tito and the other members of the gang. He felt that he had won a victory. He felt proud of himself. Inside, he felt absolutely no remorse. Just the opposite. A sense of power and control was building. Each day while lifting weights in his bedroom, he took a ritualistic peek in the mirror to measure the growth of his arms and shoulders. Each day he would feel a new glow in the changes apparent in the mirror. Big meant strong. Strong meant power. Power meant doing what you want. That meant pleasure. Pleasure meant no more pain. No more, no more.

In July, a meeting was called by the DSS worker with the Miculskis and Billy. There was an air of tension and uncertainty. Billy was not convincing regarding compliance with the rules.

As it turned out, the decision by DSS and the foster home, which was delayed, did not really matter. In the middle of August, he was arrested in his home and sentenced by a special judge dealing with drug trafficking to six months in a youth detention center.

The foster home phase of Billy's life was over. Because of his age, he was not sentenced to a county or state prison, but rather to a detention center for teenagers. It was a major turning point in his life, however. He began a period of troubled times that would include imprisonment and probation. A series of altercations, first in the detention center and then in a maximum security facility for youth offenders, placed him in clear view by the correctional system as a dangerous person who needed long-term confinement.

Sarah Smith

"Nana, help me! I'm bleeding. I'm going to die. Come upstairs! Hurry! Make it stop! Hurry!" Despite Sarah's prior exposure to school yard and locker room jokes about the mysterious menarche, she was totally unprepared for the real thing.

Grandma Gertrude lumbered up the creaky stairs yelling loudly for her precious ward to calm down. No, she wasn't going to die, and what would the neighbors think with all the yelling and screaming?

Gertrude tried to calm her down but firmly refused Sarah's request to sleep in her bed that night. As drunk as Judd was when he stumbled into bed, he insisted on having his woman beside him.

Sarah's own mother arrived home from her new waitressing job in Lynn around 1:00 A.M. Sarah was desperate. She ran downstairs and fell into her arms sobbing. Melanie was shocked. It had been more than three years since they had embraced.

Sarah told her mother of the horror of her first period, and added that Nana was mean and rough and didn't care about how scared she was. Melanie reeled from the emotional onslaught and her feelings were in a whirl. Instinctive anger toward her own mother competed with the sudden longing to take this child of her flesh into her arms and comfort her. And this is exactly what she did. She poured Sarah a glass of milk and they sat on the sofa in the parlor for over an hour comforting each other. Melanie shared her own early experiences. Sarah was not listening to the words as much as warming to the feel of the mother she had once had.

They talked about the course of their lives and what might have been. They cried over the loss of Billy to incarceration because of his behavior. Finally, when the crying had subsided, Melanie walked her baby upstairs and did stay the night with her in her own bed.

The next morning Gertrude burst into the room, cursing and swearing and demanding that Melanie go downstairs immediately.

Sarah recovered from the initial trauma of her menarche and resumed her role as "Grandma's little girl." Melanie was hurt and angry. She felt that she had been betrayed after she had let her guard down and tried to reclaim an emotional place in her daughter's life. Her growing sense of indignation and hurt rekindled a thirst for the bottle and she slowly but surely began drinking.

The toll of Sarah's emotional slippage led to absenteeism at school. Gertrude called to intercede on behalf of her baby and finally went to the

Adolescence

school itself to ask for a few more days of recovery. It had already been two weeks. Her teachers were unyielding in their demands that she come back to school or get a doctor's note explaining why.

On the day Gertrude went to the school, she arrived home that night feeling weak and dizzy. She went upstairs without talking to anyone and lay down on her bed to fall asleep. The next day, Judd could not rouse her and an ambulance was called. In the emergency room they diagnosed it as a stroke affecting her speech and the strength in her left arm and leg.

Without Gertrude in the apartment, things deteriorated quickly. Judd was completely lost. He could not provide his own meals and turned to a reliable liquid diet. Even when he wasn't falling down drunk, he was sullen, nasty, and removed from all responsibilities. Melanie took leave of her nighttime job to be with Sarah and soon discovered that her presence during the daytime was needed also. Sarah now had a better reason to stay home and only returned to school when a suspension notice was issued stating that she would not be promoted if she did not appear.

Melanie picked Sarah up at school and drove to the hospital daily. Judd visited the first couple of weeks, but when Gertrude was transferred to the rehabilitation floor, he cut down to twice a week. The two women in the house heard him crying in his bedroom during the evening. The only other sound emanating from the room was him falling to the floor or knocking down his rocking chair.

Sarah was a devoted grandchild. She held her grandma's hand for hours on end, crying and pleading with her to come home. At home, it was different. She reverted back to her fasting style, and her weight began to drop. Gradually, Gertrude regained her speech and some partial strength in her limbs. The discharge planner said that she needed to stay downstairs if she did return home.

One day the visiting nurse remarked to Melanie that Sarah's weight was bordering on critical, and explained that such organs as brain, heart, and kidneys could shut down if the level of her nutrition and hydration diminished much further.

Melanie brought her to the medical clinic at the Children's Hospital where once again the diagnosis of eating disorder, anorexia nervosa type, was made. The pediatrician did not feel the crisis was imminent, but warned that it was in the making and strongly recommended that she correct her eating habits.

Before she left, a psychiatrist was called in to review the case, but Sarah refused to talk with him. She screamed that she was not crazy like her mother and wanted to go home. Melanie was crushed by the outbursts and wondered if she could cope with it much longer.

Gertrude did come home for a short while. She suffered the second and final stroke between Christmas and New Year's. Sarah was inconsolable. Few people attended the wake, just her remaining family and a couple of friends.

The arrangements were made by Gertrude's second child, who inserted herself into the crisis when Melanie began drinking heavily. Anne Diamond was the second child born of Gertrude's second marriage. She had married well, given birth to one daughter who was making a name for herself as a teenage figure skater, and seemed to have it all together. She was married to a successful real estate broker. They lived in the newer section of South Salem and avoided Gertrude and her problems for many years.

Anne stepped forward not for any ulterior motive. There was no inheritance. But she wanted to avoid the embarrassment of a shabby wake and funeral, as it would reflect on her and her husband's business. Also to be preserved was the family name that was becoming quite well known on the sports pages.

She insisted that Melanie take more charge of her life but avoided committing herself to any more help at the time of the funeral. However, by spring, she was drawn back into the pathetic world of Melanie, poor Sarah, and an incapacitated Judd. Social Services contacted her as the only stable relative after evaluating an episode of attempted sexual abuse by Judd toward Sarah.

The episode was so traumatic to Sarah that she again required an evaluation in the emergency room, whereupon she was transferred to the Boston Children's Hospital critical care for what was now a major physical crisis. Her weight had dropped to eighty-six pounds. She required three days of intravenous fluids in the hospital. The final evaluation ultimately led to the plea by DSS that Anne consider temporary custody of her niece.

The convincing argument was the alternative. If Anne did not volunteer for this service, Sarah would be sent to a state-sponsored foster home similar to her brother's. Melanie was declared an unfit mother and had nothing to say about these dealings. The workers and the doctors explained to Anne and Cliff Diamond that if Sarah was sent away she would likely stop eating altogether and die.

Several preliminary meetings were held in the hospital prior to the move. Sarah was introduced to her older cousin, Holly, the figure skating star.

Holly openly protested the decision to invite her cousin into her family. She was an only child, an only daughter, and an only star. She felt that her career could be jeopardized by mother's divided attention. She was on the verge of breaking into the top echelon of her division. Anne and Cliff

Adolescence

reassured her that they had enough love and loyalty to her to share with the pathetic situation of her cousin Sarah Jane.

There was no sense in Sarah reentering the school program upon her release from the hospital. The school authorities advised her to stay home and repeat the eighth grade the following year.

Sarah's presence at home did require Anne to spend much more time during the day at home. She still found time, however, to go to the early morning and weekend practices with her daughter. Cliff went out of his way to welcome her to the family. Initially, she and her cousin Holly shared little time or talk. Holly's constant devotion to skating practice, gymnastic classes, and trips for competition filled the time. She was three years older than her cousin and quite image conscious. To hang out with a younger teenager wasn't cool. But there was more to it. She resented sharing the spotlight. She saw herself not only as the only child but as a true star worthy of total attention from her parents.

It was only a matter of time before Sarah began to regress in the setting, even though she realized that the Diamonds had saved her from a worse fate. She could not shake loose from the utter despair over losing her Grandma. The more attention Anne and Cliff gave to Holly's winter competitions, the more Sarah reverted to her ultimate refuge, her eating disorder.

The DSS worker met with the family and requested that Sarah consider the mental health clinic at the Children's Hospital. She absolutely refused and left her aunt and uncle and the worker totally frustrated. None of them wanted to kick her out with the inevitable consequence of starvation and death.

The crisis in the Diamond family around Holly's failure to graduate brought another regression. Sarah was brought to the emergency room of the Salem Children's Hospital and admitted once again for replenishment of food and fluids. The doctors and her aunt and uncle refused to take no for an answer. This time psychiatric treatment was necessary and Sarah had no choice but to accept it. The psychiatrist took time to explain to Cliff and Anne that the eating disorder was also a psychiatric disorder. Instead of being a depletion of food substances in the body, it was also a form of emotional malnourishment.

He traced the source as related to the years of family instability and dysfunction prior to her grandmother Gertrude entering the picture. The death of her grandmother around the time of her adolescent changes was too much for Sarah. In her confusion, Sarah equated the changes of her adolescent body with death. Growing older was perceived by her as coming closer to death itself. In her own confusion, she sought to avoid this by avoiding physical growth by starvation. To not eat was to slow her body's growth and therefore stay small and not die.

At first, Sarah refused to accept her eating disorder as her fault. It took many weeks of working closely with her counselor as well as her aunt and uncle. Anne and Cliff were losing their patience. They saw her problem as more willful and deliberate and insisted that she become more a part of the family rather than a preferred and spoiled one. They set out to offer her a list of simple household chores which Anne explained were part of her own responsibility as a family member. Cleaning up her own room, helping with the dishes at night, and once-a-month total housecleaning was something that had been a tradition in the Diamond family.

Sarah made a feeble attempt to comply, then Anne truly confronted her with her refusal to pick up her end of the deal. Sarah began purging her food after eating and taking to her bed, claiming weakness and inability to work. Both Ann and Cliff stated that the welcome mat was going to be pulled out from under her if she truly didn't turn her behavior around.

A family meeting at the clinic was long overdue. Sarah herself seemed to have blocked the attempt by her therapist, a sensible woman named Carol, for an update on the family dynamics.

Sarah was more forceful than anyone expected during the first half hour, releasing feelings of discontent with her family structure. The meeting was going nowhere. The counselor Carol called for a time out where upon she pleaded with each party separately out in the corridor to soften their attitudes. When the meeting resumed, she pointedly reviewed each family member's major gripe in a clear but slightly humorous way. By the end of the session, all parties were relaxed and relieved of their pent-up resentment.

Carol explained to the Diamonds that she herself may have been a party to the crisis. She said that she had been working with Sarah for several weeks to develop more trust and more self-esteem from a goal-setting plan she had devised. Apparently, it had partly backfired in Sarah's staunch refusal to comply with the household rules.

Sarah and Carol had developed a working relationship that did blossom at this meeting. Part of it was her own revelation to Sarah that Carol had a serious eating problem herself during her teen years. She shared with her the depression that she endured that led to a serious suicide attempt. Gently but firmly, she led her patient along a path of more self-esteem and assertiveness. Carol's plan was simple. Establish goals and reach them.

She had developed a new wrinkle on how to do this with patients and it worked. She would enter the goals in a notebook that Sarah would bring home. On the same line as the goals, there was a column marking achievements, and next to that another column marked "ounces." Carol and Sarah were to establish a goal for the week or the month, and when it was accomplished, they would write next to it the points (ounces) that she had earned. This was to identify her goals and her newfound strength that they measured by the pound or the ounce. It was no coincidence that the choice of terminology was also the name that had been used to identify her failure in terms of sustaining weight.

Things got better in the Diamond household and also in school. As the spring of her junior year approached, Sarah brought to her counselor her dilemma over the upcoming junior prom. She realized that she had never dated a boy, and felt that this was a goal that she simply could not accomplish. Coupled with this discouragement was the fact that Carol had cut her hours at the clinic because she was now in the third trimester of her first pregnancy. Sarah's confidence in herself and Carol had grown to the point where the termination of their sessions was expected to be a healthy event and not a source of failure. Carol openly expressed her wish that her patient offer her the best prize of all, and that was to accomplish the goal of finding a date for the junior prom.

Unfortunately, two events occurred that threw Sarah's plans off track. Neither of them were of her own making.

The first was the eruption in the Diamond home of the confrontation between Anne and her husband over an affair that he had been hiding. This coupled with Holly's failures during her winter competition spread a pall over the Diamond household.

But perhaps the most traumatic event was Carol's precipitous delivery of her first baby three weeks before she was due. There was no time for the planned termination meeting between Carol and Sarah. Sarah was deeply saddened that she could not say goodbye to her friend and mentor. Carol was more than a therapist; she was a dear friend and a number one role model.

It was around the same time that her uncle Cliff Diamond left the home and the marriage forever. No explanation and no goodbye for Sarah. He just walked out the door. Another disappointment, another rejection. Anne talked to her girls separately. Holly was inconsolable. She accused her mother of ruining her father's life as well as her own. Sarah overheard a particularly ugly confrontation one night. Holly yelled out her rage at being a "skating doll" for her mother's benefit more than her own. She lamented the lost opportunities to be like other kids, to be normal. She ended her tirade with a vicious attack on Sarah herself. In Sarah's confusion, she totally misinterpreted Anne's view of Cliff's infidelity. She began thinking that she was the cause. That she was the intruder. Was Holly right? The men and women in her life seemed to go away. Was it her fault? Was she bad? Sarah wondered what would happen to the family now that Cliff was gone.

The old feelings swept over her in the ensuing weeks. More changes in her life; more apprehension; more instability; and again a renewed sense of futility, helplessness, and guilt. Her depression and anxiety snowballed and led to the familiar pattern of disrupted eating. Only now her guide, her friend, and her savior was not around to help her.

Carol did not reject her phone calls, despite her own busyness with her brand-new daughter. She agreed to talk with her nightly for half an hour until she could find another therapist in the clinic.

The new therapist at the clinic introduced herself as Janine. She was a few years younger than Carol, but had a nice smile, a warm handshake and an inviting personality. Most importantly, she was well schooled by Carol in the dynamics of Sarah's emotional problems. Twice-a-week meetings were arranged for the first month with the option of continuing same or going back to the once-a-week pattern. Janine wasted no time in picking up where Carol left off as far as going to the roots of the eating disorder problem.

Her interpretations went a step further than even Carol had dared to. Janine talked about Sarah's part in the eating disorder program, not in a blaming or accusatory way, but in a way where her subconscious mind was directing the course of the illness. She talked about the "worry factor" that was at play in her interactions with other people. She pointed out to her that her difficulty in trusting people and accepting real love was being translated into expecting others to worry over her weight loss, which seemed like care and attention. It took many visits for Sarah to buy into this interpretation, and only after she had placed much worry on the shoulders of Janine did she begin to see how it worked.

Janine explained that her kind of manipulation, as subconscious as it was, was keeping her from appreciating real affection and real love from other people. Sarah resented this interpretation so much at the beginning that she threatened to pull out of the therapy. It was only a phone call from Carol one evening that turned it around and allowed for Janine and Sarah to move forward with the therapy. Sarah courageously determined that she would not slip back into her old ways of anorexia and bulimia.

Her new therapist represented a new role model for Sarah that was now imperative, since she had returned to the home of her mother after the breakup of the Diamond household.

Her next major challenge lay immediately ahead. This was the senior year syndrome. Was she ready?

It started out okay. September of the final year of high school is an exciting time. Enthusiasm is contagious. There is a sense that the final year will bring a wave of nostalgia, a sense of pride, and an expectation of accomplishment. The last time that friends will be together. The final year of schooling that began in kindergarten brings all of the above feelings and yet a sense that time will not wait for the growing process. This sense of responsibility and apprehension is much more palpable at the start of the second semester. The clock does not stop ticking.

Sarah was eighteen when classes started. Despite being one year older than most of her classmates, she entered the year with a sense of doubt and apprehension. In the background was the instability of her home situation. Her mother was still only working part time and supplementing her income with a welfare check. In addition to that, her mother was dating more and bringing men home on occasion for an overnight stay. Sarah managed to enter the classes with a determination to do well in her studies. Despite the distractions, her marks were tolerable. By Christmas she had achieved a B average.

It was shortly after the Christmas vacation when her mother came home one afternoon and announced that the doctor had made a diagnosis of cirrhosis of the liver. Melanie assured her that it was not fatal but it was a warning that she could not drink at all. Sarah received another blow a few weeks later in the form of an announcement by Janine that she was leaving for another clinic. It was a dark time for Sarah. Fortunately for her, Janine had been in communication with her old counselor Carol, who announced that she was coming back to the clinic on a modified schedule. A happy reunion. The two of them picked up where they left off and both of them thanked Janine for the wonderful job that she had done in helping Sarah to keep her balance and head for the finish line of graduation.

Sarah indeed did graduate, despite anxieties and despite some temptations to regress into her eating problems. By the time she had graduated, she had accomplished another goal set up with her beloved Carol. She had a part time job as an aide in a local nursing home.

Ruth Malone Reardon

Ruth was almost a clone of her mother Rita. Not only did she look like her, but she had her temperament as well. The temperament included the Italian feistiness as well as the affectionate and compassionate giving quality. They had truly bonded from an early age. The two of them could spark off but they would end up hugging and kissing and crying. Most importantly, Ruth trusted her mother. Rita could not lie or deceive her. She was always there.

The rites of passage went smoothly. No surprises. Just as predicted, with Mom in her corner all the way. What was a surprise for Rita was the sudden blossoming of her little baby. It seemed to happen overnight. By the time she was fourteen, she stood 5'8" and showed the beginning of a stunning figure. Jet black hair, the high cheekbones, full lips. The only thing that separated twinship with mother was deep blue eyes and fair skin, Eddie Malone's contribution.

She had plenty of offers for dates, even in her freshman year. She was shy and hesitant and waited until her sophomore year before she began going out with some of the high school kids. As a football cheerleader, she stood out from the crowd. It seemed that every member of the football team, and even the coaches, would take a time out on occasion to look at the practicing beauty on the sidelines.

What was so important was her basic sense of her own worth as well as a sharp sense of humor. She never took herself that seriously and, as with her mother, kept her eye on what her goals were and what her values were. She did not want to engage in sexual activity, but she was not a prude. Many an eager young swain was put down sharply when it was apparent that he wanted to cross over the line.

Her academic goals were fixed. She admired her stepfather, Joe Reardon, and her mother for their chosen careers. She became interested in medicine after hearing so much talk at the dining table and on the occasions of their completed tasks each day. She told them that she would either become a nurse or a doctor someday.

With all the popularity, peer pressure, and the offbeat invitations to join protests and secret cliques, she clung to her parents as the prime role models. Dr. Joe was funny, fair, attentive, and affectionate. He introduced his new family to the little social extras that made life in Marblehead unique. Family memberships at the yacht club and country club expanded her acquaintances, but she never got sucked in to using them for popularity or prestige.

Ruth Angelina Malone Reardon graduated in the top five of her class. She chose mother's old school, Boston College, as her next challenge.

Alan Malone Reardon

Alan took the jock route. It started early. Although his father Eddie Malone was never truly close by his side, he was never far away. His law career and his second marriage took precedence, but his son's athletic prowess did not go unnoticed. Snapshots and videotapes were presented to little Alan all throughout his Little League career.

Alan wanted his father's love and approval right from the beginning. But he realized, particularly during the overnight stays in Boston, that Dad's new wife came first, and even before her, Dad's career. Dr. Joe Reardon complicated things by being a fairly nice guy. But he wasn't Alan's father, and he wanted Mom more than he wanted another son. Alan was not without role models as his adolescence approached. But he simply did not trust his father or stepfather to be the number one person in his life.

Along came Pete Saunders. Pete was a legend in the town of Marblehead. All-everything in high school, he then distinguished himself at Syracuse University as the greatest running back since Jimmy Brown. Married with two daughters, he drifted back to his roots as a high school math teacher and eventually as athletic director.

He started out as a young coach in the Pop Warner league along with his job as a math teacher at the high school. He already had his eye on a career back at his high school and wanted to develop some young players that could move into the school ranks. The local touchdown club was a demanding group and his eventual career depended on developing talent. He spotted Alan immediately as an unusual raw talent. He stood head and shoulders above the rest. The kid could run, tackle, and throw the ball better than the rest. He listened attentively to his coach, worked hard, and warmed to the praise of his mentor. Alan won the freshmen team MVP award. Even though Rita and Joe attended most of the home games, it was Coach Pete's praise that counted.

The stage was set for a one-dimensional passage through the changes and challenges of adolescence. Alan grew bigger and stronger and copped one prize after another. In his junior year, he was the first-string quarterback and led the team to a state title. The townspeople awoke to this new talent and savored the presence of a latter-day Pete Saunders.

College scouts showed up at the games. Phone calls were made to the Reardon home, intercepted by Joe and Rita. They told Alan that it was much too soon to get involved in the recruiting game. Even Coach Saunders feared that his protégé would be distracted from the ultimate goal of his final year.

And how big a year it was. Another perfect season. Another armful of trophies. The recruitment flood gates opened. He could pick his college. The list narrowed down to three. One East Coast, one Midwest, and one West. He chose Harvard over Notre Dame and Stanford. His mother was delighted; he would stay close to home. Joe Reardon was neutral but happy for his stepson. Coach Saunders was not happy. He saw Harvard as a dead-end street for athletes who could make it to the pros.

Perhaps it was the advice given by his father, Eddie, that turned him off from choosing a big time showcase. Before his decision, Eddie took him out to dinner and told him that a good education was not the name of the game. After school let out, no matter whether it was the sporting world or the business world, it was not what you knew but who you knew.

But there was another compelling reason. And that reason had to do with Alan's growing doubt in himself. As graduation approached, he suffered serious moments of anxiety and depression. He felt alone. Without warning, he was struck by anxiety attacks. He was confused and did not know what to do, but he was too proud to tell anyone or ask for help. He simply did not feel ready to leave the environment that had been so protective to him. Something inside was missing. He had no real solid friends and he doubted his honesty and integrity even with his own family. Life had been too easy for him. He had not given much to anyone in return. The little boy inside was afraid and was surfacing into his conscious mind.

It started in February of his senior year when his classmate and girlfriend Linda told him that she was pregnant. What was he going to do about it? He was shocked and confused. He begged her to keep it a secret until he could think it over.

They had started dating early in the football season. She was a cheerleader. Despite the other opportunities, Alan and she felt that this was the real thing and became an item at school. She had sex with him a half a dozen times, mostly unprotected. They were in a dream world. They truly believed that they were special and nothing could go wrong.

Who could he turn to? He was too ashamed to talk to his coach, and he did not feel close enough to his stepfather. His father Eddie did not give him much satisfaction: How could he be so stupid? No precautions, no protection. Didn't he realize that it could screw up his career? No woman was worth it. He advised an abortion. All so simple. Just like a messed-up school paper. Just erase it and start over. Alan felt sick to his stomach after he hung up the phone.

It wasn't that simple. For the first time in his life, he had screwed up big time off the playing field. A couple of close friends gave him little consolation. He did have genuine feelings for Linda. What about this new life inside her? What about her family? Sooner or later he would have to tell Rita and Joe. Better sooner.

They were startled and hurt, but they did offer him the best advice of anyone. They arranged a meeting with the other family. It took place in Linda's home. Her parents were cordial but visibly angry and resentful. These "kids" could not have picked a worse time. Both of them were on the brink of graduating and moving on with their lives. Both were headed for college, Mount Holyoke for Linda and Harvard for Alan.

Everyone had something to say. There was no particular order and there was no leader of the discussion. The comments were offered spontaneously and at times it became repetitive.

What did the kids really want? Should Linda deliver the baby? If so, what then? Should she postpone her educational plans to take care of that child? Should she go to Mount Holyoke and leave the baby with the family? Should they get married and defer their college opportunities? Should they marry and live off campus at one school or the other? Should she get an abortion and continue their educational plans without a child? Should they put the child up for adoption?

Despite all the discussion, they handed the decision to Alan and Linda. One thing, however, was clear. That was the different opinions regarding abortion. Linda's parents could understand that choice and live with it. Rita and Joe, on the other hand, cited their religious and personal beliefs against it.

Linda had the abortion at Brigham and Women's Hospital in Boston. Things did not go completely well following the procedure. After she came home, she slipped into an emotional decline, losing two weeks at school. Alan visited her at the house and received a cool welcome from Linda and her parents. She finally told him that she would like to take some time apart from him to sort out her feelings. One month before graduation they officially broke off their relationship.

Alan was not accustomed to rejection. His teammates and classmates loved him. The whole town of Marblehead had him on a pedestal. He knew of at least ten girls he could sleep with anytime he wanted. But this girl wanted no part of him. It was a shocker. In addition to that, Rita and Joe could not hide their disappointment in his support of the abortion.

As much as he resented their stand, he respected it. He thought a lot more about his mother. The more he thought the more he realized what a good woman she was. She stuck by him when his father cheated and abandoned the family. She fed him, clothed him, and took him to all the practices and games. She had never betrayed him. Nor did she now. But had he betrayed her?

For the first time, he looked back over his life as an adolescent, not in terms of measuring his athletic success, but his success as a person with the people around him. He realized that he had used the girls around him to pump up his ego. He fed off the flattery. But had he turned away from his own family? His fans seemed to be all the family that he needed during those years.

Now, it was coming to an end. The Malone era at Marblehead High would become history. Another school, another team, another season. So what! Who really gave a damn about him? Who was he anyway? He had talent and good looks, but did he know what life was really about? Did he have the heart and guts to take on new challenges and changes without playing the role of the super jock?

Jessica Reardon

The death of a mother is the most devastating loss a child can suffer. The why of it is incomprehensible. Reassurances of mommy's presence in another world are untenable, unacceptable distractions. Mommies are "now" persons. Here, real, giving, hugging, kissing, laughing, crying. If they are gone, then it should only be for a while. Mommies may go to the store, mommies may go to church, mommies may visit a friend, but they cannot be gone permanently.

The grief of a child over a mother's death leaves serious scars. The child simply does not have the emotional tools to make the adjustments over a period of time that an adult might. For a child to let go of the most important person in the world is one thing, but for a child to be asked to attach to another person as a substitute is a much harder task and requires a much longer period of time. Jessica, in addition to all this, went through the ordeal of witnessing a long, slow dying process and was left with horrible images of a weak and withering body that finally expired.

As she was confronted with the terrible challenge of adolescent change, she did regress and was evaluated and treated by the mental health team. That team understated in their records their own personal and group conclusions mostly for the sake of her father, Dr. Joe Reardon. They said that she was suffering from major depression with psychotic features.

Dr. Reardon insisted on a meeting with his colleague and the two spent over an hour discussing Jessica's problems. Joe was confused and angry about the details concerning Jessica's problems around the time of his wife's death, which had not been revealed to him by anyone at the time. In the course of her treatment at the hospital, the staff had put together a lengthy history of this traumatic event in her young life.

One thing that he did know was that Rachel hastened her own death. The autopsy report listed several lacerations around her neck and abdomen. She literally bled to death one night in the company of her mother and a West Indian cook. The family doctor arrived minutes after she expired. Joe himself was en route from Marblehead after receiving an emergency call at the hospital. The cause of death was officially recorded was ovarian cancer with metastases. He now realized this was not the immediate cause of death.

What he didn't know was the extent of exposure of his young daughter to these horrible events. According to the psychiatrist, she was quite aware of her mother's final hours. She was also caught up in a confusing and chaotic behavior, not only of her mother but of her grandparents and the household staff.

Reginald and Agatha Bromfield regretted their invitation to their daughter to stay the second summer. There were two reasons. One, her cadaverous, physical condition boded ill for a lengthy survival. Second, they had to postpone moving to Belgium where Reginald had recently been posted as the new American Vice-Consul. His retirement had opened the door for long-overdue payoffs from his political friends.

Agatha's staff was depleted by layoffs and intra-staff squabbles in anticipation of the closing down of the estate while abroad. Although she herself was capable of administering to her precious daughter's needs the previous summer, she found herself overwhelmed with the advanced state of physical illness. Rachel's health had slipped away gradually but seemed to take a precipitous course that summer. Agatha insisted that her only remaining servant who also doubled as a cook help her with the bathing and linen changes. The cook asked for more money and was refused. It was not a good situation at the manor. Tempers flared.

Meanwhile Rachel's behavior began to take a change for the worse along with her physical demise. Shortly before she arrived at Bromfield Manor, her oncologist told her father that a recent MRI showed some metastatic spots in the brain. As the summer wore on, she became more forgetful and more irritable and was given to terrible outbursts aimed mostly at her mother.

Jessica's visits to her mother's bedroom, also known as the princess room, were reduced from three times a day to twice a day, and in the final week, to ten minutes each evening. Jessica sensed that the end was near and the level of her own grief increased. She came to dread the evening sessions, as brief as they were. It was as if the darkness outside the room was creeping into their souls. Mother was leaving her. Mother refused to turn on the lights. She was so weak that she could no longer sit up. More and more Jessica became frightened of her uncontrolled ravings about visions filling the room. One night she claimed that a strange bird flew into the room and hovered over her face, fluttering its wings. She begged the animal not to hurt her. She told her daughter that she could not sleep for fear that the bird would return to devour her.

A few days before she died, she asked Jessica to lie down beside her because she felt a terrible cold in her body. She knew that she was dying, but her damaged brain was not functioning. With Jessica at her side, she began spewing out a mixture of rational and bizarre thoughts. She talked of her parents and her husband, but not her daughter. She ranted over her parents' plans to abandon her and go to Europe. She talked of her husband, Joe, as being unfaithful because he did not come to visit her more often. She insisted that Jessica do all she could after she died to keep her father from fucking another woman. Jessica was stunned. She had never heard the word before.

Jessica could not sleep that night. Her thoughts were filled with the horror of being abandoned and the worthlessness and emptiness of her life. She also thought about Mother's callous neglect of her. At no time did she talk about what would happen to Jessica. How could she be so cruel? So selfish? In her dreams that night, she heard her own voice saying words that she had never uttered, words that were inconceivable. "I hate you, I hate you."

In most mansions and manors, there are two worlds: upstairs and downstairs. Jessica found some relief from the attention and affection she received from Carrie Cordero. She was the irascible cook, chauffeur, gardener, and companion to Queen Agatha.

Carrie took Jessica under her wing almost from the moment she arrived. The senior Bromfields had neither the time nor the inclination to comfort their sullen granddaughter as they watched their precious daughter slip away.

Carrie's kitchen offered her a safe haven amidst the sounds, sights, and smells created by this colorful enchantress from the Caribbean. Jessica loved to hear of the manners and mores of Carrie's island homeland. As Rachel grew weaker their sense of helplessness drew the two of them together. Carrie's humor, however, gave way to obsessive thoughts about death.

One night, Carrie told Jessica that in her island home the soul of a dying person could be claimed by good spirits or evil spirits. The devil often tried to enter the home and take up residence to stake his claim at the time of death. He would appear as a bird or large insect in the room of the dying person. Sometimes he would take the form of a simple breeze or wind that blew in the window from outside.

To keep the evil spirits away, her native kinfolk in Trinidad turned to rituals. They offered prayers and invocations to the good spirits. Special candles were lit and lasted all day, both during the prayer sessions and in the absence of any person in the dying person's room. Stuffed dolls and animals were crafted, and their role was to be the objects of needles and pins that would be stuck into them deeply to penetrate any essence of an evil spirit.

The psychiatrist concluded his chronicle of horror by describing the final scene to Dr. Joe. On the evening of Rachel's actual death, Jessica was not allowed upstairs. She could only hear Agatha screaming and crying. Carrie kept running up and down the stairs replacing blood-saturated towels. When it was over, they found little Jessica huddled in the far corner of the kitchen crying. She was clutching her favorite stuffed animal Missy in one hand, with the other hand she repeatedly stabbed the dog with a dining fork.

Joe Reardon relayed all of this to his wife Rita, who was horrified. She felt an overwhelming sadness and sense of protection for her stepdaughter. Joe also relayed the psychiatrist's advice, which was to take things slowly. Another school year was approaching. Despite her marginal progress through the early grades, they enrolled her in a private school in the neighboring town of Beverly. Boarding school was dismissed. They wanted her home at night.

Both felt that despite her emotional distance, they would not give up on this child. She had been through too much. And as members of the medical profession, they knew there was hope when a family stuck by a child in a loving and consistent manner. Separation from them was the worse choice of all, and they would not hear of it. Joe agonized over his daughter's failure to develop like other kids. Rita, despite her persistent efforts to engage her stepdaughter on a girl-to-girl basis, felt shut out and rejected. She vowed she would not quit on her, however.

Ruth and Alan fared no better. Ruth's weekends home from college were few and far between as the year wore on. However, she would shower her with souvenirs of Boston College and make an effort to invite her to her room to talk.

Alan invited her to attend football games and pep rallies, but gave up after repeated excuses. He was baffled by the remoteness of her mind, the plastic smile, the strange quality of her conversation. She never appeared agitated, never sad, but never quite in sync. When he was asked about his sister by friends and teammates, he refused to talk. Discussions about Jessica within the family left him confused and frustrated. Too many medical terms. More than once he told Ruth that Jessica was really weird.

Jessica's IQ was above average, but her grades continued to be below average throughout high school. One teacher described the dilemma as driving a car with the brake on. This teacher took a particular interest in this shy, remote child with the bland look. Despite hours of extra help after school, her grade level never wavered.

As she was finishing the third year of high school, the same teacher sat with her pupil and inquired what her plans were after she graduated. Jessica did not have a ready answer, and thought for a while. She then responded that she had no definite plans. The teacher would not accept this and kept prodding her to come up with some idea of a life after high school. Desperate for some spark of interest or ambition, the teacher invoked a few clichés. When asked if she didn't want to make something of herself, Jessica gave a puzzled look, hesitated for a few moments, and said that "there was nothing of herself to make." The final question to her pupil received the most chilling and baffling response. "What will you do next year when you graduate?" Jessica smiled, "Stay home, of course."

Her fear of growing up, of accepting change and challenge was manifested by some clues that were unmistakable both at home and at school.

Since she refused to go to the shopping malls with Rita or with Ruth, dresses, shoes, leisure wear were picked out and handed to her, usually with some sales pitch about the color and style. Invariably, she would store anything new under her bed or in the back of the closet. Only when her customary apparel was tattered or beyond repair would she concede to Rita's insistence to change. Rita would then accompany her to her room where she would discover the whereabouts of the unused clothing. She refused to be watched while putting on clothes, such as sweaters or coats. The teachers reported that she absolutely refused to undress in the girls' locker room. She would wear her gym class attire under her regular garments and then pull those garments back on after the exercise period. No one was allowed to see her body. Rita noticed once that she would truly avoid standing in front of the hall mirror.

At Christmas or birthday time, she refused to state a preference for a gift. She repeatedly informed the family that she needed nothing and she did not want anything new. She never read a newspaper and avoided watching the evening news. Around the supper table she would respond to direct questions politely but never initiated a conversation. If a news item of tragic proportions was discussed, she tried to leave the table to go up to her room.

Somewhat paradoxically, her bedroom was spotless and well ordered. After her mother died, she insisted that no one enter her domain without her permission. Her father refused this demand, and reminded her that she was still a member of the family and that she was still his child. He insisted that despite her right to privacy she simply could not refuse any family member who asked to see her.

The harmony and tidiness of her room furniture and possessions did not reflect on the state of her mind. No pictures on the wall, no clock, no radio, and only a small TV set in the corner. Rita noticed that the dial was repeatedly pointed to public broadcasting or Disney channels. She seemed to want no information of the real world around her. She did her homework at night at a small desk which rarely showed any clutter or disarray. Each morning her papers were folded into a school bag which she zipped tightly and laid in the hallway while she ate breakfast. One morning Rita invited her to open the bag to slip in some cookies. Jessica ran over and grabbed the bag and told her not to put her hands in it. Rita smelled a awful odor as the bag passed under her nose. She quickly fingered her way to the bottom and pulled out the smelly remnants of her favorite stuffed dog, Missy. She had not seem the animal since the week of their wedding. At that time, Jessica insisted on bringing it to the wedding ceremony and her father had refused.

The pattern of remoteness and avoidance continued. The summer before her senior year of high school, Jessica showed additional signs of trouble and emotional distortion. She absented herself from the walks on the beach with her father. She refused to have dinner at the yacht club. More and more she was late for supper and at times absent.

After she had been holing up in her bedroom for three days, Joe and Alan forced themselves through the door of her bedroom. She ran to a far corner of her room and cowered like a frightened animal. She screamed at them to go away and leave her alone. In the emergency room it took three staff members to hold her on the stretcher while the doctor attempted a perfunctory physical exam. She spit and clawed and shouted fragments of unintelligible words. Finally, in an exhausted state, she lay on the stretcher and stared up at the ceiling. The decision was to transfer her to McLean Hospital in Belmont. As the doors of the ambulance closed, her screams could be heard even in the emergency room. "You are the evil ones, you are the devils. But you will not have me. You will not enter me."

CHOICE

No time of life presents more change and challenge, and no time of life such an abundance of choices. As in the preadolescent year, the early choices of the adolescent do not really affect the serious course of their life.

In early adolescence, one decides what to wear, eat, who to hang out with. Choices on what subjects to take in school, choices of athletic or extracurricular activities, choices of friends, choices of movies, music, heroes, heroines, choice of role models, choices of scapegoats.

All of these are stretching exercises for the bigger, more meaningful decisions. As the teen years come to an end, other choices will shape the contour of one's character. Decisions must be made about certain values in life and certain pathways to take beyond high school. And most importantly is the issue of how to deal with one's sexual drive.

The "to be" issues of young adulthood are close at hand. Therefore, the choices of late adolescence take on a more somber tone. And as in the early childhood years, the decisions about one's future are greatly influenced by the advice, example, and genuine love offered by the primary caregivers, one's parents.

Let us now review the changes, challenges, and choices that affected the lives of seven children. Quite clearly, these children did not start out with the same amount of love and limits. The Smith children were the victims of serious parental neglect; in distinction, Rita Malone worked diligently to spare her children from the ravages of a divorce and abandonment by their father. What becomes apparent from the lives of these children are the unpredictable forces outside parental influence that certainly may alter the path of their adolescence. We begin to understand the dangers of being overprotected, as with Holly Diamond, as well as the terrible trauma that was suffered by Jessica Reardon around the death of her mother.

Finally, special attention will be paid to Jessica's struggle with a major mental illness. And I will offer a more detailed description of the most serious of our mental illnesses, schizophrenia.

Billy Smith

The one thing that the Miculski family offered was stability. Secretly, Billy admired Joe. He was solid and predictable. He did not love him, but on occasion he found himself liking him. Jeanette did not trust Billy and vice versa. Richie was okay, but just enough older to be out of reach as a big brother.

Early in his life, Billy was cheated of the two most fundamental expectations with parents. Love and limits. With the Miculski family he found limits but not love. They never quite defined their reasons for accepting a foster child. It was more than a good heart. The death of their daughter left a void that remained unfilled. Consciously they knew that Billy could not replace her. Then there was the more natural problem of midlife—the empty nest syndrome. With Richie going off to college, they were apprehensive about living in a house with one more unoccupied bedroom.

The Miculskis were okay. They were kind and generous to Billy. They did include him in family gatherings and traditions. They never referred to him as a foster child. Joe offered a measure of genuine affection with some occasional roughhouse behavior and even a bear hug. It was spontaneous and part of his nature.

Billy knew that he had a good deal, a heck of a better placement than in Medford. Despite that knowledge, he could not cross over the invisible line and surrender his pent-up feelings of hurt and betrayal. He had learned not to trust grown-ups. His father rejected him, his mother seduced and abandoned him. His first foster home used and abused him. His social workers lied to him. Worst of all, he could not trust himself. Billy had no gauge of his individual worth. No standard to measure himself by. He did not know what it was like to freely, openly give affection and receive it back. His only experiences were sexual in nature, and he always came out the loser.

He had never felt good about himself. From his earliest recollections, he was always being scolded and punished. The residual anger and resentment fueled a desire to get back at an unfair mommy, grandmother, teacher, or foster parent, thus ensuring another act of uncivil disobedience. No one had ever given him expectations to live up to; just the opposite. If they really thought he was that bad, then he'd show them.

Joe and Jeannette set up some reasonable rules as a member of their family. Billy complied as best he could. For good reason. He was safe for the time being. But at no time did he allow himself to feel good or proud of his behavior. Why should he? Being good only got you hurt.

Complying with the Miculski rules gave him some control of his life. But identifying with them was difficult. Before he could emulate good people, he had to somehow even the score with the bad ones. He had to empty out the hurt and rage. For Billy there were no acceptable role models during the early years of his adolescence. The closest he came to admiration and respect was watching professional wrestlers. His interest in weightlifting allowed him to work at something and feel the results. Big, strong men were worth copying. Out of it would come power.

His teachers at the special education classes were neuters—nice people who knew nothing of pain and suffering. The technical school staff were mostly men. Tougher and gruffer, not much else.

Ramon Hidalgo was a friend. No pretense, no judgment. Just a school acquaintance who liked to do the same things. The two felt comfortable together. Neither one wanted to be like the other, just be together. Ramon's older brother Jose was cool. He was tough. He was smart. He protected himself. He made things happen. Illegal things—that was great. He knew how to handle girls too. And he had big muscles.

More and more, Billy's masturbatory fantasies involved the theme of hurting others and being hurt. In many of the scenes he saw himself initially as a small, helpless victim of sadistic men and women. The theme ended up transformed and reversed into him being the big muscular man who gained revenge by hurting them. These fantasies took a different twist after he met Terry Brennan. The deep yearnings of the lost little boy would come to the surface with this wonderful girl-woman who, like himself, had been rejected. He allowed her to draw him into her life and her body and to end the awful sense of emptiness. For those brief moments at the beach, he was loved, he was important, he was somebody. And then it ended.

He was consumed by the hope of meeting her again to relive the golden moments. But he began to despair and then felt the old feelings of rejection and worthlessness. Her cold rebuff at the crack house made something wither and die inside him. No more trust.

The final months at the Miculskis were spent trying to control a growing sense of anger and frustration. He needed action and he got it. The assault in the park and the hurt inflicted on the young girl sent a thrill through him.

He became more reckless with his friends, falsely encouraged by the expectation that he would not be punished. The youth detention center did nothing to discourage his newly acquired sense of invincibility. Instead it thrust him into an arena of angry, vengeful peers of which he was one of the toughest. Tough led to hurting others and being hurt. He felt a strange peace. He was with his own kind. He understood his fellow residents. Brute force ruled. No mixed messages.

Billy entered adolescence psychologically bruised and survived the experience by developing a protective attitude that had as its base intense resentment and rage. He learned to wait for opportunities. He could conform when necessary. He finally did make choices that were of great importance for his future. But they were the wrong ones. Billy's self-worth and identity revolved around strength and the ability to survive by hurting others.

The prison psychiatrist labeled Billy with a character disorder, "dissocial personality disorder with explosive conduct." Another word for character or personality disorder is an attitude disorder. Unfortunately, an attitude disorder is not an illness but a habit of thinking that allows persons to cope and survive in an antisocial way. More importantly, an attitude cannot be healed by an outside person or force. The only person who can alter or change an attitude problem is the person with the problem.

Psychiatric treatment for Billy was a threat. It could only weaken the defenses he had built up. He was therefore outside the reach of any treatment efforts.

Sarah Smith

Gertrude was the boss. She was the kindly boss who protected her precious granddaughter. But she was also a cruel boss who put down her own daughter repeatedly. She grabbed Sarah for herself in her later years and continued to reject her own child.

Melanie's broken marriage, financial plight, affinity for alcohol, and depressive moods allowed Gertrude to divide mother and daughter and truly control both. It was Gertrude's second chance to be a good mother. On the first go-around, she did not give the nourishment that Melanie needed, and by sheer dint of her authority and personality she could now rearrange roles so that she could gain the love and affection of Sarah while dismissing her own daughter's bothersome protests. Depressed and discouraged, Melanie fed into her sense of worthlessness. Mom was right. She wasn't a good girl, but her own daughter was. With these roles rearranged, Sarah nestled into her grandmother's life and home, glad to be protected and spoiled. The early challenges in the preschool era were met largely to please grandma and bask in her love and attention.

Sarah predictably panicked, however, when faced with the challenges of adolescence. Despite her early awkwardness, despite the emergence of an eating disorder, she did recover enough to resume school classes. Gertrude's death was a mortal blow to her sense of security. The breakup of the household, the awkward placement in the busy Diamond home, and her demotion to second-best daughter produced a recurrence of her eating disorder.

Eating Disorders

Let us take a brief look at the phenomenon of eating disorders.

Most mental health workers agree that an eating disorder is a child's response to a changing environment that is overpowering and unacceptable. The second point of agreement is that the child, usually a young teenage girl, is going through a reaction involving her body but not involving her thought process primarily. An eating disorder is quite separate from two other illnesses which we shall discuss in more detail, schizophrenia and bipolar disease. A shared observation by mental health professionals is that the child is actually in control of the intake of food, either by refusal to eat, anorexia, or by rejection of food already eaten, bulimia.

Although this affliction may be short lived, it is not uncommon for most adolescent girls to suffer from the problem throughout the entire span of their teen years. It is less common in young adulthood and beyond.

There are different schools of thought as to the cause. One group emphasizes biochemical disturbances. Another insists on genetic factors. But more and more, the inequities of early parental nurturance are considered the core problem. The clinical manifestations of this problem seem to support this theory more than anything else.

As the problem progresses through adolescent years, certain facets of the child's behavior become more and more predictable and repetitive. Once the chronic malnourishment problem reaches critical levels, family, friends, and health professionals play a part in its continuance. The part that is played is well intentioned. There is a reflexive sympathy and affection and worry that reaches out toward the suffering child. It is this obvious "worry factor" that keeps the problem alive and even brings about recurrence.

The hospitalized anorexic girl is the center of attention. The visits, the cards, and the phone calls are welcomed. Tension, depression, and aggravation diminish in the presence of loved ones who bring with them an abundance of worry. It is as if love has been transformed into a warm and protective gesture. Soothing passivity sets in. No responsibility. The seriously ill anorexic child smiles, relaxes. It is the closest thing to the adulation and attention of infancy. The patient feels like the precious object that it once was. And does not have to give anything back. The expression on the faces of the well-wishers says, "Just don't die on us. We'll do whatever you want."

The recovery is usually gradual and everyone feels better. The teen begins to be normal and the weight goes up. After repeated episodes such as this, the friends and loved ones become confused and feel sort of cheated.

Sarah Smith

To fight off the unacceptable changes and challenges of adolescence, Sarah Smith had few choices. She could not stop the march of time, but she could try to stop her physical growth. Her second choice could have been to end her life. Her third choice was that she could have an emotional breakdown and temporarily leave the real world behind. Sarah was not emotionally wired for this event and was therefore left with the other two. Suicide was thought about, but she was too tied to the real life with her grandmother's love and protection to consider it. Thus, slowing down the physical growth was the one option she had.

The first few years of adolescence were tough. The loss of Gertrude was certainly the biggest. What no one anticipated was the infusion of emotional strength over the years from the tough grandma. Sarah had picked up some healthy morsels of strength and determination from this woman. She even developed through her adolescent years a sense of humor reminiscent of Gertrude.

Her mental health therapist Carol discovered that deep within the frightened soul there was a spark of courage and common sense. She was hardly a chip off of grandma's block, but there was enough to work with. Carol was not a con artist, but she worked the psychological confidence game to perfection. Once their relationship became solid she allied herself with her patient and slowly but surely guided her along the lines building a sense of worth. It was painful for both parties at first. Gradually, however, Sarah began to feel a sense of pride in what she was accomplishing.

The formula was simple. Set goals and reach them. Get to school on time. Finish your homework. Help mom with the dishes. Go to the grocery store on occasion. Come to therapy on the bus by yourself. The scoring system took on a life of its own. The agreed-on tasks were weighted with a certain value and incremental confidence gained was assigned a weight spelled out in ounces. Sarah was well acquainted with the language of weight measures, as she had lived through the endless measures of her weight loss for years. She now found herself in control of her emotional growth using the same dimensions and measurements. Carol used another term that was appealing. With each accomplishment, she told Sarah that she was developing a mental muscle, not just weight.

Surviving the senior year of high school and advancing beyond that point was by far the steepest challenge for Sarah. Carol's temporary departure for her own special experience of motherhood coupled with Sarah's awkward return to the company of her own mother made the task more difficult. Carol's replacement was just as sensible and just as firm and the continued growth away from regression and eating problems continued. Despite the ghosts of earlier problems, Sarah showed a tremendous amount of courage and faith in graduating. Carol's return allowed her graduate and face her future with more confidence than anyone could have expected.

Sarah made one choice during all of these turbulent years and that choice was the most important one. She chose to keep growing and not shrink.

Her clinic record at the time of her graduation showed a revised diagnosis: eating disorder, mixed type, in remission, prognosis good.

Holly Diamond

Most teenagers dream of being a star. The fame, the headlines, the adulation of the fans. It's okay. It's natural. It's part of a teenage identification process needed to finally find one's own identity as a young adult. Holly did more than dream. She and her parents set out several years before she became a teenager to make their dream come true. Anne and Cliff Diamond invested a lot of time and money in their future Olympian.

Helping her daughter through the early adolescent changes did not seem to be a great task for Anne. She talked about her own right of passage as a youth and kept her daughter's eyes firmly on her practices and competition. Her body development and her monthly periods seemed more of an annoyance than a major change-of-life issue. Skating was the main thing.

As the competition stiffened, the pressure on the Diamond family increased. Finally, Holly and her mother realized that achieving a number one position nationally was not in the cards. At that point in time, things seemed to come apart as Holly approached the end of her adolescence and the beginning of her young adult years. The dissolution of the marriage was a shock to both mother and daughter, and the aftermath of that was ugly and troublesome for all.

Holly had never taken full responsibility for her life, only her skating. When the family started to come apart, she turned her rage on her parents and also on her cousin whom she felt had usurped much of the attention and even the money in the family. In a state of confusion and anger, Holly decided to make up for lost time in terms of her teenage social life.

There was a dramatic difference in the way Holly entered her adolescent years and exited from them. Her bubble had burst and she was confused and unprepared for her young adult life. She became quite depressed over her lack of friends, lack of accomplishment, lack of job, and finally lack of a cohesive family.

Since she had never seen a psychiatrist or entered in to any mental health program, there was no recorded diagnosis for Holly Diamond. But if there had been, it might have read like this: adjustment disorder of late adolescence with anxiety, depression, and a lack of self-esteem.

Terry Brennan

Why did they let me go? Why not keep me like other parents? Who were they? What were they like? What went wrong? Did they marry? Were they divorced? Are they dead? Will I ever see them?

Who am I? What was my original name? Did I have brothers or sisters? Are they alive? Have I seen them somewhere? Where did I get my red hair? Where did I get my temper?

Was I bad? Was it something I did? Did I cry too much? Did they hate me? Was I too sickly? What was wrong with me? Why was I not worth keeping?

Her parents told her about the adoption just as she was entering the early stages of her adolescence. The results were devastating. She was crushed, she was angry. She was depressed. And she did not reverse these feelings over the next few years.

Terry turned her rage and frustration onto the closest persons in her life. Most teenagers do this in a natural way, since their parents are the only ones they can trust to take their rage. But it did not work that way. The parents became so battered and so frustrated that they began to recoil from the emotional assaults. It was at that point that they themselves began to wonder if she really was a bad child from a bad seed. Privately, they talked about her not being their blood relative; therefore, they really weren't responsible for such outrageous behavior.

Once Terry sensed this, it locked her into behavior that was designed to prove them right. If they thought she was a bad child, then she would indeed live down to their expectations. This led her on a pathway of self-destructive behavior with some immature adolescent friends.

The week at Hampton Beach with Billy Smith was fateful. It was not a good sign. For a few moments, she seemed to let down her guard and share the pain and longing of her life with a kindred soul. Billy was her other self. He had been hurt and betrayed by his parents. Instead of respecting the sameness between herself and Billy and sparing him more hurt, she seduced and cruelly rejected him. He was as worthless as herself. He deserved it. So did she.

The official diagnosis entered into the court records by the consulting psychiatrist after she had been arrested was "adjustment disorder of adolescence with a addictive and dissocial features."

Ruth Malone Reardon

Rita was her mother. And Rita was her friend. She never lied. She never misled her. Despite the natural mother-daughter affinity, there was from the beginning a blend of personalities. Ruth was not perfect. She had a will of her own and there were times when she could be obnoxious. Like her mother, she could flare up, and like her mother, she was quick to forgive and forget.

She met the changes and challenges of adolescence as they came. She was well prepared for the hormone blitz. Rita was always there for the girl talk. Never critical, never histrionic, always supportive and sensible.

School was a breeze. She was bright and handled all the courses required. She made friends easily and cultivated one or two special ones. By her senior year, she was a member of the National Honor Society and co-captain of the field hockey team and had the number two part in the school play.

She handled boys easily and carefully. Although enjoying the attention that started in her freshmen year, she did not take the romance scene too seriously. Party invitations were screened carefully, and she refused to date anyone who tried to push drugs or tried to push her into bed.

Just before graduation, she became more interested in a boy, Dana Broderick, who apparently was too shy to even approach her. He was not eligible for most popular boy in class, but he was honest and funny. She decided to go to Boston College and told her mother and father that she might just become a pre-med major.

Ruth Reardon came about as close as you can to enjoying a normal adolescence.

Alan Malone Reardon

Alan did not touch all the bases. He took a shortcut along the pathway of adolescent changes and challenges. The pubertal rites were a bit awkward and disturbing. He would not go to his stepfather or his mother for any advice. Like most boys, he picked up bits and pieces of information about sex and body changes in the locker room and on the playing field.

He felt alone and felt cheated in terms of what he saw as insufficient family intimacy and trust. But he once again turned his attention to athletics and rode out the uncertainty of the early months.

As he saw his sister Ruth progress through her adolescence and on to college, he realized that something had been lost, particularly with his mother. Even though she gave much attention to him after his father Eddie left, he himself had chosen to be the selected one in terms of his father's attention on weekend visits. Somewhere along the line, a coolness developed between himself and his sister because of this exclusive right to his father. He also felt that his mother, at times, resented the contact with her ex-husband.

Coach Pete Saunders filled the void. He was the closest thing to a father figure Alan had at the time. Alan idolized him. Alan's extraordinary athletic ability earned him the praise he so desperately needed. The two of them, coach and player, entered the high school ranks almost simultaneously. They would become legend as a duo that put Marblehead High School back on the football map.

In essence, the high school career replaced the home during those critical years. Alan actually spent more hours in the locker room, in the gymnasium, and on the playing field than he did at the Reardon residence. Between that and the time spent in the classroom, he might as well have been in a boarding school. But high school was not his real home. It was his stage. As long as he performed on that stage, he was admired and pampered—but not loved. He fell in to the dreamy expectations that are so much a part of the adolescent yearnings. Sex equals love. By the time he graduated, he had scored with six different girls. The final fling resulted in a pregnancy. For the first time in his life, he had to stop and ponder what he had done. He was forced to make a decision regarding the future of another person and the life within that person.

It was then that he realized how fragile he really was. He felt impotent, lonely, and frightened. He had developed an identity in his hometown as a superjock, but that was it. His reflection in the mirror of popularity now appeared faulty and misshapen.

Panic attacks came his way and he was more than frightened. He was afraid that he would completely lose his confidence. By graduation, waves of depression and a sense of helplessness and weakness took a solid hold. His childhood and adolescence were coming to an end. Except for a couple of teammates, he had no one he could really trust, least of all himself. He was a superhero to his fans and classmates, but he was not even close to becoming a man. He realized that something was missing, badly missing.

He rode the crest of popularity during the waning weeks of his high school career. But there was a drumbeat inside him of depression and anxiety that he simply could not shake, and freshmen football at Harvard was only two months away.

Jessica Reardon

Jessica kept it all to herself. She did not wish to return to a hospital again. If she remained silent, no one would know what she was thinking.

In truth, she herself did not know what she was thinking. She had lost her way in terms of separating reality from unreality. She could not form her thoughts, and she could not find the words to describe the horror.

And then came the defining moment, her first period.

Perhaps it was that above all that brought a major breakdown of her thoughts and feelings. The death of her mother and the emotional scars that were inflicted from the bizarre circumstance of that death came back to her in a flood of disjointed memories.

The specter of devils and evil spirits first described by the cook at Bromfield manor were erupting into her conscious mind. Thus the experience of the menarche and the evidence of the blood coming from her own body sent her from her fears into her worst realizations. She felt that she was going to die, as her mother had died, in a blood bath. And if she died, she would be nothing and there would be nothing around her.

Her stay at McLean Hospital was brief, but it did make an impact. The medications and the counseling served as a solid reference point during the early months of her recovery. But Jessica feared that a continuation of this therapy was a connecting link to the horrible experience of psychosis, and that she could not risk. So she gradually severed her ties with her counselor and her psychiatrist. Doing so left her quite vulnerable during the bulk of her adolescent years to a return of the troubled thinking that could never quite reconcile the world of the real and the unreal.

Each year of high school advancement brought more changes and challenges outside the classroom that she simply could not accept. She saw herself as different from the other kids, and she saw herself as different from her own family. She was a wanderer in a world where she could not cry out for help because she did not know what kind of help she needed. She avoided all social events and refused to participate in any extracurricular activities at school. She became the butt of classmates' jokes because of her aversion to undressing in the locker room.

She retreated as quickly as she could into the safety of the Reardon home. Although she was never truly comfortable in that home, she realized that the terrifying events that came her way outside the house were avoided.

She respected her stepmother—Rita was a genuinely good person. As for her father, she carried a latent mistrust. Where was he when mom was dying? Why did he let her go through the ordeal at Bromfield Manor?

And there was another terrible obstacle to their relationship. She could never forget Mom's dying words, as disjointed as they were. Mom had told her to do all she could to prevent Joe Reardon from taking another woman. Oftentimes Jessica would lie awake at night pondering that request, and she felt that she had failed her mother and that is why she died.

But there were other nights. Her thoughts became so jumbled that she simply would fall asleep unable to cope any longer. In addition to the nightmare voices and visions, she occasionally experienced body sensations that were even more frightening. In her deluded state and in the half-sleep of her torment, and particularly around her monthly period, she imagined that her mother did not die. Instead, her mother had come back and entered her body and the two were reunited. The blood of her dying mother was now flowing through her veins and they were together again. Her mother's voice came back to haunt her.

Rita and Joe burst into her room one night in response to a horrible series of cries and shrieks. When they asked if she was all right, she sat up in bed, looked them both in the eye and said, "We are doing just fine. Please leave us alone."

The graduating year of high school was too much for Jessica. She knew at the beginning of the year that the challenge was too much. The uncertainty of life as a young adult, the expectations of family and teachers to commence with the next phase of life, were unacceptable. The breakdown was inevitable. But the dogged determination of her parents and the timely intervention of a mental health team at McLean Hospital minimized the pain and began to set her life in some sort of order.

After looking at Jessica and her ordeal, let us take a much closer look at the problem of schizophrenia.

Schizophrenia

Schizophrenia is a most misunderstood affliction and, as a result, a most maligned and mistreated disorder. This has been going on for centuries. Ignorance and fear of contagion has caused its victims to be shunned, mocked, and punished.

Even today, the bizarreness of its manifestations leads most societies to draw a line between being normal or being nuts. This craziness is like leprosy and smallpox. Quarantines have been instituted to protect the "us" from the "them."

We are now in the 21st century, and the mystery and the myths of schizophrenia still exist. Fortunately, because of the use of antipsychotic medications and enlightened treatment methods, the so-called "nuthouses" have been emptied. Unfortunately, there are some victims of this so-called enlightened movement to empty the mental hospitals. Several of the older, chronic patients in these institutions have been literally dumped out onto the streets and now are renamed the "homeless."

In the 1970s, the growth of community mental health programs brought with it a zeal to empty the state institutions of the "wrongfully" segregated mental patients. Local resources were deemed adequate to assimilate this population. Suburban areas were more successful than the urban and inner city in accomplishing this task.

One theory was true. These poor souls, many of whom had been confined for up to a quarter of a century, were not inherently dangerous. But they were confused and many were socially helpless. Picking up the thread of their former lives was extremely difficult.

Some had lost complete contact with family and friends. To house them, the acquisition of big old houses in quiet neighborhoods was considered the best route. But neighbors became anxious and angry. Left with only a house to live in and without any technical or educational skills after all the years in the hospitals, patients seemed misfits in the neighborhoods and the towns.

Those who had spent the least time behind the bars of the state institutions fared better. Many of them were able to rejoin some families in the towns where they were born. But many others simply became wards of the towns and were forced into what are now called "shelters."

Law enforcement agencies were alerted to the problem, but what they found surprised even them. Schizophrenics by nature abhor violence. They may react to a misperceived threat or attack on themselves, but they do not precipitate it. Their vulnerability to the outside world brought on by delusional thoughts does not seek to challenge sane people. Rather they instinctively wish to withdraw from that which they do not understand. Violence is rare and usually the result of a perceived imminent risk to themselves.

We still tend to use a broad brush in painting the sick population of our society with the colors of criminal behavior. It makes good headlines. People tend to listen and read when the words "wackos" or "crazies" are presented. The monstrous crimes of world leaders have often invited the careless use of the words crazy and nuts. Hitler and Stalin were excellent targets for these common judgments. But what kind of nut are we referring to? The mind of the sick, suffering schizophrenic is not capable of plotting, executing, or covering up serious crimes. On the other hand, the rational minds of angry, vengeful persons—such as dictators, psychopaths or contract killers—can accomplish just that. And they are not insane. Let us differentiate, then, the emotional core of the schizophrenic who is "sick-sick" from the predators of our world who are "mean-sick." Fortunately, our courts of law are much better equipped now to distinguish the two.

What about the illness itself. Let us now look at causes, courses, and consequences.

Causes

In biblical times, the devil was the culprit. Demons possessed the body and soul of the insane. Holy persons were called on to purge or exorcise the demons. Until that happened, the afflicted remained a source of contagion to those nearby. This same concept, advanced into medieval times, brought about the idea of confining these people away from normal people. Bethlehem Asylum in Britain, otherwise known as Bedlam, was one of the more famous institutions. Punitive care seemed to be the answer. Compassionate care had yet to be discovered.

Sigmund Freud introduced a radical theory in the early part of the 20th century. Although not completely ignoring the problem of schizophrenia, he concentrated mostly on the neuroses and left many unanswered questions about major mental illness.

It was in the middle of the 20th century that a new dawn of compassion and enlightenment arrived regarding attitudes of treatment for schizophrenics. After World War II, an army of physicians, psychologists, and social workers set out to make a difference in the lives of the emotionally disturbed. It was none too soon. By the 1960s, it was estimated that there were more hospital beds occupied in the United States by mentally ill people than all other medical/surgical beds combined. But as to a single cause to this serious illness, most mental health workers even now agree that there is none.

Let me offer my own thoughts. I do not believe that there is a single cause. A combination of biological and experiential factors must combine to produce the problem. Neither the geneticists nor the biochemists have presented conclusive evidence that a person is absolutely destined to be schizophrenic. The physical or organic damage to the young brain that correlates with mental retardation or autism is lacking as a solid predictor of adolescent- or adult-onset schizophrenia. On the other hand, the success since the mid-20th century of antipsychotic tranquilizers offers some evidence of an anatomical or biochemical disfunction within the brain itself.

The schizophrenic is not a robot or only a mass of anatomical material. Somewhere along life's pathway, events of a damaging or traumatic nature may touch the life of such a victim in combination with some brain dysfunction already mentioned. The disease of schizophrenia may then become apparent.

Jessica Reardon in her young life experienced terrible emotional trauma. The foundation of her grip on reality and trust was shaken. However, her own unique brain chemistry combined with these events is a mystery.

The Course
There is no single course of schizophrenia. It is as varied as the number of persons who suffer from the disease. Jessica Reardon knew at an early age that something was wrong with her thinking. Like Jessica, many children learn to live with thoughts and feelings that are bothersome but not debilitating. Impairment of social and learning skills is not a clear indication of a budding psychotic process. Teachers of young children expect a certain percent of so-called normal grade school kids to be a slow in these areas. More worrisome symptoms and signs do appear when the child enters the adolescent period. Physiologic changes as well as enormous peer pressures can place the mind of the impaired child in a precarious position. Even at that point, there may not be any overt signs of psychosis.

Withdrawal and avoidance are two features that should be watched. The more natural responses to change and challenge, which are anxiety and depression, may not be manifest. Instead the mind of the disturbed child struggles valiantly to hold on to a sense of what is real and what is not. As the weeks and months wear on, this struggle intensifies. More changes, more expectations to keep growing work on the mind of the child to produce private thoughts of a bizarre nature. This is the child's only defense against the unachievable challenges. Coping with the real world of adolescent turmoil gives way to another world. Much of this emotional turmoil simmers until the late teenage phase and particularly the challenge of graduating from high school.

While on the subject of the course that the disease process takes, let us explore a few of the more common problems of thought and perception experienced by the person with schizophrenia.

Hallucinations and Delusions
At the risk of oversimplifying, a hallucination is a false perception. We perceive the world around us in a most natural way using our five senses through our eyes, ears, nose, tongue, and skin. Each of these parts of our body contains tiny nerve fibers that through a series of connections called neurons relay information about the world around us to our brain. The brain records the information for the future so that a similar perception can be confirmed. In some cases, the information is sent to other parts of

the brain so that immediate action can be employed. An example: a big red fire truck. The optic nerve recognizes the size, shape, and color of this familiar object. Each time we see the truck, whether moving or standing in the firehouse, the message of the perception reaches our brain where it is compared to previous perceptions and then validated. This is a nice orderly mental exercise, but what if the same fire truck en route to a fire swerves out of control and heads directly toward us? Now the perception is one of danger and the brain cries out a warning to "get the hell out of here."

So it is with our ability to hear, smell, taste, and touch. These precious body antennae allow us to take pleasure in our world, but they also warn us of dangers.

Using the example of the fire truck, a person suffering from schizophrenia might perceive that they see the truck and hear the sirens when such a truck does not exist. Thus, their hallucinations are described as visual or auditory.

Auditory hallucinations are the most common type, and the sound of nonexistent voices the most common subtype. Visual hallucinations come next, followed by olfactory (smell) followed by tactile (touch) followed by gustatory (taste). For whatever reason, misperceptions of smell seem to signal the onset of a much sicker and more regressed form of schizophrenia.

It is no wonder that the schizophrenic cowers behind the fragile wall of misperception. One can no longer recognize familiar cues. Size, shape, color, and texture are not what they seem to be. If one cannot trust what is perceived, then one cannot trust in oneself.

Which leads to another common aberration of thought: delusions. Delusions are the schizophrenic's defense against a senseless, untrustworthy, and threatening world. In its simplest definition, a delusion is a false belief. This does not begin to describe the process itself. Normal people function every day believing in something or somebody that in reality cannot measure up to their expectations. That is not a delusion. Examples: my team is the best baseball team in the country. My girlfriend is the most beautiful girl in the world. My political party is the only party that will help the poor.

The delusional system of the schizophrenic is not meant to idealize a system or a person. It is not a mechanism to identify with a winner. It is not Disney World either. It does not invite the victim to wish upon a star. It is a mental mechanism used by the schizophrenic to help their scattered thought process gain some control.

The most common type of delusion is called paranoia. In the paranoid state, the schizophrenic uses a thought process called projection. Lacking a solid grip on one's thoughts and feelings, the blame for the totally chaotic state of mind is shifted to other persons. *I am not sick. I am not bad. I am not helpless. It is you. You out there. You are evil. You did this to me.*

This state of mind can be dangerous under certain circumstances. Mental health caregivers are likely to be perceived as a threat instead of a help. When they try to advance their treatment efforts, the schizophrenic may misperceive and interpret help as an attack.

Less common but easily recognized is the delusion of grandeur this person needs for protection, not so much from a perceived threat from others, but from a horrible sense of inadequacy. As the world around them deteriorates, as the lines between reality and unreality melt away, as their own self-images shrivel, they concoct the belief of invincibility or omnipotence. Leaders of various movements and cults down through the ages have been accused of this affliction. The difference in such persons from a schizophrenic is that they can control their grandiose schemes when necessary. The schizophrenic has no stop buttons.

Somatic delusions or distorted beliefs about one's body are rarer. Physicians are more likely to encounter this. I once treated a girl who was having a difficult time in the senior year of high school and who told her parents that she could not continue her final year because of an eye problem. Her pediatrician and a consulting ophthalmologist could find nothing wrong. When I asked her to describe the problem in more detail, she angrily replied, "It's like I told the other doctors. My eyes are just too big."

I commented that they seemed to be of normal size and shape, to which she replied, "It's not that. It's the holes in my eyes. They are too big."

"What holes?" I asked.

"Can't you see? The holes where the lights come in."

I reassured her that a certain amount of light was necessary so that she could see. She once again replied, "But you don't understand. Too much light comes in to my head. And that means that people like you can see inside me."

Such a fixed distorted belief is in sharp contrast to the reasonable complaints of itching, blurring, or even double vision.

A further guide in understanding the delusional process is to consider the difference between two figures of speech that we all learned in our earliest English grammar lessons, similes and metaphors. We were taught that the two are close. A simile is a comparison of objects using the words "like" or "as." A metaphor compares objects without using these words.

The schizophrenic high school senior did not say, "It's like I have too much light coming in." But rather, "I have a hole and too much light is coming in." It's not "like you can see inside my head" rather "you are looking inside my head."

Such a fixed distortion of reality is frightening. No amount of reason nor logic can correct this thought. And the more one tries, the more confused the sufferer becomes.

In the acute stage of a schizophrenic breakdown, other disturbances of thought may be evident: incomplete sentences, pressured speech, and bizarre word patterns.

Consequences
When talking about the consequences of acute schizophrenia, we must review briefly the dramatic changes that occurred in the mid 1950s, particularly with the invention of helpful medication.

Shortly after World War II, the drug Thorazine (chlorpromazine) was made available. It was to the mental health workers what penicillin was to the World War II Army medics. The population of the state and federal mental institutions began to decrease, and within twenty-five years, the majority of those hospitals closed their doors forever.

Shorter stays in general hospital units have replaced the old state hospital system of long confinements. Most persons are able to return to their families and reenter society within a matter of days, not months and years.

But there are other possible consequences. Because of the nature of the illness, there are certain things that are not likely to be available to the recovering schizophrenic. One of those things is high-stress employment and the other is marriage.

The chronic schizophrenic learns to avoid certain stressful situations, such as the workplace. Another problem can be competitive social circles that are present in some communities. The noise and the repetition that go with factory or assemblyline situations are likely to test the schizophrenic's mental organizational skills beyond their endurance.

Marriage, unfortunately, is not a venture that is highly successful. Most schizophrenics have either never married or have married only once and been divorced. The biggest problem seems to be intimacy. Intimacy in a successful marriage is that intangible ingredient that allows each party to open up the deepest reaches of their soul. To share their innermost secrets and accept each other for the good and the not-so-good parts is the stuff of intimacy. Intimacy requires trust—trust in each other's assets and trust that the flaws will not destroy the marriage.

The schizophrenic lives constantly with the memory of previous breakdowns and the specter of possible regressions in the future. It is almost impossible for that person to share the horrifying memories and experiences with another. There are some successes, however. There are some whose suffering and recovery can transcend the risks of exposure and form a solid union with another person.

Finally, I would like to compare schizophrenia with a medical problem, diabetes mellitus. Like that disease, schizophrenia is a lifelong affliction. It can be controlled but not cured. Thus, the antipsychotic medications may be compared to insulin, and the compassionate help of others may ensure a long and satisfactory life.

As life goes on into the later years, there is less likelihood of breakdowns, since the person has already survived changes and challenges that certainly were more intense and more traumatic.

Jessica Reardon received timely help and an enormous amount of love and support from her family. Both of these gifts boded well for her travel through life and the inevitable encounter with other changes and challenges.

Chapter Three: Young Adulthood

CHANGE

"To be or not to be."

That is the question that faced Shakespeare's young prince Hamlet, and that is the question that confronts every young adult before their mid-twenties.

More specifically, the not-quite-ready-for-prime-time post-adolescent must grapple with lonely decision about "who-to-be," "what-to-be," and the big one, "if-to-be."

It is lonely because no one but oneself can make such a choice. Parents can pressure but not insist on a pathway to adult maturity. There are no laws demanding that one continue schooling or get a job. It is lonely because with newly acquired freedoms come serious responsibilities that no other person can accept.

The emotional rollercoaster ride of adolescence is over. The excuse of being just another "crazy teenager" doesn't fly. Older adults hold young adults accountable for their behavior.

The lazy summer days seem to pass quickly. The congratulatory glow of commencement day rushes all too quickly to the "now what am I going to do with the rest of my life" day in September. It is unfortunate that the events that flow from September for the next half dozen years receive such little attention from the experts in the behavioral sciences. For the unavoidable struggle to put the finishing touches on our early growth and development is truly one of the most pivotal phases of life.

Everybody understands the terms " terrible twos" and "terrible teens." We tend to expect and excuse the bothersome behavior of these periods as part of our life. There are no cute clichés for the early twenties. To become an adult or not is a private personal challenge. And excuses don't matter anymore.

The most prominent feature of this next chapter of human development is the inescapable responsibility of choice, of having to make decisions by oneself and for oneself. These choices are not about what to wear, or what to eat, or what television show to watch. The important decisions come about gradually and are the product of what each young adult measures as worthwhile in life. These decisions lead to the answers of what-to-become, who-to-be, and if-to-be.

The "if-to-be" question is the most crucial. For if the young adult decides to play it safe, stay home, and cling to the apparent security of childhood, then the other challenges of "who-to-be" and "what-to-be" cease to be issues.

But if the person takes the chance and continues to explore the new world of responsibility and reward, then the three questions of "being" turn into three wondrous invitations to own and control one's life.

If-to-Be

As with early childhood, late childhood, and adolescence, life's natural challenges to accept change and grow are presented over a period of years, not in moments or in weeks.

In our culture, the high school graduate has two choices: further education or work. As we follow the young adult along these ventures, two experiences stand out. One is the familiar challenge to leave behind the lifestyle that is relatively safe and predictable, and the other is to take on something new.

Taking on something new at this point in life requires a major developmental step of finding a philosophy for life itself. For a growing child, dependent on adults for sustenance and knowledge, the question of life's meaning is irrelevant. The child is too busy accepting or rejecting parental dictums governing everyday behavior. Not so in the late teens and the early twenties.

Here we go again! Change and challenge. Leaving home to find another home. And with it all, our reflexive, emotional responses—depression and anxiety, the two natural and inevitable human reactions to loss and change.

In our earliest experiences with change and challenge, tears of sadness and screams of protest announce our displeasure. In young adulthood, these primitive biological tools must give way to more elaborate behavioral patterns. These we will soon explore.

But the question of "if-to-be" remains the biggest question of all.

What is the purpose of my life? Is there life after death? Is there a higher power? Is there a caring God? What will happen to my parents when they die? How will I get along without them? They've always been here.

Is my life worth living? Why should I struggle? Why work or go off to school? Why not stay home where it's safe? What's the hurry? Who really cares about me other than my family? Why not take what I can get? Everybody else does.

I didn't ask to be born, dammit! Why do I have to put up with all this pressure to do something with my life?

These concerns are very much a part of young adulthood. They persist until each person begins to construct a personal "raison d'etre," a reason for being. There are no card-carrying atheists at this stage of life, but there are many agnostics. To be convinced that there is no God, no hereafter, and no purpose in human existence is the first step in personal annihilation.

It takes an awful lot of faith to be an atheist. For most young folks, that's much too risky. On the other hand, to struggle with the questions of what kind of purpose there is in life is a much safer, though unwanted, course at times.

This brings us to a topic that rarely graces the pages of psychiatric treatises: the issue of human spirituality. I use this term to introduce an important dimension into the process of our natural growth and development in the early adult years.

Developing a solid sense for the "Why" of our own life is essential at this time. Without it, the "How" to live becomes frightening and unimaginable, as we shall discover when we explore the various maladjustments to life as we go on.

In measuring the challenges of adolescence in the last section, we used as references the physical, intellectual, social, personal, and sexual growth patterns. Now, as we follow the young adults' choice of school or work, we must add the vital factor of spiritual growth.

But before that, a word about the other "to be's."

Who-to-Be

The "who-to-be" question is related to the identification process discussed extensively in the chapter on adolescence. The main thrust of that discussion was around the issue of "who-to-be-like." Of great concern was the day-to-day struggle of the teenager in copying desirable adult traits and values. The identification process gradually gives way to the inevitable task of owning an identity. Of being someone! Unique! One of a kind! Not like anyone else!

For better or worse, the building blocks of our personality come together by the mid-twenties. It is interesting to compare the comments of fellow alumni at reunions from high school and even college. The high school group usually laments the problem of how unrecognizable or different we appear. On the other hand, the college and graduate school friends rejoice in how little we have changed. Their focus is on personality and not appearance. Only minimal changes seems to occur after college graduation.

Acquiring a personal identity in the twenties is complex. But once that identity is established, it is permanent.

What-to-Be

In the Middle Ages, "what-to-be" was simple. Sons followed in their fathers' footsteps; daughters did the same in accordance with their mothers' examples. Perhaps we will never know the job satisfaction index from this tradition, but it was all that they had. The only escape was to rebel and run away from home to the monastery or the convent or the circus. Not so today. An incredible array of occupations and professions await the high school graduate, and this includes both genders. "What to be" is more a problem of the right selection rather than the limitation of choice.

Unlike our medieval counterparts, today's parents, at least in intact families, tend to guide, support, and even push their kids into their favorite choices. This phenomenon may create a different form of rebellion.

Not all high school graduates are prepared to make the absolute right choice immediately. For many, issues of finance, health, or family obligations force them into more immediate or practical ventures. The persistent ones may pursue career changes later on.

The "what to be" question is not limited to a choice of profession, job, or that elusive star called a career. When we come to the chapter on marriage, the role of parent and spouse represent responsibilities that all too often force us to look in the mirror of the soul and ask, *What kind of spouse or parent am I?* These questions have nothing to do with the paying job or career.

The "to-be" questions are not disconnected or unrelated to each other. The issue of "if-to-be" is the central question. If this one is resolved during the early adult years, the "who" and "what" questions follow in the successful passage through young adulthood.

School

Further education beyond high school is traditionally obtained in college, although technical and trade schools are increasing in number and importance. We will now examine the challenge that awaits the high school graduate on a bigger campus.

Thus far we have used the term "leaving home" to distinguish that time of life from birth onward when a certain phase of our growth reached a point when another change and another challenge disrupted our sense of comfort and security. The souvenirs of those adjustments were the rattle, the potty, the school bus, and the pubertal fluids. Now the college freshman must leave the house as well as the home.

Being left on the college campus by one's parents on that fateful first day is a repeat of the Day of the School Bus. Sure, the parent-child ties have loosened tremendously. And the confidence gained from meeting the challenges of adolescence and high school must offer a certain comfort. But, nonetheless, there is a singular moment in the parking lot of the college at the time of the kiss, hug, handshake, or just simple eye contact when each family member realizes that childhood is over, that letting go is essential, that each one must lose something to gain something. It's lump-in-the-throat time. For the parents the drive home is terrible—sadness, apprehension, and the nagging question, *Did I do enough?* For the new kid on campus, the heavy climb up the stairs to the dorm room is accompanied by similar musings. But whereas the petrified little tike wondered if he or she would ever see their parents again, the grown-up collegiate orphans ponder the notion of whether they will ever see the parents again the same way. They realize that something has happened on this fateful day.

Thus, the journey of life begins anew. This time for much higher stakes. To be somebody and not just to belong to somebody.

The first semester away from home is critical, and the early days of that semester the most important. Thank God for the telephone. And thank God for weekend visits, either by the home folks to the college or the student back to home itself. The phone calls and face-to-face contacts delay that sense of abandonment and isolation on that first day of college. The reassurances help with the gradual adjustment to college life, particularly with one's classmates and most importantly with one's roommate.

For the college authorities, it requires a Solomon-like wisdom to perfectly match all incoming freshmen in terms of complete compatibility. Such information as temperament, sensitivity, maturity, and ability to leave behind childhood entitlements are conspicuously absent on the admissions office computer disks.

For the fortunate few roommates, the bonding chemistry is immediate and is the stuff of lifelong friendships. Most roommates, however, have to work a little harder. What helps is the kinship factor. The awareness that emotionally we are all in the same boat. Everyone shares the natural uncertainty and homesickness. Quite soon the awkwardness promotes a give and take—a need for some understanding and support from another person and a willingness to return it. Learning to get along with the roommate is an important challenge. A certain number of new students will find this adjustment of sharing a room impossible. For the child who simply is too ill prepared for the home separation, the challenge of giving and taking will prove too much. For the unlucky roommate of such a student, the chance to fashion a healthy partnership is diminished.

Aside from the roommate issue, there is need to adjust to new friends and classmates. Once again, there is strength in numbers and there is time to develop these friendships. Being on the low end of the college caste system, freshmen instinctively search for both anonymity and support within the frightened herd. The diversity of personalities offers a more generous selectivity in the search for "someone like me." Thus it is not uncommon for roommates to accommodate each other quite well while securing equally close relationships with other classmates.

The personality of the college student is ever developing. En route to an adult identity, one still needs to identify with others. Whereas the parents were the most important models during adolescence, now the focus is on other young adults thrown together with a stated goal and an unstated challenge. The goal of attending college is to learn much data and to graduate. The bigger challenge, however, is to learn how to become a responsible adult during these precious formative years. Let us now look at the academic roles first.

⇝

A highly structured learning process awaits the new student in college. One will enter school at a certain time and one will graduate from school at a certain time. During these four years, the sun will rise and set each day, the school day will begin and end on time, the seasons will come and go, holidays and vacation times will be observed. All of this, come hell or high water!

Students occasionally criticize the rigidity of this process. But inwardly they appreciate the predictability and the discipline that it entails. The luxury of childhood excuses is gradually replaced by the responsibility to get the work done on time. And most importantly, the senior year students come to realize that the reward for all of this has been earned by themselves and for themselves.

The selection of courses is often difficult in the earliest months. Few freshmen are absolutely convinced about their ultimate goal in college. Exposure to other student interests and the impact of certain faculty play a part in the final pathway of majoring in a subject. Intellectual growth is automatic in this process. If the student does the work and perseveres, they will gain the ultimate goals. Such growth and maturity is directly related to the question of "what-to-be."

The role of one's college teachers is extremely important. The college professors are well aware that they shape the student in ways that go beyond the classroom. At this vulnerable stage of life, perhaps no other adult is positioned to influence the intellectual hunger of the young adult and the craving to be somebody special. Many colleges and universities encourage the tutorial system for this purpose. In a not-so-subtle way, the teacher resembles a good and trustworthy parent. In that role the teacher, who also personally cares about the student, bridges the gap of loneliness and homesickness while at the same time inspiring the young adult to reach beyond the books and the grades. At a time when one is seeking to establish solid values in life, this relationship is vital. However, a problem may arise when the ability or integrity of the trusted teacher does not measure up to the task. The power of this model adult to influence the vulnerable younger adult may be misused to feed the teacher's selfish ambitions or appetites.

I will now turn to the other part of campus life, the part that relates to the questions of "who-to-be" and "if-to-be." Outside the classroom, time spent on campus is usually divided into three areas: a social life, a recreational life, and a spiritual life.

Social Life

Perhaps the first thing the new freshman realizes is the variety of choice of campus activities. When not in class or laboring over the books in the dorm, student life is enriched by the availability of concerts, lectures, mixers, outings, movies, day trips, faculty parties, dances. Special events are usually arranged with group trips to the big city theater or arts. The local shopping mall is appealing as a reminder of the life just lived. Throughout the four years, the assortment of social opportunities multiplies, feeding the student's appetite for experiences that will stitch the fabric of the developing personality.

However, the most important social experience is with people, not events. Those people are peers and occasionally elders. The important elders that come in contact with the student are members of the faculty, dorm supervisors, coaches, or club leaders. Unlike the high school experience, the adults, both intimate and distant, were imitated and sometimes rejected in the "who-to-be-like" process. The maturing college student may find at the end of the four years a rewarding kinship with selected adults. This is a good sign that the generation gap is closing. Through hard work, trust, and the resulting confidence acquired with the older person, the student begins to feel more comfortable with adults than with kids. And in this process the student becomes more adult themselves.

As the freshman student begins to consolidate friendships with classmates and roommates, there may be an eventual extension of the search for friends among older college students. The need to associate with older peers is a healthy sign, as it portends the wish to again imitate people who have already "been there." Not all match-ups are healthy, however.

Friendships and acquaintances form a solid foundation for growth and maturity during the early twenties. But the real testing ground, the real opportunity to grow from childhood to adult, is in the one-to-one relationship.

College romances are natural and necessary. Going off to college means leaving the house and home of our childhood. The absence of love and support screams for relief. The replacement for this is most understandable. Falling in love at the college level is not the same as teenage puppy love or "the crush." The feeling of walking on air may be the same. The sense of total warmth and joy, the giddiness, the specialness, the naughtiness, the hopefulness, the godliness is the same. The sense that there are only two really important people in the world is the same. The conviction that life will never be the same, the future holds nothing but pure happiness, is the same—all of these make up that wonderful event "falling in love."

But one thing is different.

Falling in love is by definition time limited, and at some point, the bubble must burst. For the young adult as compared with the adolescent there is no safety net in the form of family. When one returns to earth there is loneliness and the realization that one is truly on one's own. The stakes are higher for one who has already left the house and is trying now to leave the home.

In the next chapter on Marriage, we will explore the complexity of blending two lives, both searching to extend the good parts of home and make up for the missing portions. For now, let us examine one of the more misunderstood challenges along the pathway of becoming an adult. And that part is sex.

Sex

Confusion was the key feature during the earliest adolescent sensual stirrings. For the college student, the problem is choice. What to do with our sexual urges? The glands are in overdrive, pumping out hormones that in turn awaken desires you never knew existed. The habit of adolescent masturbation is not enough. Both genders are affected by this rush of emotion and physical energy, and both genders are drawn closer to each other because of it. Given the choice of solitary sexual pleasure or the natural drives to share it with another person, let us examine the phenomenon of young adult sexual expression using as a guideline an old-fashioned concept called "sexual intercourse."

Nowadays, this term is rarely used other than in stuffy legal struggles or in theological discussions. It is too correct, too proper, and too limited. Not vulgar enough, like the four-letter words. Don't let it fool you. The word "intercourse" is loaded with a variety of meanings. Dictionary definitions differ ever so slightly. Essentially they describe "intercourse" as a connection of dealings between people or an exchange of thoughts or feelings between people.

If we are to truly understand the workings of sexual intercourse, we must revisit some of the features in the last chapter having to do with sexual satisfaction by oneself. The simplest activity, masturbation, has two components: physical and mental. The physical component is the least complicated. The sexual fantasy portion is more intricate. Without reexamining all the details of that subject, we will focus on the important elements as they affect the choices of sexual expression available to the young adult.

The entire purpose of masturbation is too produce an orgasmic pleasurable feeling the satisfies the body and the mind. The recipient of that feeling is also the producer of that feeling. The Freudians call the experience "autoerotic."

The fantasy part of this act involves a necessary control of another person or object to produce total pleasure to the dreamer, whether that fantasized person is willing or not. None of this is real, just imagined. An important point is the repetitiveness of the fantasy situation as it plays out in the pleasurable manipulation of another person. In other words, the themes of each person's sexual fantasies are quite often reused and recycled in familiar playlets. They represent, on a subconscious level, the most intimate workings of the persona. The fantasies are necessary plays, much like our nightly dreams. The central character is always oneself, but it is a self with many faces and many desires. One of those faces, as incredible as it seems, is the face of the tiny infant within us who blissfully expected years ago to have total love and attention in the service of providing pleasure and avoiding pain. Other elements of our personal sexual fantasies contain a mixture of hopes, yearnings, and desires that were unfortunately never realized in our childhood, whether it was in the early stages, the middle stages, or adolescence. Thus, the repetitive themes of our sexual dreams and fantasies are truly a reflection of the darker and unfulfilled side of the still developing character of the young adult. The one thing that is different from the masturbatory phase of adolescence is choice. How to harness the unsettled parts of our personality is the dilemma.

All of this comes together in the potential adventure of sexual intercourse. From the day the young adult arrives on campus, it is necessary to engage in a variety of activities with other students and faculty. All of this in a general sense must be considered as a form of intercourse if we use the definition of dealings with other people—verbal intercourse, social intercourse, business intercourse, recreational intercourse, and political intercourse. The topic now is that most vital one-on-one emotional and often sexual intercourse.

During the college years there are at least five separate possibilities for engaging in sexual intercourse: Saved Sex, Scattered Sex, Sad Sex, Solo Sex, and Sadistic Sex.

Saved Sex

Saved Sex is becoming a rare item in our culture. Saved sex is the old-fashioned kind. No complete organ-to-organ sexual intercourse until marriage. Kissing, hugging, touching, squeezing, and handholding are okay but not all the way.

Most surveys gathered from the responses of college students place this behavior in the distinct minority. But not completely abandoned. So why do some young folks make this choice to wait for sexual intercourse? The answer would appear to be somewhere in that fuzzy Nevernever Land of spiritual growth which is part of the young adult's concern. This is the land where values-in-life play a part.

The challenge of developing a relationship with a member of the opposite sex in college is a mighty serious one, given the incredible variety of personalities and the differences in personal values, hopes, dreams, and ambitions. But it is a magnificent challenge! If successful, the rewards will last a lifetime. If one is able to fuse the maturing pieces of one's adult personality to the like parts of a love object, then growing into adulthood and leaving childhood is so much easier. Falling in love at this stage of life is natural. Emotional, intellectual, and social intercourse follow as a way of becoming even closer and establishing a blissful intimacy.

But falling in love is not the same as LOVE. It is wonderful precursor to the real thing. In the next chapter on Marriage, we will explore the differences. For now, it is important to examine one crucial difference in the emotional intercourse that takes place between the in-love couple and the learning-to-love couple. That difference has to do with the phenomenon of "respect." Respect in this setting involves both self-respect and respect for the other person. Self-respect first.

Self-respect is earned and not received from others. In the late stages of adolescence, it begins to develop in a much more tangible and important way. Self-respect is the result of achieving goals that we ourselves set, of doing what we told ourselves we were going to do. It is a feeling and knowledge of oneself that develops slowly and gradually, up until that time of our young life when we are compelled to measure our self-worth by our reflection primarily in the judgment of adults. Peer approval counts somewhat but is suspect even by ourselves because of our knowledge of our peers' imperfections and flaws in judging others. The journey from high school to the end of college encourages us to build on confidence and self-worth because of what we do, not what we say.

How, when, and why two people fall in love at this time of life is a puzzle. The kismet, the chemistry, and the celestial alignment perhaps all play a part. But after the magnetic forces have played themselves out, other events must occur for the relationship to develop. Much of this furtherance of the relationship depends on the maturity of each party, their own self-respect, and that important respect for other people. The confidence and sense of self-worth by one member of the romance instinctively seeks something similar from the other. Sooner or later, as the fever and the fervor grow amid the emotional and physical attraction, the two parties must make a decision, *Is this for me?* Two young souls groping with intense emotions, sexual urges, and wanting their precious love to last forever must come to grips at some point with the concept of forever.

A further word about the importance of respect for others. One is not born with a respect for other persons. The tiny infant is incapable of feeling for the welfare of other people. The newborn quite naturally just feels, and not for others.

Respect for others is learned. It is learned firsthand from the parents and within the family. How each member of the family treats each other, in particular how the parents give and take between themselves, is a vital part in developing a respect for other persons. The attitude parents have for nonfamily members, neighbors, even strangers will affect the growing child's hunger for norms and values to live by. Respect for the privacy, integrity, and values of the in-love partner in college plays a significant part in the decision to make a serious commitment and perhaps to delay sexual intercourse in the service of this respectful commitment.

Obviously it is much simpler for those lucky young adults who are brought up in a respectful atmosphere than those who are deprived of same early on. The child who witnesses the support, love, and affection exchange between parents builds a sense of what emotional intercourse is all about. It is basically about the consideration of others' needs, not just our own. From this, the child who is struggling as a young adult to deal with sexual urges will undoubtedly be reminded of this same principle in terms of the value of others and not just one's self.

Sexual activity that is saved for the purpose of a lifetime commitment may not be popular on the college campus. Regardless of the culture of the times, the concept of true love and respect for others will guide that young adult into a private, personal decision to contain urges. Such control combined with a deep sense of love and commitment will bode well for the next major challenge, marriage.

Scattered Sex

The hit movie "Animal House" portrayed a certain element of the college student body as playfully primitive. The theme of their sexual high-jinx was acting out some post-adolescent masturbatory fantasies. Humor turned into hilarity when the absurd pranks challenged the stodgy traditions of the elders. Even if it is one weekend a year, most college frat houses attempt to be "Animal House wannabes."

The phenomenon of scattered sexual behavior occurs more commonly because of a search between two lonely persons to make up for some missing pieces of their childhood experience. Parents are entrusted to provide love and limits for the precollege child. The results of this commitment are always imperfect. The college student longs to fill in the blanks with another person using the tools available: mind, heart, soul, and most importantly, body.

Sexual intercourse on campus is a means of communicating this need. The problem is that taking love and comfort from another person is not always matched by a giving component. This then may lead to a number of potential encounters in this search for relief.

What is the part that is missing? What is it that drives some young students to demand a completion on their unfulfilled emotional needs?

The missing ingredients, particularly in the area of love and nourishment, will be examined in much more depth in the next section on Choice. But for now it should be noted that if there are missing pieces in childhood that cry out for some satisfaction at the college level, then they are likely to be the components of the depressive syndrome that we have discussed earlier. Those components are made up basically of sadness, madness, and badness.

The college student feels an incompleteness and some emptiness if insufficient love came their way as a child. They may also have been the victim of some abuse or anger. This could color their sexual appetite. The sexual partner is quick to pick up messages of anger and hurt. And last but not least, the sense of badness or inadequacy may drive the unsuspecting college student to feel better and to feel like something even though the sexual experience is short lived and without any healthy emotional value.

An honest respect for the other person is missing in many of these ventures. In its place is a hunger, demandingness, and sense of entitlement. The guiding principle is *I deserve it. It is owed to me.*

A variety of behavioral patterns take place on campus given the transitory nature of the relationships. The more timid individuals blend in to the group. Inevitable panty raids, pot parties, dorm orgies allow some anonymity. For the more aggressive and daring individuals, one-to-one relationships are preferred. Particularly on the male side, there is a sad arrogance that accompanies these events. It is not uncommon for the shallow thinking participants to brag about their lists of conquests.

Sad Sex

Gay sex is sad sex. It is sad for at least two reasons.

The first is the conscious realization by the young adult that a decision to embark on a lifestyle of same-gender sexual intercourse sets the course through the perilous waters of rejection and ridicule that most often is irreversible.

The term "coming out of the closet" has assumed cliché status in our modern vernacular. But a closer look at the metaphor suggests serious losses that are likely to be experienced. The "coming out" part announces to one's personal close friendships and family that they have heretofore been deceived about the essence of their loved one's persona. The "closet" part challenges them to accept or not accept the behavior. The fallout in terms of damaged personal relationships creates an inevitable sadness.

The second reason has to do with the misguided search to make up for prior love experiences that went wrong. To understand this point more clearly, we must refer briefly to the childhood experience of imperfect parental love and limits and the resulting legacy of residual depression which is made up primarily of madness, sadness, and badness. Choosing to make up for the traumas or inequities of childhood with a member of the same sex means that one truly abandons the hope that the missing components of love endured in childhood can be compensated for in the natural order of adult love.

Thus, the major facet of childhood depression, which is sadness, is perpetuated, not resolved. The emotional scar remains constantly within reach for the picking. But instead of insufficient love being at the center of the sore spot, it is now replaced by imitation love.

The madness part of the depressive syndrome has a safe and convenient outlet in the arenas of social and political protest. The smoldering rage contained within the heart of the homosexual finds an available outlet with the vigorous demands for rights and nondiscrimination that are popular either by demonstrations or in the media. These activities tend to offer anonymity and at the same time neutralize the residual anger and nagging sense of low self-esteem left over from childhood.

All in all, homosexual intercourse developed in the young adult years may indeed dull the pain of the emotional unfinished business of childhood but it does not allow for an adequate exchange of feelings, hopes, and dreams that one can build on in coping with the future changes and challenges of life.

Solo Sex

Solo sex has a ring of sadness to it also. Young adults on campus suffering from crippling shyness and little confidence tend to avoid any meaningful social contacts with persons of either gender. The solo existence is safer. One's feelings are not exposed. The chance of rejection is minimal. But the reward of the bigger gamble, the give and take, the sharing with other human beings, is forfeited.

Such a shy person may not be entirely lost in the battle for growth and maturity beyond adolescence. For a significant number, it may only be a delay in the process. Not quite ready for prime time but not hopeless. For others, however, who will not emerge in more healthy ways, this shyness may portend a lifestyle of loneliness and emptiness gaining little and relying on oneself to meet the inevitable challenges ahead.

The sexual style for such a lonely person is usually masturbation, simply for relief if for nothing else. But rather than the natural experimentation of adolescence, this behavior may now show signs in young adulthood of a stunted and sterile adjustment, not only of one's sexual development, but of one's social, personal, and spiritual growth.

Sadistic Sex

If homosexual intercourse fails to compensate for inadequate nurturing in childhood, then sadistic sexual habits aren't even close. Hurting others has no growth potential at all. Sadistic sexual acts are driven not by the unresolved sadness of childhood depression but by the madness. Revenge for old hurts is the purpose. Whereas anger and cruelty may spice up masturbatory adolescent sexual fantasies en route to orgasm, sadistic sexual acts use real people for the twisted pleasures.

Such choices and patterns of behavior challenge the essence of healthy intercourse. The perpetrator of these acts has no interest in an exchange of feelings. That person only wants the victim to feel pain so that they can feel pleasure. The young adult on the college campus developing this primitive and unacceptable sexual behavior may not be conspicuous. The cauldron of steaming rage left over from childhood may indeed be quietly channeled with athletics, particularly contact sports. The overly aggressive athlete, however, may not be able to leave the anger on the field of battle.

Young Adulthood

The term "date rape" is used more frequently on campus nowadays. Incidents of gang rape are increasing as are complaints by women of physical assault. Once again, the goals of such practices are uncontained perverse pleasure.

For the college student about to graduate into the real world of responsibility, with the fair expectation of mutual respect and sharing, this choice of sexual expression is an indictment, not only of serious character flaw, but of an attitude of dangerous disregard for the worth of other human beings.

This concludes the issues of "who-to-be." The discussion has only brushed the major concerns of young adulthood life. We will reexamine these topics in a more detailed way as our stories continue.

Trust

There is a regimented quality to college life. A time to enter, a time to graduate. Five days a week of formal classwork. Sessions begin and end on schedule. Athletic and social diversions are posted for certain dates and times. The student's brain must cognitively recognize these demands and steer through the maze of events.

But the young adult is more than a brain. There is a heart and soul that feels, yearns, and hopes. So what is it all about?

The "if-to-be" questions have already been raised earlier in this chapter. But what about the answers? The big question of whether life is worth living must now be resolved by each young person, alone, with no one else to decide and no one else to blame. Adrift in a sea of confusion and insecurity, lacking a sense of self-worth, sensing a loss of support from parents or family, the emotionally undernourished student faces a grim prospect. Going home is not an option, for home in the first place was not sufficient.

On a deeper level this unfortunate person, unable to trust themselves or others, will no doubt have a difficult time trusting a supreme being or God. This only complicates the sense of confusion and abandonment. For owning such a trust would give them some compass to steer by, to put them in touch with someone or something who represents a purposeful life and life after death.

Unfortunately, a certain number of these young adults begin to die in spirit during the college years. More tragically, a certain number just die. For without a meaning to life, what difference does it make.

Suicide during the college years presents at least two familiar patterns: active and passive. On the active side, intentional overdose is the most common choice. Body lacerations next. The passive mode features single-passenger auto accidents, alcohol toxicity alone or with a group, "chicken" challenges, and one of the most insidious, newcomers to the self destructive scene, and that is the eating disorder phenomenon.

Once again, the quality of emotional nourishment in childhood is put to the test. A sufficiency of love and limits enables one to accept the challenge of adulthood, even though the road is not smooth.

The most vital legacy from an emotional nourishing family is trust. This gift from parents to child is crucial at this delicate time of decision. As we discussed earlier, the trust of the parents by the child depends on their consistent behavior as well as sensible love and limits. The child learns to rely on those parents who stick by them. The parents' reliability is sorely tested by the troubled adolescent, but their ability to remain loyal strengthens the growing trust.

Basically, parents sow the seeds of trust in the earliest years. And inevitably, the child returns the ripened product to those same parents. This gift is not wrapped or packaged; it is a most sincere offering. It is earned by the receivers, and it leaves the giver enriched even more. The college student about to tackle the mysteries of life beyond the academic shelter is strengthened by this ability to trust not only their parents but those colleagues around them who share the uncertain college experience.

After trust comes values. Both are the intangible by-products of a healthy childhood.

What are values? For the lack of a better definition, values are standards to live by. Values affect our attitude toward ourselves and others. Values guide us in our choice of friends, religion, political party, career, and last but not least, in how we measure ourselves. During the four years of college life, the values instilled in us by our parents will shape our ability to get along with others. At times the young adult may be forced to stand up for something that is valued by them, risking disapproval or even rejection from colleagues. In this crucible of choice and growth, one's values become more solid and reliable when challenged.

But nothing is perfect. The student who brings to campus life arbitrary and uncertain values runs the risk of making choices that may lead them further away from a sense of self-worth and a diminished sense of what life is worth.

Thus far we have concentrated on the college background as the setting for young adult growth. For those who choose not to continue their formal education beyond high school, the issues are the same, but the challenges may be somewhat different. We will now examine some of the differences.

Job

The first major difference is the continuation of family life, and the second, the entry into the job market instead of going to school. One is not exposed to the shock of being transposed abruptly from hearth and home to the big college campus. Absent the full commitment to education, the same person usually confronts the reality of work life where the biggest jolt comes from realizing that no one owes you anything other than what you earn. The child who leaves home for college is forced to work through the separation pains immediately. The child who stays home may still be nourished by the comfort of home life where family roles continue and childhood expectations change ever so gradually. Food and laundry services are expected to continue.

The first intrusion into this comfortable existence comes when the parents dare to suggest something in return, like board money. No more free lunch! Obviously lunch is not the issue. The real meaning of this request is that the parents intend to treat the child as an adult and introduce the nasty notion that their child now owes something back for services that heretofore were expected.

A sobering moment, but a necessary one! It does not have the cataclysmic boom of the Day of the Rattle, but this moment in time sends a message about a new era of parent-child relations. The challenge now for the young adult is to enter another natural period of change where a responsible person will begin to replace the entitled child.

The young adult who ponders the rewards of previous expectations presented by the parents will accept this challenge without much fuss. However, parents themselves may balk. It is much easier to keep the status quo and hang on to a dependent child. On the other hand, parents who truly realize the importance of teaching the child new responsibilities will begin the awkward task of instituting some payment for services rendered.

If parents sometimes have misgivings, there is certainly no timidity on the part of employers to make this point clear. The young adult faced with the prospects of a day's pay for a day's work soon realizes the same questions as the college student about where their life is heading.

The harsh realities of employment and responsibility soon lead to the question of what-to-be. Is this all there is? Will I do this for the rest of my life? For those young adults either unmotivated or ill-equipped with further training or education, the answer may indeed be "yes." Sooner or later, a decision must be made to better oneself (or not) in the job market.

Back on the home front, another conflict may develop. The young adult who is reluctant to give up the entitled "goodies" and who is still struggling with some residual adolescent turmoil may challenge the parents' rights vis-à-vis their rights. An ill-conceived declaration of independence may follow, complete with an angry departure from the house. The classic parting shot goes something like this: "I don't need you folks anymore. I can make it on my own."

Sooner or later, it becomes apparent that boldly leaving the house is not the same as leaving home. Impulsively declaring one's independence from family is not the same as achieving it. The emotional unfinished business with parents will inevitably resurface in new settings and be played out with other people who will have varying degrees of tolerance.

A final word about the subject of work. Basically, no one really wants to work. We are born into this world expecting others to work for us. Mom and Dad are expected to provide food, clothing, toys, entertainment, tuition, and vacations for free. They, however, must work to get money to pay for these things; thus the basic reason for labor is bread.

Were it not for hunger pangs, prehistoric man would not have wandered out of his cave in search of food and some leafy fabric to cover the cold skin. Career ladders were not in vogue in those days. Whether one is self-employed, unionized, professional, or free lance, the basic motivation to get out of bed each day and sell the labor of mind and body to another for money is still food and clothing and a place to live. If one enjoys one's job and is fulfilled, so much the better. But if one equates one's self-worth to rank or prestige, there is some danger of a letdown.

For most high school graduates, the first job offers not only money but a chance to graduate into the world of adults. It is new, challenging, and a bit exciting. It is a chance to prove one's worth by accepting a task and completing it. Boss approval is welcome, but peer approval is even better because one's peers are often a mixture of young folks and elders and therefore a more valid mirror.

For the young adult, still clinging to the entitlements of childhood, the work challenge may be rejected. The series of job failures will be rationalized as "their fault, not mine." The success of a job after high school does serve as a measure of one's maturity and capacity to continue growth into adulthood. A job invites one to develop tenacity, commitment, purpose, consistency. These are solid elements in building the character of an adult.

Life is more than one's job, but the acceptance of the work ethic by the high school graduate allows them to grow and develop confidence, which makes the task of meeting the challenges and opportunities of the adult world easier.

Young Adulthood

Now, back to the stories. The challenges that await the young adult will lead to clearer patterns of adjustment or maladjustment and, in the section on choice, a more detailed discussion of the more common mental illnesses.

CHALLENGE

Billy Smith

Billy served his time. The parole officer from Lynn had visited him earlier in the week, the prison psychologist the day before. As part of the parole obligation, he was to check with the parole officer once a week for the first six months and submit random urine specimens twice a week. If the tests were positive for any illicit drugs, he would be subject to arrest and possible return to prison.

Before leaving, she put him in touch with the owner of a rooming house in Lynn and offered to hook him up with a part-time job. The only job available was loading cartons of milk onto a truck at the West Lynn Dairy. He had already refused to consider the possibility of schooling or job training.

Billy just wanted to get outside the dirty gray walls and breathe some clean air. He had dreamed of going to the beach, any beach on the North Shore. The one he really wanted to visit was Salem Willows, where as a child he rode the flying horses and ate the cotton candy. It was all gone now. He had to put it out of his mind.

He wanted no part of his family, particularly his mother. She visited him a few months before his release. She was a mess. Rumpled clothes, matted hair. She cried throughout the visit. Gertrude had just died. Sarah was with Anne Diamond. Melanie was stuck in a one-room apartment. She continued to work at the bar and kept part of the welfare check.

Within a week of his release, Billy became restless. He realized how alone he was. Despite his freedom, he felt confined. The job was dull and repetitious. His co-workers were sneaking joints and invited him in. He refused. One of them said he looked like a guy who had done some time. Billy wanted to punch him out but thought better of it.

He had no money, no car, no friends. And the parole bitch had him on the end of a leash. Nights were the worse. Without a TV or radio, he would sit in his third-floor room looking out at the people and cars moving along the Lynn Common. Sleep came hard. Dreams were filled with bad memories, coupled with nightmares. Familiar themes—being alone in the dark, people laughing, teasing, sitting on him, beating him.

He was a frequent patron of the local McDonald's. It was better after midnight. No one to bother you. Plus they had day-old newspapers and endless refills on coffee.

Two nights in a row he found himself sitting opposite two guys who looked to be high on something bad. The second night they showed some interest in the white dude chomping on a hamburger at 1 o'clock in the morning. The message was obvious—alone and nowhere to go. They smiled, said "hi," and asked if they could join him for just a minute.

A shiver of fear passed through Billy's body and brain. If it was money that they wanted, forget it. If it was fun and games, then he was overdue for a fight. The guy behind the cash register smiled as they pulled up their chairs. He yelled over to Billy to relax. "They're nothing but two pussycats. Just watch out they don't stiff you for a burger and fries."

Their intentions were not to get a free meal. They introduced themselves as businessmen—the trading business, high-priced commodities. But not like the stock exchange. They wondered if Billy needed a job. He said he was interested. The conversation continued outside the restaurant on a park bench across the street.

"Big money, Mr. Smith. No waiting and no checks. Hard cash. All you gotta do is make two or three deliveries a week. Our customers usually hang out at some whitey bars. Places we ain't welcome. How about it?"

Drugs! He knew it was drugs. Here we go again. The Lawrence scene all over again. He needed time to think about it.

"No big rush, man. Take your time. We usually drop in for a burger a couple of times a week. See you round."

Billy was ready to break out. He was fed up with his new prison without walls. He craved the excitement outside the system, the legal system, the cop system, the prison system, and the parole system.

Three weeks later, he met the commodity traders at McDonald's. They discussed his first assignment. He turned on the overhead light in his smelly room and counted out the twenty-dollar bills. Fifty in all. One thousand bucks in advance. He slept through the night for the first time in months.

The parole meetings came and went. He peed into the cup twice a week and the tests were just fine. She commended him on his behavior and asked how the job was going. He replied that even though it wasn't much money, it gave him something to do. She remarked on how well he was budgeting his money, since he had just acquired a sharp new wardrobe. He claimed that his mother had loaned him some money for clothes. She winked and said, "Thank God for moms."

One week later, Billy skipped his urine test and failed to show up at the parole office. A warrant for his arrest was issued, but he was long gone. The previous weekend he met with his business partners at their pad in Saugus and got stoned on booze and coke. He stayed over for the next few nights, drowning himself in the magic relief that bathed his body and brain.

He knew the rules. One strike and you're out. His friends wanted to stash him quickly. He was a hot commodity, soon to be a fugitive. They did not trust his loyalty under the pressure of a little chat at the local police station. The first stop was a safe house in Roxbury. The following day, a sullen man named Jocko drove him to a dilapidated brown stone building in the Bronx. The fugitive from the North Shore of Massachusetts would blend in nicely with the fugitives in the Big Apple.

He was introduced to his roommates and offered a lumpy mattress in a corner of their family room. The family itself was made up of three adults with no blood ties, a white man and woman and a strange spooky-looking man who looked like a mannequin with the latest ill-fitting robes. He was a small-time pimp; the girl, a would-be actress and Times Square hooker; the other guy, a recent graduate of Attica Prison.

Tiffany offered to share her bed with whichever guy got home first at night. The loser got the pull-out sofa. Their advice to Billy was to stay in the apartment for the first week until the local cops moved on to a new batch of mug shots and wanted posters. He thought he'd go crazy. Their TV was on the blink. At night he wandered around the neighborhood a few times just to keep his sanity. He was close to the breaking point. They were all using coke and the pimp was into heroin. None for their guest. He couldn't be trusted. Might pull a nutty on them.

Billy did not last a week. On the sixth night, he read himself to sleep before midnight. As was his custom, the first couple of hours were fitful. He heard the sound of footsteps in the inky black room.

He started to get up but Tiffany gently pushed him back onto the floor with her foot. She quickly knelt down beside his mattress and issued a couple of giggles and a couple of burps. She smelled awful. He guessed that she had turned a couple of tricks and got drunk into the bargain. The next thing he knew she was straddling him around his waist. She leaned over and pressed her lips on to his face. The booze was whiskey, cheap whiskey.

Maybe it was the suddenness, maybe it was the darkness. Maybe it was the crushing weight of her body on top of him. Whatever the combination, his immediate reflex was to strike out. No more play thing. No more victim. With stiffened arms he lifted her up and threw her heavily across the room. In the darkness, he could hear her body strike the corner of the couch. As he crawled over, he saw the blood oozing from her forehead and immediately turned on a light. Despite his rage, he grabbed a bath towel and ordered her to press it against the wound to stop the bleeding.

Suddenly, he felt like punching and kicking. He was almost out of control. As he moved towards her, he halted as her sobs reminded him of another woman, his mother. So often he would hear her gulping deeply to get air into her lungs after bouts of crying. So many times he feared that she would die. Was this bitch dying? God! What had he done. He slowly walked across the room, sat on the floor, and began to cry.

The menfolk arrived home around three in the morning. Tiffany met them at the door. They had brought an overnight guest with them, a former New York Jets linebacker interested in a career change. They bounced Billy around the apartment as quietly as they could. When he was almost unconscious, they lifted him down the stairs and dragged him into a nearby alley where he slipped into a coma from the numerous kicks to the head and ribs. The next day some kids found him lying next to a trash bin. He awoke in the intensive care unit two days later and left the hospital within a week.

The best that the social worker could do was a shelter on the west side of lower Manhattan. Billy was an easy find for the NYPD. Everyday they checked the guest lists of the local shelters. When they arrested him, he was eating supper. Despite the cuts and bruises, they recognized him from the mug shots sent from Massachusetts.

The extradition papers arrived within two days and he found himself in Walpole State Prison twenty-four hours later. Billy was big, but he wasn't tough. His reputation at the youth detention center and the county jail didn't count for much in the jungle habitat of the state prison. At twenty years old, it was just a matter of time before he received his first lesson in prison etiquette. Within a month, he was attacked by three inmates in the shower area and repeatedly sodomized.

Reparative surgery was performed by a contracted local surgeon who bragged to his colleague that he was becoming an expert in this procedure. Billy remained on the prison medical floor for a few days and then transferred to another cell block where the danger was supposedly minimal. Nevertheless, he was petrified.

Before leaving the medical ward, he talked to Harold, the physician's assistant. Harold had some compassion and listened carefully to this young man who was so frightened.

Billy returned to the medical dispensary a week later. The stitches were ready to be removed. His surgeon had been called to the hospital for an emergency. Harold explained that in such circumstance he was deputized to do the job.

When it was over, they again chattered about life in the new cell block. Billy broke down and cried. He hadn't had a solid night's sleep since he arrived and was having suffocating panic attacks whenever he went into the shower or cafeteria. Harold put his arm around him and spoke of a possible solution. The orderly who worked in the dispensary was due for parole in a few weeks. Would Billy be interested in the job? Prior experience wasn't necessary. Harold promised to teach him all that he needed to know within a week or two. He couldn't guarantee a transfer from the current prison quarters, but the job did require four to six hours a day on site. Billy received his orientation and training a few days before the other guy left. He was delighted. Finally a good night's sleep. He was grateful to Harold. Except for Richie Miculski, no other male had been that kind to him. Harold warmed to his enthusiasm and attitude. Billy had found a home of sorts. He hated to leave at four o'clock to return to his steel cage.

The two got along well. Despite the ten-year age difference, they didn't lack for conversation. Once a week, usually on Friday, Harold brought something special for lunch. The kitchen was small but had an adequate refrigerator and microwave. It was the height of Billy's week. By the end of the first month, Harold made his move on his young assistant. He presented him with his medical record and explained that he would like to close out his notes on the recent surgery.

Under the guise of manually exploring the surgically corrected rectal laceration, he added gentle massages. When Billy asked why, he whispered, "Because you are so beautiful."

Billy was released from prison six months early. With the assistance of Harold, he hired a lawyer who convinced the judge to dismiss the drug possession charges. Although his Lynn friends implicated him at the time of their arrests, he had never been found with the goods. Breaking parole was the only real remaining charge, along with flight from the scene.

Harold found him a room in Somerville within walking distance from his own Cambridge suite. An entry-level job in the housekeeping department of Cambridge City Hospital was arranged and Billy gratefully accepted it. His supervisor was a good friend of Harold's. Billy entered the brand new world of gay society in Boston. Along with his mentor and lover, he visited the bars and lost himself in the world that was pleasurable and, most importantly, safe.

In the beginning he felt both excited and relieved. But there was a certain amount of detachment with the sexual acts. He desperately wanted to separate from the brutish life of a prisoner. Harold had rescued him, and he had genuinely cared about him. That was perhaps more seductive than anything else. In his fantasy life, he created many different roles vis-à-vis his friend and lover. But ultimately, the non-role was the most comfortable and reassuring. He was no longer a victim. He did not hurt. And for the first time in many years, he did not have the urge to hurt others.

Holly Diamond

The first eighteen years of Holly's life were spent on her skating career and not on growing up. She was shielded from the normal changes and challenges by her ambitious parents and coaches. Special schools and tutors catered to her busy schedule. Afterschool activities with other kids were not permitted. Her only playground was an ice skating rink. And one day the ice melted.

It could not have happened at a worse time in her life, but it could not have happened at a more predictable time. The end of childhood and the beginning of young adulthood is an inescapable moment that demands both reflection on what had been and a wonderment about what will be. It is the subject of all valedictory graduation speeches, as the audience sits in rapt attention.

The winter competition was over. Holly returned to her classes in preparation for graduation. The principal at the private school called a family meeting to break the bad news. Holly had fallen way behind her classmates and would not receive a diploma.

Her screaming and crying filled the offices, the corridors, and some of the classrooms. That night all sat in the parlor to console one another. It didn't help. Holly's wailing and moaning provided background music for a bitter exchange between her parents. Who was more to blame was the topic.

Holly refused to return to the school in September and insisted on resuming her skating program in preparation for the North American Competition. Another parlor meeting was had. Another disaster. Cliff said that the well had run dry. No more money for her skating career. It took both parents over two hours to calm her down. At one point, Anne tried to call the police, only to have the phone slapped out of her hand by her husband.

For two weeks, Holly retreated to her room, claiming that her life was over and that her parents were to blame. On the occasion of her brief appearance at the supper table, her parents noticed a strange pattern of mood swings. She had adopted a tendency to shift from moody to giddy very rapidly. They offered a visit to her pediatrician but she angrily refused.

By now, Anne and Cliff were barely on speaking terms. Even that was about to change. In early October, Anne found a pearl earring in the crease of the car's passenger seat. Cliff admitted to a year long affair with his secretary. He was not sorry nor defensive. He intended to file for divorce.

Holly's bubble had completely burst. What was happening? Her career and her father were about to disappear. Who was she? What was she? The mood swings became more intense. From mute catatonia to fiery rage. Anne was beside herself. She insisted that her sister resume custody of Sarah to reduce the tension and chaos in the home.

Holly was hospitalized overnight after swallowing a hand full of aspirin. She convinced the psychiatric consultant that she was not an immediate risk and adamantly refused treatment.

As the Christmas holidays approached, the two women reached an uneasy truce within the confines for their condo. Anne needed money and began working as a secretary in a downtown real estate office. At first Holly welcomed the change from mom's prying eyes and ears. By the end of the year, it all turned around.

Mom began spending time with a coworker, the boss's brother. Greg was Hollywood handsome, two years divorced and ready for some action. Anne announced that she was spending the new year holiday weekend at Greg's condo in New Hampshire.

Holly was crushed. It just wasn't right. Another confrontation, another round of coldness and bitterness on both parts. Holly felt she had to get away. She was suffocating. The walls were closing in. She called a skating buddy from one of the national tournaments and arranged for a two week getaway in New York City. Anne objected. She wasn't strong enough. Holly's reply was, "What do you care?"

She and Danielle hugged and kissed and stayed up late retelling the funny and not so funny exploits from the last skating competition. Danielle was three years older than Holly, street smart, brought up in Brooklyn, and wise to the ways of the big city. She began introducing Holly to her friends and fellow cast members from the off Broadway play. Most of them lived in the same apartment building or neighborhood.

Holly soon found out that she was hanging around with a party crowd. Late night gatherings with booze, drugs, and sex were commonplace. Danielle announced that she had promised to visit her parents in New Jersey for the weekend. She knew Holly would be okay. Holly was not so sure. She needed her friend close to her.

The day her friend left to rejoin her family, Holly sat in the room for hours on end with the lights off. She called her mother around six o'clock. Anne was buoyant and at the same time, insensitive. She was caught up with the excitement of her engagement to Greg. The wedding would be scheduled after Easter. And yes, they're moving into his condo in Nahant. Holly hung up the phone and began to cry bitter, angry, helpless tears.

The party noise came from down the hall. She was not sure what time it was, but she knew she had fallen asleep on the couch. She rose slowly, put on some slacks and a bright red sweater and moved as in a trance down the hallway to be with people, no matter who they were. Vodka on ice for two hours. A few joints but no coke. By midnight she was the life of the party. She found more laps to sit on, kissed more faces, noses, and ears, and had more hands shoved up under her sweater than anyone else. The next day she had vague, ugly recollections of what had happened. She recalled being under a large bedspread rolling and tossing with three other naked bodies. There was an awful smell. Apparently she had vomited in the bed. She remembered being dragged across the floor into the bathroom where the guys angrily stuck her head in the toilet and left her sitting on the floor. How she got back to her apartment, she did not know. She awoke around four o'clock in the afternoon on Sunday, lying on the floor of her apartment with the smell of vomit stuck to her clothes and clogging her nostrils. For the first time, she truly wanted to die. It was not a question of ingesting pills and being rescued anymore. But she was afraid to die. And yet what was there left for her on this earth? Mom was out of her life, as was her father. She had two choices—to live in a world where she was all alone and rejected, where she was a failure, where she could not defend herself or support herself and had no real friends and no money; on the other hand, she could kill herself for real, not just try. Either way, the horrible black abyss was waiting for her. If she descended, no one would ever know or care. The noise of a police siren came and went from below her darkened room that Sunday night. It startled her and broke her dismal reverie.

There was a third choice. Why hadn't she thought of it? She smiled to herself. There was some hope. She had once been somebody. She could be somebody again. She was good. She had talent and she had style, and no one could take that away from her, ever.

After a long, hot bath, Holly lay down comfortably on the top of her bed and dozed off. She needed some rest before her performance that evening. At ten o'clock she woke. It was time. She had packed the bright blue skating outfit from her last competition and had laid out the pretty colored garment on the back of the chair. She put it on and looked at herself in the mirror. Real good, real fancy, and real professional. Next the bag with the ice skates. She walked out into the frigid late winter night and slipped into the subway station a block away.

People gawked and turned away. What was this young woman doing with no coat over her costume. Her legs must be cold. The poor thing didn't have enough money to buy a coat. They smiled at her and she smiled back. She felt that she had already gained her attention even before her performance.

The lights at Rockefeller Skating Rink were turned off when she arrived. Undaunted, she sat and slowly laced on the skates. With no effort at all, she glided on to the darkened ice surface. A security guard called to her but she paid no attention. A few people who were passing by stopped to watch the performance. They were enthralled by the professional beauty of it all. Periodically, she would bow and curtsey to their applause.

By midnight the crowd had grown into a sizable assembly. Her performance was superb. They were caught by the rhythm of it all but also by the bizarre nature of a single skater showing her wares in the dark and in the freezing weather. She seemed possessed by her own performance and there was something eerie about the fact that there was no music.

By one o'clock the police cars arrived and four heavyset well-clothed policemen walked through the developing snowstorm onto the ice. She would not leave her performance and they had to carry her into the car. They noticed that her skin was covered with frost and that she was totally exhausted. Within seconds she fell asleep in the warm vehicle en route to the hospital. When she arrived at the emergency room she again slipped into unconsciousness, but only after demanding that they return her gold medal which she believed they had stolen from her.

Holly spent three weeks on the psychiatric ward of the Bellevue Hospital before returning home to Salem. Her diagnosis was bipolar disorder, mixed type. Medication had been offered and was successful, allowing her to recover. Plans for both counseling and medication therapy were forwarded to her mother Anne after lengthy phone conversations during Holly's hospital stay.

Sarah Smith

Her job and her counselor. These were the two things that Sarah depended on very much. After high school, Sarah began working full time in the nursing home. She was appreciated and she was rewarded with a goodly amount of support and friendship. She continued to see her counselor Carol and as before was guided slowly but surely into a mature young woman who gained confidence by her actions more than her words. Setting goals had been the rule of therapy during her teen years and continued to be the guiding principle as she moved into her young adult years. Her main goal was to secure her job and make enough money to support herself and help her mother Melanie run their small apartment.

Melanie had remained sober for the past two years and made a special effort to provide a home for her long-lost child. In her own way, she was proud of Sarah, especially the way she plodded through the last years of high school. Both mother and daughter were well aware of their limitations and the difficulty that had shaped their life without a man around to help. Melanie preferred not the think about Sarah's complete lack of male role models as a child. No father to speak of, a sullen, selfish Judd, and then Cliff who was cheating on the side.

Sarah told Melanie that of the three men, Cliff was the one that she liked the best. He tried hard to make her feel wanted in their home. When the ladies of the house were on the ice-skating circuit, he took time to be home at night, to do the cooking, and to get the groceries. Sarah genuinely missed him when he left home for the other woman. He continued to call her about once a week to support and reassure her that she would be all right.

The nursing home was on the Salem-Marblehead line. Sarah could walk to work. While in high school, she started working in the kitchen helping to prepare the supper meals. Afterward she graduated into a full-time employee, ostensibly for summer replacement help. By the fall, she was a full-time person who truly loved the closeness with the elderly patients. Many of them called her by her first name and complimented her on her good manners, good looks, and sparkling clean uniform. She devoted herself entirely to their care, which included bathing and dressing. In addition, she offered them kind words and moral support through their tribulations. She often thought that she saw her grandma Gertrude in some of the women patients particularly. She was somebody now. She was needed and she was important, and she began to feel important to herself.

The guiding hand of the counselor, Carol, was always there. Although they had cut back on the appointment schedule, twice a month seemed to be enough. Carol was proud of Sarah, and indeed thought of her at times as her own daughter.

Carol suggested that she develop a more active social life. Sarah was hesitant at first but realized that she truly was grounded in a pale work-and-home existence schedule. Carol reminded her that her social life in high school was nonexistent and even suggested that she consider a boyfriend. Sarah confided that she certainly had a yen to meet a young man but was not quite ready at that time. Carol was encouraged and knew that in time that her protégé would develop a much broader taste for life around her.

Terry Brennan

The Brennans still had some love to give. They needed to fill the gap. The kids were grown up and had left home and they felt the pain of the empty nest.

Terry Brennan's life might have been different. But the Brennans did all they could, certainly in the early years, to share their home and their love with her. Inevitably, however, all parties had to deal with the crisis of adolescence and all of the wonderment and uncertainty that it brings.

The early years went smoothly. They doted on the little redhead with the beautiful smile and the feisty temper. She wore the best of clothes at Easter and Christmas gatherings. And she was indeed bright. The teachers said she was the smartest one in the class but also the most rambunctious.

Oddly enough, it was to her father Jim that she turned for affection, for fun and games, and for forgiveness at times. Marie gave her what she could but did not seem to have the same warmth or patience. The older Terry got, the more the two women seemed to develop a communication gap. During her preadolescent years, the women had many tiffs over what clothes to wear, TV selection, and even her choice of friends.

In truth, Marie was struggling with midlife problems that included several family deaths and losses. Her mother and father died within a year of each other, and a sister was diagnosed with cancer of the breast. Her husband Jim was beginning to talk about early retirement, and money issues became an item in their marriage. Thus the stage was set for an unusual and unique series of events that none of the parties could have anticipated. The problems ahead of Terry Brennan following the knowledge of her adoption were indeed critical.

In the earlier discussion of adolescence, we traced the serious challenge of growing from a kid to an adult, of grafting on traits and values from idealized persons so as to someday have a solid identity—over a period of years searching to be somebody, not just an unsure, unreliable geek.

This starting point for most kids is membership in a family where the roles are clear even if not completely accepted. There is a mommy and a daddy, and maybe other children of certain age and gender. Most kids wish they were some one else. But at least they know who they are and most importantly they know that they are loved no matter what they do. Being a member of a family means belonging to parents and siblings.

For the adopted child, however, it is different. From the moment the child is told about its true heritage, questions of worth creep in. Adoption agencies differ as to the right time to discuss all this. What they do emphasize is the importance of building a trust between parents and child. The preschool years are where this begins. By the time the child reaches the latency years, the bonding and sense of belonging bode well for the child's acceptance of the unavoidable questions of rejection.

Just telling the child is not enough. Adoptive parents must work through the issues and be prepared for some unsettling moments where the basic feelings of madness, sadness, and badness surface.

In an unhealthy or dysfunctional family structure the issues of adoption may create havoc.

Terry Brennan was crushed. It was bad enough to go through the menarche without her mother Marie to help out. At the time she and Jim were on a two-week vacation in the Caribbean. She was too embarrassed to tell her aunt Jeanette with whom she was staying.

The night they took her back home, Terry pulled a tantrum. Jim and Marie were shocked. They were then angry and resentful. They deserved some time away. And she was telling them that they were cruel and insensitive parents. That angry confrontation served as a starting point for a contentious relationship during the early part of her adolescence and indeed throughout Terry's challenging teenage years.

All parties went to bed angry, but they resumed the discussion the next night. Terry was subdued but not apologetic. She burst into tears upon hearing about the adoptive process. She had been only one year old. She wanted to know everything. What agency? What city? Did they know who her real parents were?

There was a lull in the conversation. Several minutes of silence. She then jumped up and ran into the kitchen crying. "Oh, this is terrible. This is awful. Why did this happen to me? Why did they do it? Why did they let me go? I didn't do anything wrong. What am I going to tell my friends?"

Jim and Marie followed her into the kitchen to comfort her and she pushed them away.

"Don't come near me. Don't touch me. You're not my real mother and father. I hate you. I hate them."

The Brennans went back to Catholic Charities out of desperation. They needed some advice and needed it now. Fortunately, the social worker who had helped with the adoption was still there. She was quite supportive and quite eager to be involved again. Terry's response was not unusual, she said. What it took was some patience on everyone's part. She arranged for an appointment so that all could meet in person and discuss the project of trying to work out a better relationship. Terry adamantly refused to attend the meeting.

Other attempts were made by the Brennans to soften the blow of the news delivered to Terry. She repeatedly rejected their efforts, however. This in turn caused some hardening of their attitude and they began to feel betrayed themselves after all that they had offered this child.

Terry was an angry young adolescent, and took her anger into the schools and into the streets. Her rage at times seemed unbounded, and for some reason she would not see the other side and take responsibility for her actions. This set the parents and the child further apart over the ensuing years. Terry found kids she could identify with and they were not healthy identifications. By her senior year, she had an abortion and two arrests for drug possession. If she was bad and rejectable, she was living out this role and in a somewhat perverse way, trying to show people how bad she really could be while at the same time looking for some love and protection.

Young Adulthood

She drifted through the streets of Lawrence and then Boston. Messy relationships with drug lords and some runners left her with a sense of excitement and an odd fulfillment. The fact was that she turned ultimately into formal prostitution when she did move to Boston itself.

She had told Billy Smith during their beach stroll that she had hired a lawyer to find her real parents. He came up with no hard evidence, but sadly reported that her real father had been sent to prison for armed robbery and her mother had turned to prostitution. He had no idea where either parent was. Both had changed their real names a couple of times.

In Boston, Terry was in too deep to get out. She was consumed in the dangerous world of prostitution and drugs. Her one security was provided by a pimp from Roxbury. He kept her in his stable as long as she brought in the money. It was indeed a cruel and dangerous life that she lived. At first, she was a star prospect with top price. Between the customers, the competition, and her master's paranoia, her attractiveness inevitably faded.

Billy Smith recalled seeing her with her "man" at a gay and lesbian protest in Dorchester. Even from a distance she had changed her appearance drastically. She was haunted and haggard. No longer robust. She also seemed to be limping. What was noticeable was her bright orange hair and an ugly jagged scar that stretched from the left side of her lip to her cheekbone. The smile was still there but in a contrived and labored way, and two upper teeth were missing.

Genital herpes put her market value as zero according to her pimp. He reluctantly allowed her to stay at his pad until she could pick up another line of work. One month limit! She was expected to clean, cook and make herself scarce whenever he brought a new girl home for a "training session." One night, he changed the rules and insisted that she participate in a menage-á-trois, after which he kicked her off the bed onto the floor with orders to get her disgusting hide out of the room. An hour later, as they lay sleeping she returned to the room holding the pimps revolver. In rapid succession, she shot each of them in the head and then arranged their bodies on the outer edges of the bed with a space in between. Her final act after climbing in between the couple was to lie down facing the ceiling and shoot herself through the mouth.

According to the newspaper reports, the police were baffled as to the meaning of the scene. Clearly a murder-suicide. The gun was in her hand. But why? They guessed that somehow it had to do with revenge or some weird ritual. They wondered if she had been hurt or rejected by the man and the woman lying on either side.

Billy Smith read the newspaper account. The cops had guessed right. But there was so much more to it. She had found who she was looking for and it was no different. She was a reject once again, but this time she would stay with them and not be separated.

Billy put the newspaper down and cried.

Ruth Reardon

Boston College was a good choice. Sure, it was her mom's alma mater. So what. It was still a sensible institution of higher learning and it represented old-fashioned values. No big campus protests, riots, or orgies. Plus it was an hour's ride from Marblehead. She shared an off-campus room with Karen from Danvers, which was next to Marblehead. They would often share rides during their freshmen year.

It was not much of a separation or a culture shock. She loved her new friends and her new digs. Weekend visits home the first couple of months were a relief from the classroom drudgery. She had carefully selected her courses from the catalog before arriving. General liberal arts stuff and some introductory sciences.

There was plenty of social life available. Just to meet people, she went to some parties during registration week. The football pep rallies were fun. Gigantic and noisy, but a place to be seen. Her thoughts, however, drifted down Commonwealth Avenue to Boston University, where her high school classmate was enrolled.

She and Dana Broderick continued their close relationship beyond their senior year. No big commitment and nothing binding, they actually went to the prom with different partners during their final year. It was only after their graduation that something clicked. They met again at the yacht club dance one night and got reacquainted. They were the only under-thirties in the crowd and left early to be together. They sat on a rock wall at Devreaux Beach and just held hands while they chatted.

Once a week, one or the other made the phone call from one end of Commonwealth Avenue to the other. Quite often they would impulsively jump on the trolley and visit the other's campus. They fell in love quickly during that freshmen year. They developed a deep respect and solid love for each other as time went by. Comfortable in each other's company, they could laugh and relax with ease. They hugged and kissed but stopped short of sexual intercourse. Ruth said it went with marriage and not before. Dana agreed.

Ruth made the Dean's List from the first semester on. Despite her pre-med major, she made sure she took liberal arts courses to satisfy her mother's advice. Mother said if you cannot read and write in your own language, you haven't been educated.

A particular fascination was the philosophy course given in her senior year. The student-teacher discussion groups were her favorites. Serious questions about religion and the meaning of life were encouraged. By the end of her college career, Ruth had a solid grip on the faith and values she grew up with.

Ruth graduated from Boston College cum laude. She was accepted at three medical schools and chose Tufts University in Boston. College was a good time for her. She grew into a mature young woman and had a solid sense of confidence.

The changes and challenges were not overwhelming because of her own and her family's preparation. They stood by her all the way and she trusted them. She was not an overachiever. She stayed within her limits, but those limits were quite vast. She had fun along the way. She did not need to be number one, as her mother had told her over and over again, "You don't have to be the best, just do your best."

Alan Reardon

They were bigger, faster, tougher. They were all heroes back home. Freshmen football at Harvard was a surprise. Alan Reardon had not anticipated the level of talent on the practice field. It was an Ivy League school. You didn't have to win, just fight fiercely.

Pre-season tryouts and conditioning started in mid-August. On Labor Day, he had run into enough people to sport a sprained ankle as well as a sprained left thumb. He was ranked number two quarterback when the season opened. Number one was three years older, three inches taller, and a recent discharge from the U.S. Marine Corps.

His academic schedule was a typical first semester waltz, tailored to the demanding hours of the football, soccer, and rugby squads.

He was assigned to a "jock" dorm. His roommate was a rugged linebacker from New Jersey, who was All-State. On the field he had the ferocity of Dick Butkus. In the dorm, he was quiet and serious about his studies. They got along right from the start. He was the first black student from his town to go to an Ivy League school. He was not about to screw it up.

The coaches warned them about jumping right into campus social life while the football season was on. His quarterback coach warned him of jumping in after the season also. He claimed there are some good people around and there are some bad ones.

Alan was in no hurry. Responsibilities of herohood still lingered. He was not a big man on campus, and at least for the time being, he liked it that way. His mother Rita called him once a week and he did manage to get home for a few overnights in the fall. He surprised himself by opting to stay around the house rather than go out. For the first time in his life, he felt more comfortable just hanging around and seemed to take a renewed interest in the affairs of his family. He was amazed at how his parents had matured. They were really neat. They cared about his early career at Harvard. They asked questions about his friends and his studies. They even attended a couple of home games in Cambridge. Joe usually slipped him a hundred dollar bill on Sunday nights just before he left to go back to school.

He was puzzled about Jessica, however. So strange and withdrawn. She had refused follow-up treatment after her first breakdown. She was barely passing in school and had no friends. Maybe he could take her out to the campus some weekend and show her around.

While playing football or practicing, he felt calm. But the Sunday night trip back to Cambridge was a bummer. There were times when he wanted to turn the car around and go back to Marblehead. He had a strange sense of weakness and helplessness at times. He still felt that he had no solid identity, no solid grip on himself.

Where was he headed? What did he want in life? What was life all about, anyway? Why did his mother and his sister have it all together? What went wrong? Why couldn't he feel for other people? Was he really that self-centered?

He returned from the spring break in Florida with the same empty feeling. The sex and the booze parties at Daytona left him morose. It was a repeat of high school. The girls were bigger and hungrier and the booze was occasionally laced with some designer drugs. Lots of war stories to brag about back on campus. But who really cared?

His father Eddie dropped over to spring practice and Alan introduced him to some teammates. For the first time, he was actually embarrassed. Eddie's eyes were bloodshot and his speech slurred. He knew he was drinking too much but mid-afternoon was a no-no.

As a sophomore, Alan's chances of starting as quarterback were nil. He was now number three on the depth chart. He shifted to wide receiver at his coaches' urging. Instant star. The same talented hands that could throw the ball could catch it. But something happened en route to the hall of fame. His own teammate stepped on his foot while coming out of the huddle. Three bones fractured and no surgery required. They simply never healed over the next few weeks and months. He was out for the year. He still couldn't bear weight by the start of the following season. Apparently the bone chips had not healed properly and had impinged on some nerve endings. The pain was excruciating.

In his senior year, he felt distracted and unsure of what to do upon graduation. He had switched too late from a physical education major to business. Harvard Business School turned him down. Not enough courses and not high enough grades.

Except for Jessica, the family showed up at his graduation. His father Eddie sent regrets, however. Business trip to Tokyo. His sister Ruth looked great. Marriage suited her. He had always liked Dana Broderick. A good guy, no phony.

The family went home and he stayed on campus that night for one final fling with his buddies. He made an early exit from the beer bash downtown and laid awake for a couple of hours just thinking about the graduation ceremonies, the hugs and the handshakes, and what it all meant.

Certain thoughts kept coming back. What have I accomplished? Four years after high school and I still don't know where I'm heading. An ex-jock with a broken foot. Is that it? Where the hell am I going? And the most frightening realization of all. Who really cares?

Jessica Reardon

No violence, no major resistance. Jessica entered McLean Hospital as a sad, lifeless, and sick young woman. However, the staff members at the hospital were sorry to see her leave one month later. She was a good patient, and she did benefit from their efforts. She responded quickly to the staff's sincerity and kindness as well as their straight talk. The initial care plan called for high doses of antipsychotic medication. But the real difference was the effort by the people around her. Predictable routines were arranged so that she could gain some sense of scheduling in her life. Verbal reinforcement of reality was a high priority.

The hospital staff offered her relief from a world that threatened to engulf her, five years of coping with changes and expectations that only confused and tormented her. She was never in synch with the flow of teenage changes, whether they be style or language. And the worst of it all was that she knew it. She realized that the mirror of her mind was cracked. The distorted reflections of herself and the world around her were overpowering.

Prior to discharge careful plans were made for after care. Weekly visits for one month back to the hospital itself were seen as the backbone of the plan. During these visits she would receive both counseling and medication management. Unlike the prior occasion of hospitalization, she embraced this aftercare plan and saw it as vital to her survival. She actually felt bad leaving the hospital, because she had managed to reach out and make friends, both on the staff and among other patients.

By the end of the summer, her counselor felt that she could engage in some work and called the director of volunteers at the Salem Children's Hospital. Jessica agreed to volunteer one morning a week as a receptionist in the waiting room outside the pediatric intensive care unit. She greeted parents and relatives and quietly fetched them coffee and pastries. In addition, she managed to take charge of the waiting room's magazines and flowers and took a real interest in this challenge. Although her person-to-person contact was minimal, it seemed rewarding. The director of the hospital himself received phone calls and letters complimenting him on the kind and beautiful young lady who was so helpful. She proudly showed copies of letters to her counselor and to her parents. She began to smile around the house.

Joe and Rita welcomed the information gathered from the hospital staff and doctors. It helped them to shape their own plans for support and encouragement within the family. Life at home became much easier during the autumn months. The continued treatment in Belmont plus the volunteer job seemed to offer Jessica just enough challenge coupled with the gratification that came from knowing she could function in the real world.

Her parents began to notice something else. She was beginning to develop a little personality. She expressed herself more in terms of likes and dislikes and entered into the family conversation. She listened to soft rock music and became interested in films on the old movie channels. She would stay up until the wee hours of the morning laughing and giggling over old cartoons. In fact, Jessica was catching up. It was as if the high school experience never happened, and now she was hearing, feeling, tasting, and seeing the fun times she had missed. The McLean Hospital staff reassured Joe and Rita that it was a positive experience. They did caution them, however, that she should stay clear of bizarre horror shows. Unfortunately, one film slipped through around the Christmas holidays.

Jessica stayed up one night watching an old black-and-white version of Dickens's "A Christmas Carol." She was overwhelmed by the drama in this film, particularly the graphic scenes of the ghosts. The following morning, she did not come down for breakfast and stayed in her room until about noontime. When Rita went up to her room, she was lying in bed in a catatonic state and by the end of the day she had been returned to McLean Hospital inpatient unit. She came home within three days much improved. The medication adjustment and the intensive support seemed to do wonders. Both she and her therapist and her family realized that she was by no means completely cured, and they were all thankful for the rapid response that helped her get back on her feet so quickly.

There was no question that Jessica was more resilient. It was a hard-earned strength based on her determination to listen to her caregivers and her parents and accept the fact that she had an illness that could be treated. The doctors at the hospital said that this feature of her acceptance of her

Young Adulthood

illness and of the treatment bode well for her future. They were even more encouraged when they heard that she had thanked her parents for their early intervention.

If Jessica was making up for lost time regarding music, videos, and teenage interests, she was also willing to explore some girl things. Rita was attentive to this newfound interest. During the winter and spring months, the two of them drove to Boston a few times to explore the world outside of Marblehead. The first trip went well, lunch at the Ritz. Around the February holidays, the two of them again went to Boston and took in the Copley Place mall. Jessica was not as comfortable this time. It was mobbed with high-schoolers on vacation—lots of running around and screaming. Rita suggested catching a movie, but Jessica froze. She said that she was afraid to sit in a dark room with other people.

The third venture was in late spring, lunch and an afternoon at the Museum of Fine Arts. The Monet exhibit was current and Jessica was absolutely thrilled. She chattered all the way home about the beautiful pictures. She never seen anything so wonderful. Joe felt it was a good test of her recovery. If she could relate to and admire the Impressionists, then her ability to perceive life as it really is was indeed healthy.

Her volunteer job at Children's Hospital continued through the first six months of the year, and she was given more tasks. By the summer, she was doing readings for the tots and bringing them juices and snacks. She loved being with the little kids and they loved her.

The summer social scene in Marblehead was quite another story. Jessica was not comfortable at the yacht club. She felt everyone was staring at her. Rita tried to make light of it and said indeed they were—but the reason was that she was so strikingly attractive. This type of reassurance did not work. Jessica was afraid of the crowds and the highly intellectual chatter that went on at times. She began to feel that there was something wrong with her and asked if she could avoid some of the weekly cocktail hours and dinners. In a sailboat, she was a different person. She loved being on the water, and as soon as the boat had cleared the harbor, she would peel off her sweater or jacket and soak up the breeze, the salt air, and the sun. Not only that, but she was a surprisingly adept sailor.

Joe and Rita were encouraged at her continued development. She was entering the real world of busy people and busy activities and seemed to have a way of putting a brake on situations that she feared.

In the fall, she signed up for two courses at Salem State College. One of the nurses at Children's Hospital encouraged her to do so, and actually accompanied her to two of the courses. One was in art appreciation and the other in the history of modern music. She did so well that during the second semester she added additional courses and announced at the end of that term that she was enrolling the following autumn as a full-time student.

By that time, medication management and counseling sessions were reduced to monthly visits. She was determined to make a life for herself.

CHOICE

Billy Smith

With his prison term behind him, Billy had the opportunity to start a new life. He was no longer a child. The Department of Social Services had no power over him, nor did all the people that he resented. No more foster homes, no more grown-ups pushing him around.

But he walked out into a world with few resources at hand. No money, no job, no family, and no friends. Worse still, he had no game plan for his life. All of a sudden, his childhood was gone and he had never been taught how to cope in the adult world.

The one thing that he trusted, the one familiar feature of his life, was the feeling of anger and rage. Unfortunately, his anger was to determine a lifestyle that would be repetitious. For Billy, hate was a reliable feeling. It replaced sadness and fear, and certainly replaced any sense of tenderness or softness. It offered the illusion of strength and confidence, but it was a mirage. He was able to feel less vulnerable with his anger, and armed with a righteous rage, he felt it was okay to hurt others.

Dealing drugs came naturally. It put him in touch with people who had similar ideas about life. The world of adults had never welcomed him. He was an outcast from the beginning. So why not stay outside that world, outside of its rules, and outside of its laws.

It felt good to skip out on the appointment with the parole officer. Screw her and all the other stiffs that tried to control his life. The trip to New York City was exciting. A new beginning. He was in control now. There were moments on the drive down when he thought of his father. He wondered if that was why he went away. Mom told him once that he had failed to show up for some legal thing. What if he were still alive? Maybe he would find him someday. Maybe it was better if he didn't.

Billy was no match for the street-wise thugs in the big city. It almost cost him his life. Rage and vengeance are common currency in the ranks of the city's outcasts. You just don't turn it on each other. He broke rule number one with the brutal attack on Tiffany. He had a short visit to the Big Apple.

Young Adulthood

Back behind bars, he had yet another lesson to learn. Billy was no longer a kid, no longer an angry adolescent, scrapping and wrestling with other screwed-up kids. He was in a human jungle now made up of predators of every stripe. Life was cheap, loyalties nonexistent, and pleasure forbidden unless you took it from someone else instantly and brutally. He was convinced before he arrived that sex and violence were the same, but was unprepared for the level of savage satisfaction he encountered. He was a thing again and not a person. A helpless, worthless thing.

Harold rescued him from the jungle, and Harold with his attention and affection took the little boy away from his hurts. By arranging for a job and for a place to live, he assumed the parent role. Billy saw him as the missing father. There were no taboos about sex with a parent figure for Billy. As a child, the taboo about real incest had already been broken by his mother.

Billy found a certain amount of peace in his young adult life, but only if he stuck to the here and now. The business of everyday survival consumed him. He could not afford to be introspective or to dwell on all of the hurts of his life. Deep inside he was still restless. So many feelings that he did not understand. The nightmares wouldn't go away. He was still suspicious of new situations and new people. The panic attacks returned and were more crippling and more frequent. In enclosed places such as elevators and trains, he thought he would suffocate. He could not stand heights and shunned crowded shopping malls. He was afraid to tell Harold about his fears and anxiety in the crowded, noisy bars.

Despite all this, Billy's life as a young adult was better than it had ever been. He questioned, however, whether he was in real good control. And where was it all going to end up. Billy wondered and worried constantly.

Holly Diamond

The bubble finally burst. Her career was over. Family life gone forever. It was all so sudden. So final. So frightening. She had nothing to fall back on. Her skating friends were gone. Once you drop out of competition, they drop you.

The emptiness was compounded by a feeling of deep resentment. She had never taken real responsibility for anything but her performance on the ice. Even then, Holly was loathe to blame herself for her imperfections. It was the ice that was too soft, too wet, or too hard. And the judges were too old, too young, or too biased.

Mom was always available to take the heat. Now Holly turned her resentment on her best friend, her mother. She blamed her not only for her skating failures, but for robbing her of a normal childhood. In her wild tirades against her, she mentioned the failed marriage. Having spent her energies in her angry outbursts and in her sulking, she turned away from Mom and sought relief with newly discovered local friends.

But Mom was more vulnerable than anyone thought. She had ignored the early signs of her midlife changes as she paid most of her attention to her daughter. Aside from the hormonal changes, she blocked out the impact of family illnesses and deaths that had mounted around her. Sure, the marriage was not on the best footing, but Holly's career did come first after all.

Mom had dropped out of any type of social life during Holly's skating career. Thus, she stopped getting invitations to school reunions and parties. Now she lay awake more evenings wondering about the course of her life. But there was always another practice, another car trip, another competition that in the past had distracted her.

It all came crashing down on Mom when her princess, her only child, left her and went to Boston to start another life. She deteriorated into a heavy drinker, and plummeted into a deep depression, stopping just short of killing herself.

The shock of it all brought mom and daughter together for a brief time. But the virus of selfishness that had driven both to seek the glory road of fame and fortune resurfaced in the form of opportunity. Anne found a man, a guy she so badly needed. And she didn't look back. Holly was stunned by the betrayal and did the one thing that she had been trained to do—turn to the stars. Go somewhere. Perform and be the best.

But Holly and Anne had a secret that was to prove telling in the months ahead. That secret had to do with months and years of mood swings that accompanied the ups and downs of the skating circuit. Oftentimes, her mother would stay up all night after a bad performance hugging and rocking her baby. There were many rides home where the cold silence was broken by a piercing, uncontrolled scream from Holly. At times, Holly mentioned to her mother that she could see nothing but a black hole of nothingness ahead of her after a particularly poor performance.

Throughout her life, Holly had bounced back by way of driving or flying to a new place, a new arena. New York held promise. But as the miles ticked off en route to the land of opportunity, she sank into a suffocating sense of despair. She realized that she could not function without her mom. She could not live without her. How strange, she thought. Mom could live without me, but I cannot live without her. This was completely unacceptable.

Thus Holly Diamond broke down under the weight of serious losses after enjoying what seemed like a well-ordered, protected life.

Bipolar Disorder

If schizophrenia is the most misunderstood mental illness, then bipolar disorder is the most misrepresented. It is commonly overdiagnosed. Not so a quarter of a century ago—then, it was called manic-depressive psychosis, and there is the clue. True bipolar illness is a psychosis, a major, crippling mental illness. Today, however, many mental health workers mistake varying degrees of mood swings for the real thing. This is more common in the field of adolescent psychology. For good reason: the topsy-turvy emotional rollercoaster ridden by most teenagers may look crazy at times. But if we interpret these excesses of adolescent behavior as true guidelines for the diagnosis of bipolar disease, then most teens would indeed be diagnosed as bipolar at least once a week.

In the first chapter, we highlighted the central role of depression in all mental illnesses. Bipolar disorder begins and ends with this fundamental emotional response to life's changes and losses. The term bipolar refers to the opposite extremes of the depressive mood. At one end, the absolute, desolate pit of despair; at the other end, a giddy, carefree, irresponsible trip as far away from the terrible darkness as one can get. The bipolar flight is an escape from the awful pain of depression. In that context, it is also an alternative to suicide.

The manic or high phase of bipolar regression is radically different from the avoidant behavior of the schizophrenic. The other major difference between these two diseases is the locus of impairment. Schizophrenia is a thought disorder, and bipolar is a mood disorder.

A certain personality structure is common to those who suffer this illness. Some of the basic ingredients include intelligence, humor, and a muted pattern of anger. This same blend has launched many successful careers, particularly in the entertainment field. Stand-up comics on a particularly wild night could pass for a bipolar patient on a mental health ward. The difference is that they can turn it off after the show. The bipolar patient cannot.

Other similarities include the ability to aim fast, witty, sarcastic volleys that in essence are shots at other people, particularly authority figures. The verbal attacks by the sick bipolar patient are really nasty verbal grenades that contain an enormous amount of resentment and rage but happen to be wrapped in a wry and ugly humor.

The psychiatric staffs of most inpatient mental health units, if they had a choice, would rather care for ten schizophrenics then one bipolar patient. Why? The schizophrenic avoids confrontation and the bipolar patient seeks it out. And because of the intelligence and humor, they manage to strip others bare. They like to embarrass people. They loathe authority and delight in weakening it.

The bipolar patient who entertains an audience also controls that audience. It is not so much a search for fame and fortune as a desperate effort to avoid the dark shadows offstage where there is a sense of nothingness.

As we discussed at the beginning of the book, the core ingredients of the depressive mood are sadness, madness, and badness. No one feels these emotions more painfully than the bipolar patient. A penetrating sense of sadness and loneliness is offset by the need to be with other people. Being alone is unbearable. The people that the bipolar patient seeks out must hear of the injustice of life, the unfairness of it all.

The madness or anger is woven into the message sent out by the bipolar patient. In terms of the sense of low self-esteem and even badness, the bipolar turns it back onto some object, either in the audience or persons of a familiar nature. The message is simple. *You are bad. You people out there who put me in this damnable situation. You parents, you teachers, you politicians, you cops, you lawyers, you doctors and nurses.*

I'll get even. I'll taunt you. I'll insult you. I'll mock you. And yes, if I really get angry, I will punch you, kick you, and maybe even kill you.

Once the volatile mood escalates, the soaring balloon containing the gases of rage and impotence will drive the patient truly into an uncontrolled state. Hospitalization is the first step in controlling such behavior. The world is no longer the stage. Instead, the limited confines of a mental health ward become the shrunken world. That world is made up of people who are either patients or staff. And they then become the objects of the bizarre mixture of feelings.

Usually, the energy expended in the tirades simply runs out. The grandiosity trickles down with the help of reality and limits imposed by the staff and with certain medications.

Lithium carbonate has become a standard medication in the treatment of bipolar disorder. Oddly enough, this is derived from the soil as a simple common salt. For the use of treatment in bipolar disease, a chemically purified product is available in varying strengths. This medicine is not a guarantee of complete relief. During the latter part of the last century, an anti-epileptic medication called valproic acid (Depakene) has been used with much success where lithium carbonate fails. Again, no miracle, no guarantee, but a valuable agent in the treatment of this illness.

As with the disease of schizophrenia, occasional regressions are likely to occur, particularly in the adult phase as well as the middle years. Successful treatment revolves around follow-up counseling and medications. Within a few weeks or even a couple months, the bipolar patient is able to resume normal activities such as work, family, and social life. This is good news and bad news. The bad news is that a dramatic and complete recovery tends to discourage the patient from continuing the necessary post-breakdown treatment. The good news is obviously the feeling of relief and freedom to return to a normal life.

Paradoxically, the intelligence and the pride of the bipolar patient lead them away from the early signs of a potential regression. There is a false impression that working harder, running faster, avoiding the thoughts of a depression will work. Thus the breakdown may surface with frightening speed. Family and friends may be unable to head it off. On the other hand, as life goes on, the more mature person sees that they really are vulnerable and is more likely to trust family and friends with their caring advice to get early help.

Holly Diamond did recover quickly from the breakdown in New York City. She did return home, and although quite confused and quite depleted, she maintained a short-term treatment program. Her recovery over the long haul would be difficult because of the terrible insult to her self-esteem, which had been inflated and pampered during her childhood years. Holly had lived her early life in front of mirrors. She saw only what others reflected with their praise and their applause. Finally, she was all alone and she was faced with the difficult task of answering the questions of young adulthood, who to be and what to be.

Terry Brennan

Terry Brennan did not die from a psychiatric disease. She died as a result of a lifestyle that in the diagnostic manuals appears as a personality disorder. The most distinguishing feature of a personality disorder is not a disorder of thought or mood, but of attitude.

What is an attitude? An attitude is a habit of thinking and feeling. What is a personality? At the risk of simplicity, a personality may be defined as the unique character of a person that is shaped by attitudes.

An attitude develops over time. It is formed subconsciously to guide us through the uncertain pathways of our growth and development. It is not just a protective garment. It also serves as a compass to facilitate choices. Unlike the workings of real compasses that relate to a fixed magnetic spot at the North Pole, our emotional compass, our set of attitudes, can give faulty readings.

Terry Brennan gathered a collection of hurts and misperceptions about her origin and about her worth, and packaged them in to a tragically flawed psychic compass. Rather than accept the fact of her adoption and be thankful for the emotional nourishment offered by the Brennan family, she chose an attitude of resentment and mistrust. A dark obsession developed around the unacceptable rejection by her original parents. She fought off the pain of depression with the shield of rage and bitterness. She did not allow her feelings to be internalized. Vulnerability and weakness would follow and she would have none of that. She was young and strong and feisty. So why not let it all hang out? Up till now, she had to play the cards that life dealt out. Now it was her turn to deal.

As a young adolescent, she found that there was another world outside the Brennan family, a world that fit her needs. Teenage rebels are not hard to find. She chose to identify with other rejects. She felt comfortable with those who thumbed their nose at convention and did what they wanted when they wanted. But the carefree trip through the forest of antisocial protest soon led her into a jungle crowded with human predators. To survive, she used and abused others, such as Billy Smith. Finally, she got lost in that jungle.

Terry died without friends or family. The symbolism of the death tableau was not lost on Billy. In death, she ended her search for the rejecting parents and took them with her.

Before leaving the unfortunate story of Terry Brennan's life, a word about that special category referred to in the diagnostic and statistical manual, personality disorders. For whatever reason, mental health theorists and researchers during the latter part of the 20th century seemed to have minimized the impact of this problem on our society.

One of the reasons may be an aversion to introducing moral or religious norms into the pure and uncontaminated notion of mental illness. One cannot be blamed or blasphemed for acquiring cancer or diabetes. There is a need by some professionals to explain most medical problems as genetically or organically determined. And there are those who espouse the idea that all mental illness results from chemical imbalance. Choice does not enter into it. No-fault behavior.

But Terry Brennan and Billy Smith did choose their lifestyle, although not wisely. And most importantly, they chose to obliterate the personal pain of loss the change, or depression and anxiety, by inflicting pain on others.

Much research and study needs to be done before we truly appreciate the preventable precursors to character malformation. Perhaps our best hope is the rise of an army of sociologists who have moved beyond their earlier mission of relief and rescue of society's victims and have awakened to the necessity of getting at the causes. Inevitably that awakening will lead to the complex challenges that beset the vulnerable child in a dysfunctional family system.

Sarah Smith

Sarah did not suffer the hurt and betrayal inflicted on her brother, Billy. He was grossly underprotected in his earliest years. She was overprotected. Gertrude literally swooped her away from the limp grasp of her battered mother and split the two of them irrevocably. Gertrude's own suppressed guilt over parental omissions when her daughter Melanie was young was assuaged by her exaggerated nurturance of her granddaughter. The net result by the onset of adolescence was a woefully immature child. Whereas Billy would learn to cope with the cruel world of uncaring adults and foster families by plotting his own revenge, Sarah drifted into a sure-fire attention-getter, her body. From her earliest years, Grandma Gertrude's poor sick baby was excused. As she experienced her menarche, Sarah found out that Mother Nature did not accept excuses. Ready or not, the body must change.

Sarah did not consciously set out to lose weight and be sick. It came naturally. As a messenger of her fears and foreboding, her body had rescued her quite reliably during the preadolescent years. By developing the habit of not eating or eating and purging, she drifted into the fuzzy reverie of a stoppage of growth altogether. If one doesn't eat, the body will stop growing. If one stops growing, one can stay young forever. Stop the world and let me off.

Even if this were not true, as she inevitably discovered, there were bonus points that went with the eating disorder. She was allowed to continue the poor little Sarah theme into the teen years. She evoked attention and sympathy from the unsuspecting. This instant gratification, this reward proved to be a most difficult hurdle in the later years of her recovery. Sarah early on equated attention and sympathy with genuine love, and thus during her teen years never developed a sense of the give-and-take that is the core of a trusting, loving adult relationship.

By the end of adolescence, she had succeeded in surviving on the outer fringe of her peer groups, always getting by but never truly invested. Even she became tired of the old routines. And fewer and fewer people came to her rescue.

Along came a caring and experienced therapist who herself had been through the pain of an eating disorder. Sarah finally found someone who saw something deeper and stronger within her. Their relationship developed as a condensed version of a positive nurturing parent/child experience. She began to make up for lost time.

Her conversion was also prompted by the realization that fewer and fewer people were left to cater to her childish expectations. And the emotional extortion ceased to work. Her crises were more often ignored. She reluctantly acknowledged that those she had once manipulated were only dishing out emotional junk food to discourage her from self-destructive behavior.

At this stage of life, most persons with an eating disorder are faced with three choices. The utter barrenness of their existence may drive them to end their life. Few take this option. The second choice is sadly to reinvest one's energy into the further pursuit of body shrinkage, with malnutrition and metabolic crises that increase in life-threatening outcomes. They simply up the ante. The third is to find the strength and courage to begin to grow again. Sarah was indeed fortunate. She found a professional person who understood the problem and unflinchingly pushed and pulled her through the stages of depression, anxiety, and doubt until she gained ownership of her own life.

Although the job at the nursing home was a challenge, it also brought with it some appealing rewards. She was comfortable working with the elderly women, most of whom smiled the Gertrude smile of approval and affection.

Mind-Body Problems

Let us now take some time to examine in more detail disorders affecting the mind and body.

In the diagnostic and statistical manual, there are other disorders involving mind and body interactions. The most prominent are called psycho-physiologic disorders. In the last century, these were referred to as psycho-somatic disorders. Regardless of what physical organ or system is affected within the body, the common denominator is the blend of damaged body tissue coupled with emotional pressures as an accompaniment. These disorders may seriously interrupt the normal functioning of major physiologic systems such as the gastrointestinal tract, the respiratory system, the cardiovascular system, the endocrine system, and the skin. Familiar names include stomach ulcers, ulcerative colitis, Crohn's disease, bronchial asthma, neurodermatitis, eczema, hypertension, and migraine headaches.

No one has yet figured out how the emotional trigger mechanism—which is by itself an intangible and invisible entity—can lead to real painful disrupted tissue damage.

In the medical profession, there are some who refuse to accept the possibility of a mind-body interaction. To them, the psyche and the soma operate independently. Feelings and thoughts do not have the power to make the body change or break down. But indeed there is clear evidence in our everyday life to demonstrate the opposite.

The simplest example is the common experience of crying. Crying involves the visible production of real tears made of real water which suddenly appear around our eyes and then roll down our cheeks. The process is involuntary. Other than professional actors, no one consciously commands the water to flow out of the body.

A series of physiologic events must occur in lightning-fast sequence for the event of tears to take place. Basically, a message is sent to the lacrimal (tear) glands located in the rim of the eye socket. This message says, "Squirt." The message itself is carried by tiny nerve fibers which through a number of connections or synapses reach back into the recesses of the brain to the command station. No one is quite sure where that headquarters is located.

The most important feature of this neurological-glandular phenomenon is the cause: a feeling. A feeling of sadness. A feeling of sorrow. On occasion, an overwhelming wave of happiness or surprise can produce the same end product. H_2O rolling down the cheek. No one has ever seen, touched, tasted, or smelled a feeling. Nevertheless, it possesses a tremendous power to alter, even in a miniscule way, the chemistry of the body.

Sarah Smith did not suffer from a psycho-physiologic disorder. Her pattern of weight loss and metabolic change was controlled and not involuntary. It served an important purpose in her life. It protected her from the pressures and unacceptable challenges of growing up.

Good news and bad news. The bad news was the terribly disrupted life during her critical adolescent years. The good news was the reversibility of the whole process. When she chose to change her life, she could. She underwent the ravages of the disease but could reverse it. Quite different from the patient who suffers from psycho-physiologic disorders—the ravages of ulcerative colitis, migraine headaches, or chronic asthmatic disease cannot be turned off as easily.

Help is more available today for the victims of psycho-physiologic diseases. The cooperation of medical specialists and mental health professionals is vital. Most importantly, the patient must be willing to acknowledge the presence of body-mind interaction.

Ruth Reardon

The young adult years were actually enjoyable. Having met and mastered previous challenges, Ruth entered and exited this phase of her life with confidence and a solid sense of who she was. Her mother, Rita, continued to be a steady influence. Rita had struggled to keep the family together after her first husband walked out, and she watched her daughter's growth and maturity with pride and pleasure.

Rita was Ruth's number one role model. Her stepfather Joe was not too far behind. Mom and daughter had their moments, particularly during the teen years, but the Italian tempers gave way to tearful reconciliations. And they were the closer for it.

College life was not a traumatic change from family life. The campus was less than an hour away. But it was the confidence and set of values that Ruth carried with her that helped. Academics were no great obstacle. She had always been a well-organized student and possessed an above-average intelligence.

In high school, sports had been a minor part of her life. She loved the exercise and the camaraderie, but did not have to win at all costs. Her coaches in field hockey and tennis called her a grinder, steady and predictable. Her teammates trusted her. She always kept her end up. She did not have the same enthusiasm at the college level of competition. She had less interest in the demands of practice and the fulfillment of the coaches' ambitions. She ultimately settled for noncompetitive activities.

Boston College was indeed just right for her. She could pick and choose her friends, her courses, and her extracurricular activities at a site minutes away from her home. And best of all, the trolley line connected Boston College with Boston University. Although her high school friend, Dana Broderick, commuted from Marblehead daily, they quietly reveled in the knowledge that they owned Commonwealth Avenue. The two entered and graduated from their respective institutions the same year. During their stay at the colleges, their relationship grew steadily. It did not exclude separate social events, and they did agree to allow an occasional date with another person. They also agreed on something else. To reserve sexual intercourse for marriage. They built their young love on trust and respect.

Ruth's natural curiosity about her life, her God, and her religion was accommodated through the Catholic university's abundant array of courses and seminars on these subjects. She was surprised at the provocative nature of these discussions. Most of the teachers encouraged full-scale assaults on traditional beliefs, with the intention of walking the doubters back into the sunlight. They insisted reason added to faith was the stuff of adult commitment and conduct.

The "who-to-be" question was easy. She always wanted to be like her mother, but she knew that the issue of being like someone ended with being herself. She genuinely liked herself by the end of her college years.

The choice of "what-to-be" had always centered around the medical or teaching professions. At the urging of Rita and Joe, she took the premedical courses and was accepted at medical school.

Ruth Reardon is presented as a fairly normal young adult. She experienced her share of changes and losses, but enjoyed the love and support necessary to meet the challenges. Her choices during the young adult years were based on that support.

Alan Reardon

Despite the emotional jolt in his senior year, Alan partially recharged his ego by the time he arrived at Harvard. Part of the power of this recharge was simply to do nothing during the summer but enjoy the postgraduation fun and games in Marblehead. He rationalized that a recently graduated sports hero shouldn't have to work anyway. He couldn't cheat his adoring fans of their last few glory days together.

The pre-season practice sessions at Harvard put an end to his illusions of immortality. Many of his teammates were as good as, and some even better than, the Marblehead whiz. As his confidence shrank, he experienced the same nagging thoughts that slipped into his head around the pregnancy problem.

Who am I? Where am I going? Do I really give a damn about anyone? Does anyone give a damn about me?

Alan started taking long walks around the campus at night and even dropped into the chapel a couple of times after practice. He paid more attention to the family chatter on weekend visits and listened more attentively to his dormmates about their families and about their personal lives. But he still felt something was missing inside and he couldn't quite find it.

During his first two years, he turned down no invitations to parties, nor did he shun the revelry of springtime in Florida. There were still plenty of girls, but the sheer thrill of seduction and conquest was gone. Gradually he sensed a shallowness to it all.

The relative meaninglessness of his existence was reinforced by the career-ending foot injury, coupled with the sense of weakness and uselessness that came over him around the celebration of his sister's wedding. Ruth was more than an older sister. She was the genuine article. No tricks, no pretenses. How did she get that way? He had always believed that winning something was the key to success and happiness. He was a high school and town hero. Nobody in town would recognize his sister if she weren't in his company. It was all so confusing.

He actually envied her. She had something he didn't. Ruth had a closeness with her mother that he didn't. He found himself blaming his own dad now. At times, he felt resentment toward his coach, Pete Saunders. During his freshman year at college, he called Pete a couple of times during the football season, but the coach was too busy to meet with him. The current team was heading for another championship. Alan was past history. Alan was of no use to the coach now.

The male figures that he used to emulate in his childhood and teen years began to fade away. He hardly ever heard from his dad. The latest news from his uncle had Eddie on his third marriage and living somewhere on the West Coast. Coach Saunders was busy developing other heroes. He actually found himself more comfortable with Dr. Joe Reardon, his stepfather. Not a lot of contact, but what there was felt easy and genuine. Joe never pushed himself into Alan's life. No great expectations, but no put-downs either. And he was always there.

Perhaps the thing he admired most was the way his stepdad treated his mom. They shared a deep respect and fondness for each other. They enjoyed each other's humor tremendously. They had disagreements that could turn into spats, but never fights. Joe told him once that one of the secrets to a good marriage was never consciously wanting to hurt the other. Alan knew that he had a long way to go on that score. In his brief lifetime, he had hurt other girls. Not with physical abuse, but with a reckless, selfish need to take and then discard.

The college years passed too quickly. Like most jocks, he was slow to develop a game plan for life after graduation. He thought about his parents' jobs but never quite bought into medicine or law. Several of his classmates were headed for business school, but that left him cold. He had never really worried about money. He was content with his modest allowance from Joe and Rita. He finally admitted to himself that he really was spoiled and lazy.

"If-to-be" was never a serious question. The suicidal death of a dormmate in his freshman year stunned him. He had known of athletes who died in competition and even in strenuous workouts, but this made no sense at all.

Alan never fully rejected his Catholic upbringing, but he had doubts. He went through the questioning stages through high school and college. "Is there a God? What is God like?" By the time he graduated from Harvard, he read with great interest several books on subjects such as great world religions, theology, and moral philosophy. Alan finished the early stages of his young adult life with just a glimmer of some maturity and purpose. The circular pathway of his existence was beginning to uncoil into a straighter line. He knew that he had a lot of work to do. But he finally did want to grow up and not just grow older.

Jessica Reardon

The young adult years were breakthrough years for Jessica. She emerged from the nightmare existence of her childhood and adolescence with the help of family and mental health workers. For so many of those years, she cowered within the imaginary shadows of fear and mistrust. At the hospital, trust was the number one goal. And trust is not a gift. It is earned. The staff at McLean Hospital were gentle and patient. They did what they said they would do, and they were there when they said they would be.

The newer antipsychotic medications were a godsend. They freed Jessica from the neurochemical restraints that had shortcircuited her thought process from an early age. Once released, she responded tentatively and then hungrily to the offers of staff and family to taste and feel the simple pleasures of companionship and love. The medications also allowed her to use her superior intelligence in a whole new way. Schizophrenia is not a disease of the intellect, but of the normal processes of thinking. Released from the crippling distortions of reality, Jessica was ready to advance her education. One sympathetic professor at the college told her parents that she was finally "driving the car without the emergency brake on."

Her confidence was initially tested as a volunteer at Children's Hospital. The director of volunteers took a special interest in her and guided her through the scary introduction period. She loved the children and the staff and gradually gained popularity with the families.

Rita became as much a friend as a mother during these critical months. As time went on, they developed weekly schedules for lunch and shopping. Her father Joe was slower to approach his long-lost daughter who seemed to be changing before his eyes. Too many times over the years he had built up his hopes only to be banished from her presence.

Jessica began accompanying her parents to Sunday mass but seemed more uneasy there than at home. In one of her early psychotic tirades, she claimed that God had allowed the devil to kill her mother. She stood up in church once and screamed that the wine was real blood. Even as a young adult, she refused to receive communion.

Jessica knew that she was not completely healthy. She had been taught by the mental health workers that despite some vulnerabilities she could live a long and happy life. The medication was crucial. The love of family and friends came next. As never before, she felt a freedom to shape and control her life one day at a time.

Chapter Four: Marriage

CHANGE

Next in our continuous growth and development is marriage. It is the most natural experience to advance our lives in a healthy way. It is a popular choice, but not the only one. Not everyone chooses marriage—and not every person who gets wedded chooses marriage. This is the main theme of this chapter. So our first task is to distinguish the wedding ceremony from a marriage itself.

Over the years, weddings have become more complicated, more elaborate, and more expensive. Unfortunately, the "more" trend ensures only those moments of glory. The chance of success in the marriage is not guaranteed by the expense of the wedding.

The long-term success of a marriage is much more dependent on the emotional maturity of the married partners. That level of maturity is directly related to each one's success in meeting the changes and challenges of life that we have been describing up to the point of the wedding vows.

The wedding vows are spoken in a most dramatic and most solemn setting. Despite the brevity of most wedding ceremonies, the moment in time where the promises are made by the bride and groom regarding their intention to join together in love and commitment for the rest of their lives is truly the pivotal essence of that day.

Speaking these vows aloud before a hushed audience evokes an understandable panic or stage fright by the principles involved. Each member of the rapt audience instinctively listens to the quivering voice with respect, reverence, and wonderment. For those attending who have already taken these vows, there is a silent appreciation of the awesome significance of the promises.

Through our lifetime there is no pledge, no agreement, no contract that can match the marriage contract stated aloud in a sincere way which will define the course of one's life. Let us now take a closer look at that contract and that life.

The Marriage Contract

It is not customarily a written contract, although the high divorce rate in this country has prompted the use of legal documents to spell out financial and property settlements that might ensue from a failed marriage. Nonetheless, the marriage vows spoken by each party in front of witnesses under the direction of a clergyman or legal authority do constitute a solemn pact.

It is a unique agreement for at least two reasons. One is the termination date: there is none. The contract ends on the event of death of one or both partners and not on an appointed day and time. Most newlyweds would agree that even that inevitability can never diminish their eternal love.

The second reason is that the marriage contract constructed verbally at the wedding ceremony is made up of mutual promises only. There is no mention of what each person expects in return. All business contracts demand a return. Let us look more closely at this unusual relationship, particularly that missing part, the expectations.

Promises

Despite cultural, ethnic, or religious differences and despite an increasing tendency to personalize the wording of the vows, the basic promises boil down to three. To love, respect, and remain faithful. Each party intends this on the wedding day.

In the olden days, to love, honor, and obey were the standard vows. Out of respect for gender equality in our modern society such a promise of obedience (by either party) is onerous and has been abandoned. The word honor is still used at many ceremonies, but the word itself has lost some of its chivalrous charm. People honor gods, causes, and countries more than other persons. Respect is a more practical and more important expression in the marriage vows. A respect for the loved one extends the promise of love through the unforeseen and uncharted waters of inevitable change and challenge that test every union. Respect implies a value placed on the spouse, whereas the promise of love, though immeasurable as to quantity and quality, springs from the heady, intoxicating experience of being in love.

Loving someone is a learning process. Of the three promises it is the hardest to define. True love can only be measured in time. If being in love is the seedling, then the day-to-day living together guided by respect and loyalty are the ingredients that make it grow.

Back to the promise of respect. Respect is solid and practical. Love is not always practical and love requires the constant nourishment of reciprocal love. Respect for a loved one means never, ever, wanting to hurt that person deliberately. As we shall see, keeping this vow is the most essential element over the long haul in making a marriage work. Respect is more enduring than love. It needs less return from the other. But it cannot survive a breach of trust.

Thus the third promise: fidelity. A most solemn and necessary element. Without it there is no true marriage. Without it, faithfulness to the other promises is worthless. Fidelity means a willingness and intention to stick to the other partner for life—way beyond the excitement of the wedding and honeymoon. Fidelity survives all the temptations to bail out and look somewhere else for the perfect love. Fidelity endures the crushing disappointments that life can serve in the form of sickness, death, and financial stresses. Those who keep this promise are entitled to use the term "my marriage," "my husband," "my wife," and not the bland, polite label "relationship" or "significant other."

Fidelity to each other spread out over a lifetime is a most magnificent recurring gift. But at the wedding ceremony it is only a promise.

Expectations

Nobody thinks about expectations at the wedding. The wedding itself is a celebration, a now thing, a fun thing. Let the future take care of itself. However, it is the future where the other part of the marriage contract plays out. And how the silent, elusive subconscious expectations of each partner are handled determines the future of the marriage.

Before looking at these expectations it is worth reviewing a few key experiences in our early growth and development. For this is where the adult expectations are formed. The first and foremost expectation from the moment of our birth is to be loved and cared for. The infant brain is incapable of formulating this concept or any concept. But the helpless baby learns from the day-in, day-out routines with mother that it is being attended to with the welcome promptness and tenderness.

After the Day of the Rattle, the child realizes it must give a little something back even if it is just a bit of patience and forbearance. On the Day of the Potty, another change. If the child does what mommy and daddy want, there is instant love and approval.

The love supply from parents to children is a natural and endless resource to be enjoyed over and over again. As the child grows and leaves the home, even in the early years, to be educated and to meet other kids, the love of the parents may be offered in different forms. Approval for accomplishments is one. Less obvious but equally important is the difficult task of setting limits on behavior by the parents. This form of love is not the warm and fuzzy kind and is therefore rarely appreciated.

Unfortunately, in the everyday world the suppliers of love, the parents, find themselves unable to deliver it. Recall Billy Smith's experience at the door of the hospital in the first chapter. This was not a happy occasion. The bitterness between mother and father bode poorly for the success of the marriage. And the heir to that rift would soon become the victim.

The child of a dysfunctional marriage becomes a part of a dysfunctional family, and the expectation to be loved and cared for are thwarted as repeated disappointments and neglect leave a serious mark.

Thus, the unfinished emotional business of our imperfect childhood reappears on the occasion of a marriage. The wedding promises speak of a second chance to feel loved and cared for in the adult world. But the partner is not a parent. The love supply is there but it is not obligatory or unconditional. Each partner therefore has special needs that have been unfulfilled. Each partner has hidden expectations that will surface in the marriage.

Many hopes and expectations fill the hearts of the eager newlyweds, but for a truly successful marriage, three basic expectations which are quite reasonable abide in the deep layers of the psyche of each person, awaiting fulfillment in the days and years ahead.

Expectation one: "I want as much love from you as I received before I met you."

Expectation two: "I want you to make up for the love I missed."

Expectation three: "I want you to make up for the hurts that I've suffered."

At first glance, these silent, private expectations do not appear unreasonable. They form the nucleus of every romantic novel or movie that has a happy ending. The problem is that in real life neither party realizes consciously what their own expectations are, and obviously the other partner is equally unaware of what is expected.

The instinctive quest for love from the moment of birth now takes the form of some serious promises and expectations. The promises are easy; living up to each other's expectations is impossible unless an extraordinary amount of love, patience, and wisdom endures the long haul. Compromise and flexibility are needed to modify and reshape realistic expectations.

These three expectations are best understood using a marriage situation as a model and superimposing them on the interactions of the newlyweds after the honeymoon. With no disrespect for one of the most cherished love stories of all times, let's explore what hazards may have awaited Cinderella and Prince Charming regarding their promises and expectations.

Cinderella and Prince Charming

Everyone recalls the unfairness of Cinderella's life before the royal wedding. In the home of the cruel and taunting stepmother and stepsisters, she was offered little love and a lot of emotional pain. We must assume that such emotional malnourishment took its toll. Sadness, madness, and badness are familiar emotions, and the repetitive slights and insults to Cinderella became tucked away deep in her psyche waiting for a time of restitution.

Restitution usually takes one of two forms. One is the high road, the other the low. The healthier form is reconciliation with what was missing, and the lower form is revenge. Reconciling the emotional inconsistencies and inadequacies of our childhood and going on with our adult growth is the most important theme in this book. Refusing to let go of the hurts and the inconsistencies is the other theme that leads to the emotional illnesses and aberrations. Let us now peek in on castle life a few weeks after the honeymoon.

SCENE I: *The Bedroom*

PRINCE: Wasn't that a wonderful dinner we had tonight? The poached venison and the soufflé were just delightful. Just the way I remember them when I was a child.

CINDERELLA: Well, I'm glad you liked it, my darling. I had a hard time swallowing the meat. I've never tasted anything like that. Tough to chew. And the dessert was so rich, I thought I'd have to vomit.

PRINCE: Oh, dear! That's a pity. I will tell the cook to check with us each day about the evening meal. That way we can be sure of an absolutely divine dinner.

CINDERELLA: My, prince, you are so kind. I sometimes feel that I just don't deserve it.

PRINCE: By the way, my dearest, mother and father are coming over to see us next week. I invited them for the weekend. I hope you don't mind.

CINDERELLA: It's not that I mind. I just don't feel comfortable yet. It all happened so fast. We really haven't had the chance to get acquainted. One day you put on the glass slipper and the next thing I knew we were getting married. My darling, I'm not sure your parents really know me yet.

PRINCE: Oh, nonsense, my pet. How could they help but love you? You are so gentle and caring and innocent and lovable. We'll have a wonderful time.

SCENE II: *Banquet Hall*

QUEEN: My dear, you look lovely. That color becomes you. Baby blue, isn't it? It's so fitting. You're still only a child. Just between us girls I noticed that you only have one earring on. I suppose that's all right. My son is so silly he probably won't notice. He never did appreciate a well-dressed woman.

CINDERELLA: Thank you, your majesty! I didn't notice the missing earring. This is the first time I've dressed up like this for a dinner. And the table. It's beautiful. So much gold and silver.

KING: Cinderella, you look ravishing. Eat hearty, now! You'll need your strength for the big fox hunt tomorrow.

PRINCE: Not to worry my dear. It's an annual affair. All our friends from nearby castles will be there. I thought I'd surprise you.

CINDERELLA: But I don't even know how to ride a horse! At home all we had was some chickens and a pig. I wish you had warned me.

QUEEN: I'm very disappointed in you, my dear. All of my son's other companions rode so well. I know that he counted on you joining us tomorrow. He has never missed a hunt since he was five years old. That's when we gave him his first pony.

SCENE III: *The Bedroom*

CINDERELLA: My dear, I'm really ticked! This was not a pleasant evening for me. First of all, your mother spoke to me as if I were a little child who really didn't know anything. Then you pulled the hunt thing on me, which is embarrassing and unfair. And then your mother gets another dig in about how unprepared I am to be your wife.

PRINCE: Aahh, my pet, I'm so sorry. I didn't realize that it would turn out this way. I only wanted to please you.

CINDERELLA: And I you, my dear. But I'm beginning to realize that pleasing you in the manner that you're accustomed to is going to be one tough job. You've always had so much, and I so little. I feel like I have so little to give.

PRINCE: Nonsense, darling! Just becoming my bride was the supreme gift. Just be yourself, nobody else, and I will love you forever.

CINDERELLA: My prince, I don't know if you really know me. I did not grow up with all the love that you had. Just the opposite, in fact. It's not so easy to give it away. Sometimes being insulted opens up old wounds and gets in the way of loving you.

PRINCE: Aahh, my dearest wife, I believe our love will overcome it all.

CINDERELLA: I hope so. But I believe I must try harder than you. Please have patience with me.

PRINCE: I will have endless patience, my love. Now please roll over and give me sweet kiss good night.

CINDERELLA: Not tonight. I have a terrible headache.

Cinderella is more in touch with the problem of expectations than the prince. Through no fault of her own, her capacity to give love spontaneously is limited by the supply available within her, and further restricted by the conflicting emotions of resentment and yearning over the unfair childhood years.

Having been spared all of this, the prince is intent on preserving the glow of romance, oblivious to the reality that life after courtship and wedding will require major adjustments over the long haul in order build a solid marital love from the early in-love phase.

Six Phases of Marriage

Aside from the well-intended wedding promises and the unforeseen bumps in the road produced by subconscious expectations, there are other serious pressures on the married couple that derive from natural life events.

No marriage can succeed without periodic adjustments, and no one can anticipate the adjustments necessary to iron out the intimate and complex business of reconciling each other's expectations. But we can anticipate the challenges that life itself has in store. There are at least six different phases of married life that produce such challenges.

The First Year

National statistics are alarming. More than forty percent of all marriages fail in the first year and lead to divorce proceedings. In addition to that, fifty percent of all first marriages fail, including the first year and beyond. So what happens in a matter of months to bring the passion and promises of the wedding to a crushing halt? There is no one answer, of course. But the most often quoted comment by friends and family is, "They just weren't ready."

Throughout this book, we have witnessed the sad but true fact that "we gotta grow older, but we don't gotta grow up." The penalty for not maturing within certain time frames is the dragging forward of some emotional unfinished business into the next unavoidable change and challenge.

Up to the time of marriage, there is no clear-cut way of measuring one's progress through the earlier tests of maturity. But marriage is a hard teacher that presents a tough examination of our emotional growth and development. This test boils down to how ready and willing we are to engage in a love relationship where we must learn to give and take despite all the inequities and insufficiencies of our earlier years.

In the first year of marriage, the test focuses on how ready we are to give up what we did have or what we didn't have. It is doubtful that any set of newlyweds sits down after the honeymoon with pencil and paper and individually lists from memory all the events of insufficient love in one column and all the hurts in another. This is ludicrous and well nigh impossible. For the insufficiencies of our childhood are not recorded neatly in some mental ledger, but rather absorbed in the fabric of our developing persona, our soul, from infancy right through the wedding day.

A child who is nutritionally deprived from the physical standpoint is likely to show the results in a modified adult bone and muscle structure. A child who is emotionally deprived will have psychological abnormalities hidden and unmarked in the soul. So, the newlyweds return from the blissful, carefree interlude of the honeymoon still glowing from their day in the sun where the wedding guests joyfully proclaimed them number one.

Although a growing number of newlyweds have already cohabited, let us look at one basic event common to all new marriages, and that is leaving home.

Leaving home is not the same as leaving the house. Leaving the home of parent and family means giving up certain habits of daily living on the one hand and important emotional support on the other. For a woman who becomes a wife, leaving home is far different than for the man who becomes a husband. In a marriage, two individuals essentially leave a home to create another home. Although there are no job descriptions listed on the marriage certificate, the woman is the prime home builder.

Men are more capable of building houses, but not homes. The softness of home, the warmth, the peace, the meals, the clean clothes, the smell of cooking, the preparation for holidays, birthday parties, the small intimate details of daily life, the grocery shopping. Home is synonymous with Woman. So right from the get go, there is something a bit unfair about the expectations of each party in building a home. The scale of fairness and gender rights is a bit tilted.

There is still another difference for the woman who marries. Not only is she expected to take the lead in creating the hominess, but she leaves behind in her family of origin those little niceties that she received but now must provide, whereas the husband leaves the comfort of home and marries into the expectation of similar comforts from his bride. But things are not all black and white. Many newly minted husbands, recognizing this inequity, try hard to be that gentle man who can partially make up for the mothering their wife left behind.

Because of these inequities, however, it may take some women much longer to truly leave home emotionally. One of the most necessary instruments in helping this transition is the plain and simple instrument called the telephone. There are no statistics, but I suggest that the number of phone calls during the first six months to the family of origin for the average married couple would find the wife in the lead by at least ten to one. This method of communicating with loved ones back home is a natural response and is aimed at adjusting to the separation from home while building the marriage.

Despite these adjustments, there are forces at work on the negative side that do lead to the stunning failure rate of first-year marriages. At least three obstacles deserve a look: habits, sex, and in-laws.

Habits. Each party to the marriage brings into the day-to-day routines certain personal habits. There are bathroom habits, eating habits, drinking habits, dressing habits, social habits, work habits.

Habits are repetitive learned behaviors that are quite useful and comfortable in coping with daily life. All too often, however, one or the other in the marriage finds the habits of the spouse objectionable and attempts to change them. Most couples tolerate the differences and realize years later that they have both changed and have adopted some common habits.

The issue of who leaves the toothpaste cap off should not be the precursor to an early divorce. The problem is that the issue of the toothpaste cap can swell to monster size if the newlyweds allow it. Combined with dozens of other little annoyances, the couple may fail to appreciate these differences as normal adjustment problems to be worked on. But, under the heading of premarital habits, there are other things that are by no means trivial.

One of the most threatening habits or lifestyle issues is excessive use of alcohol and drugs. And it can affect both parties equally. The addictive nature of alcohol and drugs is one of the most damaging influences to the commitments made on the wedding day. The essence of such habits is a message that the love and companionship of the other partner is simply not enough. Emotional needs of the drinker or drug user can not be satisfied by the spouse. And that message cuts deeply. If both partners are afflicted, then the sanctity of the wedding promises becomes quickly sullied and a mutual distrust and disrespect surface.

Another premarital habit of significance, although less threatening to the marriage, is the tendency of husbands to insist on the rights of male bonding: boys' night out, the bowling league, tennis, golf. In some ways, this resembles the wife's need in the early days of the marriage to remain in close communication with family and girlfriends over the telephone or at lunch or at the shopping center. Many wives recognize this as part of their husband's need to readjust his habits and do not challenge these events as total rejection early on. But it may over time reach a level of serious neglect and some change becomes needed.

A final comment on habits detrimental to the marriage has to do with something much more serious for it concerns the modern phenomenon of dual careers.

Nowadays, it is quite common for newlyweds to have separate jobs. The financial demands that go with raising a family lead to a continuation of the two-income family. Most couples working in harmony to preserve the marriage and family find ways to accommodate these extra pressures, but there is a variation on this theme that is not as easily resolved. It has to do with the popular concept called "a career."

A career is more than a job. As we discussed in the last chapter, a job is something simple. It is a necessary effort to gain sustenance to survive. In prehistoric times, it took the form of hunting for food, building a fire, constructing a shelter from the weather. A career in modern times is a job plus. It includes not only a paycheck but personal fulfillment, prestige, and such bonuses as power and popularity. The most popularized careers seem to be in the entertainment industry as well as sports and politics. Unfortunately, a career can compete with a marriage, and two careers can actually destroy it. The person who insists on a career may be embarking on a dangerous balancing act. Inevitably, situations will arise where a decision must be made regarding which of the two is more important. If the choice is career, then more often than not the marriage suffers.

Sex. Sexual intercourse plays a vital role in communicating the deepest reaches of our emotional being. Attempts to profess love verbally or in writing pale in comparison to the emotional energy that radiates within the conscious and subconscious mind during sexual intercourse. If the married lovers are truly giving of themselves unselfishly, they reveal precious parts of themselves that then become additional facets to be treasured. But if sexual behavior slips in to more take than give, more demand than offer, more kinky appetite than respect for the other, then the seed of doubt is planted. If this persists, then another scenario is likely to develop in the marriage.

The spouse who is offended feels unsure and unsafe in bed and may begin to avoid exposure to objectionable sexual activity. Communications out of bed become strained and angry feelings may build between the two. During the first year of marriage, this struggle may develop into an impasse where either or both parties may simply call it quits.

Short of this, sexual incapability may lead to cheating. As we noted in the last chapter, control of one's sexual nature and developing a healthy integrated sexual life is not easy to come by. If sexual incompatibility is not resolved in the first year of marriage, then one or both parties may seek gratification elsewhere. This may lead to an irreversible breach in the young and fragile marriage contract.

In-Laws. The in-law issue often begins at the end of the wedding celebration, at that moment following the drinking, dining, and dancing. The wedding guests gather around for the final good-byes as the newlyweds, dressed in traveling clothes, cheerfully but tearfully hug and kiss their way to the door. All eyes are glued on the bride and groom as they complete this ritual. Only when they reach the parents does the noisy chatter slip into a hush. For although each guest senses that they must now share their special friendship with the wedding party, the moment has arrived where the parents will embrace their loved ones and separate from them in a manner that is quite solemn.

In-laws have become an institution in our society, thanks to some tradition, some jokes, television sitcoms, movies, and novels. A popular notion of in-law participation in a marriage goes like this: Both sets of parents will to some degree intrude and tamper with the union of their children. Why? Because it is human and natural to try to make up for their own sense of loss. This stereotype has reached a level of cliché in our culture. But despite this, most newlyweds, armed with this knowledge, will usually deflect the more obvious overtures in a kindly and sensitive manner. However, the combination of the parents "I told you so" and the child's uncertainty about the spouse in the first vulnerable months of marriage may prove to be a destructive force.

"Mama never told me it would be like this" is an old vaudeville joke. But with the telephone so near at hand, mama's advice may be repeated and reinforced to the detriment of the new union. The loneliness and yearning of the parents is understandable. The giving up of a child to a marriage is measured intellectually as a natural stage, but emotionally as a loss. Most often it occurs during the difficult time of adjustment in their own lives, the middle years, when major challenges assault their sense of security.

The magnetic pull of in-laws is strongest during the first year because of the mixed emotions felt by all parties in those early days. This is indeed a challenge for the newlyweds that, if resolved, should tend to make for a smoother relationship as the marriage proceeds.

There is a little twist on the theme of in-law intrusion that deserves a mention. Someone once told me that "God made in-laws to save marriages." At first blush, this seems totally opposite to the wisdom of the ages. Here is the explanation I received.

In-laws may be used as a convenient scapegoat by each spouse whose real grievance may be with the partner in the early days of the marriage. Complaining about one's in-laws to one's new marriage partner is not advisable in the interest of buying time to strengthen the early bonds of love and loyalty. However, making deflected complaints shared with friends or co-workers outside of earshot of the spouse is a common occurrence. Since everyone knows about the natural tensions between newlyweds and in-laws, moaning and groaning is listened to, laughed at, and dissipated by friends who one can trust. This way no one really gets hurt.

The Child-Bearing Years

If marriage is the definitive testing ground for all of our earlier growth and development, then becoming a parent is indeed the most serious challenge within the challenge.

We are born into this world as legitimate takers. In order to survive in this world, we must learn to give and take. At the wedding ceremony, we formally state those intentions as the binding elements to a lifelong union. When children are born into that marriage, the immediate realization is that we now must give. We must give unconditionally and totally. And there is no immediate compensatory take.

For the couple who have survived the first year adjustments and have strengthened their commitment to build on their love and respect for each other, the arrival of a child is more a natural addition to their life than an unwelcome challenge. But for the couple still troubled by the give-and-take balance, and uncertain of their intentions to spend the rest of their lives together, the arrival of a child is an intrusion.

When either party is actively brooding about the selfishness of the spouse or the inadequacy of their love, the challenge of parenting a helpless baby becomes enormous. The child is the immediate loser because rather than being the focus of parental love, it becomes the displaced object of parents' struggle to make up for what love they themselves are missing.

Spontaneous affection quickly gives way to job assignments. Raising the kid is a chore, not a joy. Keeping track of who does what becomes the name of the game and the subject of bitter encounters. With the arrival of the baby, each parent is forced to deal with the issues of give and take privately, for there is an invisible scale nestled deep in the subconscious mind that never stops weighing the love quotient against the capacity to give it away.

For the individual who comes from an ungiving, dysfunctional family, the challenge to give may be impossible. The impediments stem from a combination of both an unwillingness to give but more often an inability to offer such unconditional love. The supply within simply doesn't match the demand from without.

The full weight of this difficulty is not obvious in the earliest months of the baby's life. Pride in the parental instinct to nurture and protect the helpless being obscure the inevitable challenge. So within a few years of the wedding ceremony, the couple is confronted with first-year adjustment issues and then the event that will test their true intentions. Words are the focal point of a wedding; deeds are the stuff of a marriage. And the child born of a marriage cares only for deeds.

The Child-Rearing Years

The Early Years

The roles of mother and father have already been described in the earlier chapters, as seen from the needs of the growing child. At the risk of oversimplifying, once again love and limits are the key items required of the parents in rearing the child in a healthy way. The right blend of both is the trick. Not too much or too little of each—the correct recipe. But there is no cookbook to guide mom and dad, and even if there were, the incredible array of stresses, distractions, and attitudes toward children would defy a uniform product of their efforts.

Child rearing is perhaps the most difficult challenge in life because its demands are incessant and unforgiving. The day-in and day-out cries of the child for love, attention, patience, companionship, discipline, and forgiveness must be balanced by the need to work, make money, compete with others, and come home to do more work around the house. One must participate in social obligations, and maybe, just maybe, get a good night's sleep.

Once again, the quality of the marriage makes the difference. The couple that works together selflessly will find a way. The couple that loses the spirit of generosity and respect will find the burden heavy.

Adolescence

While the adolescent child is wrestling with their first big change of life, the married couple may well be immersed in the struggles of the second change: midlife. More about that shortly.

The role of each parent differs in the drama of adolescent turmoil. Each parent becomes the silent, unwitting role model for the ever-shifting demands of the child of the same gender. It is important, therefore, to be oneself during this process of being copied or identified with. Consistency is necessary to help narrow the wild mood swings of the child who admires the parent one day and rejects the parent the next.

On occasion, such steadiness is challenged openly by the adolescent, luring the parent into a trap where an inconsistent or negative emotional response is encouraged by the rebellious teenager, but at the same time is regretted.

While struggling to offer some formula of love and limits, the parents of the adolescent need each other very much, for the child is also an expert at splitting. This is perhaps the cruelest ploy. What can't be obtained from one parent may be wheedled out of the other. The net result may be a marital rift (paradoxically, what the needy, young adolescent soul doesn't want).

At the risk of being repetitious, the partners of a healthy marriage will usually tough it out and guide the unsure child through the storms, although all parties will be somewhat battered and bruised. The couple that is barely speaking or openly critical of each other, however, is likely to treat the adolescent rebel with little tolerance or respect. Marriage at this stage of life is tough enough without being assaulted from without.

Letting Go
The adolescent avalanche does end. What was silently yearned for comes to a close only to be followed by an unexpected shock: the empty nest.

The first child and the last child to leave home seem to make the biggest imprint on the parents. The reason is not related so much to the individual child as to the larger meaning of change and challenge. The married couple who have given so much, endured so much, and received so much find this to be somber moment in their lives.

The child who leaves for college after the bombastic teen years leaves behind a dull ache in the hearts of the parents. Nothing quite prepares mom and dad for the event. Even though college is a transitional experience, the physical separation of child from home portends something more serious. Time is marching on. No going back. The shadows are suddenly longer.

If it is a time for reflection, then it is also a time to consider remarriage to each other. They need to quietly join hands and hearts and rekindle the promise of love and companionship. For a brief time, the couple feel a natural sense of loneliness and wonderment. For the devoted couple, this should pass and be replaced by gratitude and solace and the knowledge of each other's love and loyalty and a job well done.

But, once again, for too many couples the empty nest may be an invitation to empty the marriage. Faced with only each other for company and hardened by endless and bitter encounters over long-forgotten differences, one or the other may broach the subject of separation and divorce. The timing of this dilemma falls within the next difficult time for change and challenge, midlife.

In conclusion, a word about the concept of remarriage. For a marriage to truly last, the couple will need to readjust to life's inevitable changes and challenges. In a sense, this is a remarriage. There is no ceremony, no blessing, and no witnesses. Periodic recommitment derives from a deep love and trust. And the marriage bonds will get stronger for this process. For most couples, this is a gradual process and not a conscious, formal event or ceremony.

Marriage is for life. And life expectations in the twenty-first century are remarkably higher than they were for our parents. A solid marriage is a tremendous aid to living through the next three phases—midlife, retirement, and late life—with health and happiness.

CHALLENGE

Holly Diamond

Rick Capitti owned his own business, such as it was. His beat up 4X4 truck, lawn mower, and cracked snowplow blade fit snugly into a rented garage located on the edge of town. For landscaping jobs, he hired high schoolkids or some hung-over drinking buddies from the Tanner Tavern. In the winter, he worked solo pushing the pretty white powder to the side of the Peabody streets. The city contracts were the best. A full day's pay for maybe a half day's work. He loved it. All alone behind the wheel. No hassles. No responsibilities for anyone else. Nice and quiet. Plenty of time to outwait the throbbing in his head from last night's fun.

His father, Tony, was a businessman, too. His garages housed four heavy-duty gravel carriers and a million dollars' worth of large earth-moving equipment. "Capitti Brothers Construction" was painted on everything he owned. He was proud of his accomplishments. He was not proud of his arrogant, ungrateful first-born son. Rick lasted two years in the business. He got tired of the physical labor and demanded an office job. The day he quit, Tony kicked him out of the house also.

Rick found a bed at the YMCA for a couple of weeks and then moved in with a high school buddy in a two-room flat overlooking Main Street. Everything was within walking distance. He could save wear and tear on his eight-year-old Chevy. The real advantage, however, was his proximity to the local hangouts. Cruising for chicks was his passion. Now they were a stone's throw away. As a high school football hero, his friends described him as a taller, slimmer Sylvester Stallone. How could he miss?

Seven years later, he was still working the downtown action. Only now he stood out as the old man. At twenty-six, he felt the sting of rejection by a louder and livelier bunch of local groupies. Most of his friends had married or moved out of town. Not only that, but he found himself trying to hide a soft paunch, just above his belt line. Even working out at the gym did not seem to help. That was when he decided to try the summer softball league. Holly Diamond was the result of that venture, and he felt quite grateful for this find. The Labor Day picnic featured a traditional softball game between the women's and men's all-star teams. Encouraged by her friends at the daycare center, Holly joined her group early in the summer and, with her natural athletic ability, rose to be the most fearsome pitcher in the league.

The giggling, beer-swigging jocks were mowed down by her effortless pitches through the first six innings of the game. Ignoring their taunts and risqué comments, she silently reveled in her dominance of the local heroes. As she walked onto the diamond for the final, victorious inning, she just couldn't contain herself. Stepping up to bat was the loudest of them all, the Stallone lookalike. He yelled that he was going to knock the ball into the next town. With his glassy eyes fixed on her, she fiddled with the ball in her glove and then let loose a pitch that caught him directly on the side of his head.

He dropped to his knees and was escorted to first base in a dazed and stupid condition. The next two batters popped up, and the third and final batter struck out. Holly went over to Rick Capitti as the teams congratulated each other. She apologized for the wild pitch. He shook her hand and insisted that she owed him one. The price tag was a dinner date and they agreed to go out that night.

They lived together for the next six months and married after she confirmed a two-month pregnancy. Rick insisted on an abortion, but she refused. A justice of the peace in Saugus performed the ceremony. Jody from the daycare center was her maid of honor and Rick's youngest brother the best man. No reception. The four of them had dinner at an Italian restaurant on Route 1 and then they were off to Cape Cod for a three-day honeymoon.

The parents on both sides were the last to know. As expected, Rick's mother cried and dad threatened to cut him out of his will completely. Holly wrote a brief note to her mother who was now living in North Carolina. No reply. She and her father Cliff went out to dinner. They laughed and they cried. They reminisced about the old days, particularly the ice skating goof-ups. Before leaving, they became sentimental and held hands across the table. Cliff wished her all the best and promised to help if she needed him.

The first trimester was awful. By the third month, morning sickness became all-day sickness. She almost lost her job at the daycare center, but they liked her so much that they hired a temp to fill in. She was able to return by the late winter weeks and started her maternity leave a few weeks before her due date in August.

Marriage

Throughout, Rick was no help at all. He constantly reminded her of his original advice and chided her for not listening. This allowed him to keep his distance, even at her most desperate moments. Having a baby was a woman thing, he said. He had man things to do. His business came first. He was the main breadwinner. Because of his heavy responsibilities, he was damn well entitled to his own time outs—Wednesday and Friday nights at the bar, come hell or high water. He managed an extra night during the dart throwing competition.

Holly felt alone and abandoned through most of the pregnancy. She cried herself to sleep many a night, yearning for the touch, sound, and reassurance of her mother. *How could things have gone so wrong? Is she happy? Why did she reject me so? Was I bad? I tried my best. God, Mom, I need you so much now.*

As the pregnancy wore on, Rick and Holly felt a definite coolness to their relationship. The sexual fervor of the early months turned into infrequent, almost obligatory coupling. In the last trimester, Rick avoided her altogether. He told her that her body was grotesque.

Whenever she complained, he responded with comparisons to the old-fashioned women, like his mother. She brought six kids into the world. Clothed and fed them all. Worked around the house from the morning until the night. And never bitched.

As the end of pregnancy grew near, she was desperate for some female conversation and company. Calls to her mother in North Carolina went unanswered. On an impulse, she phoned her long-lost cousin, Sarah Smith. They arranged for a luncheon date.

Holly was amazed at the change. Sarah met her at a downtown Salem lunch spot, garbed in a white, sleeveless sheath dress that highlighted a radiant tan and a full figure. The chatter started immediately. Most of it revolved around now things. They talked endlessly about the expected delivery and all the cute little furniture, toys, and clothes that were available in the mall.

Before parting, Sarah said that she had a surprise and flashed a sparkling diamond engagement ring. Giggles and tears followed. They agreed to meet again in a few months. Holly was genuinely happy for her cousin, unlike her disgust a few years ago when Sarah was at death's door, living a mousy existence within a cadaverous body. Good for her!

A cesarean section was necessary to bring little Louis into the world. The obstetrician feared for mother and child after twelve hours of pain and pounding. Holly was totally exhausted. The nurses were more concerned for her than the strapping eight-pound bruiser. She remained in the hospital for four days.

Holly was exhausted both physically and emotionally. She welcomed and dreaded visiting hours. She desperately needed support but was too weak to respond. Rick's mom was the first to arrive. Regardless of her resentment over the shotgun wedding, she could not resist holding her first grandchild; not so for her husband or her other sons. Cliff came each day with flowers and candy for his daughter, a proud granddad. Sarah and her fiancé dropped in briefly and left when Holly dozed off.

Rick really didn't know what to do. He had never been a father. He genuinely melted when the nurse placed his tiny, squirming son into his arms. But a strange stiffness followed. The responsibility for a pregnant wife was one thing, but the realization of facing a lifetime of obligation to another human being was another. The first night after the birth, he joined his buddies and got blind drunk.

Holly returned home physically stronger, but emotionally drained. Rick had only come to see her twice during the four days. That hurt. As she looked around the cluttered apartment, she realized the shabbiness of her home and her marriage. The following day she was unable to get out of bed, just too weak. Rick was angry and then scared. He called his mother, who came over immediately.

Maggie Capitti took over. She recognized the complete exhaustion that had reduced Holly's strength and will. But she was not a talker, she was a doer. She immediately made out a list of groceries and supplies for the little one, and ordered her son to go out and fetch them. The first hour she spent at Holly's bedside holding her hand and wiping her brow. She reassured her that things would be okay. She stayed over for two nights.

It almost worked. By the third day, Holly was immobile and appeared to be in a coma. Emergency room staff after many tests and x-rays diagnosed her as having a mental exhaustion and depression and sent her to the mental health ward.

She left a week later, tired and shaky but more alert. She reluctantly agreed to take antidepressant medication and see a counselor for follow-up support. Although fearful of probing into the events surrounding this breakdown and also the events of her first breakdown, she had to agree that the pressures of the past year had truly drained her. Just when she finally became a mother, she realized how much she needed her own mother.

The diagnosis offered by her doctors was not bipolar disorder, as before. This time it was major depression, postnatal type. The discharge planners arranged for the services of a home health aide for the next few weeks. Little Louis rejoined his mom within a day of her return. Holly was anxious to have her baby back. She felt awkward the first week with the bottle feedings and changes, but adapted well after that.

Rick was Rick. At his mother's insistence, he came home each night for supper to help out. But at least every other evening, he sheepishly excused himself and went down to the tavern for a drink. With his three-hour absences, Holly realized that he hadn't changed at all.

By Christmas, things had deteriorated badly. He rejected her demands to stay with her nights and weekends. It was her baby, and she could take care of it. One night he failed to come home at all. The next day she confronted him with her suspicions that he had another woman. After a loud, ugly scene, he slapped her hard against the side of her face and walked out. The same scene took place a few weeks later, only this time he punched her. She was too ashamed to tell his mother or her father. Instead she visited an agency in Salem, a home for abused women and children. She and Louis were accepted the next day.

In a drunken rage, Rick arrived that evening at the shelter brandishing a baseball bat. He was arrested and charged with attempt to enter illegally and with threats to inflict bodily harm. The judge placed him on probation and issued a restraining order to protect his wife and son.

Holly's father Cliff obtained the services of a lawyer to reinforce the legal mandate. He also found Holly a small apartment in Lynn close to his own condo. That summer she filed for divorce. Rick was then living with another woman. The divorce was uncontested.

Sarah Smith

Rob Carleton started out at the Green Acres Nursing Home as a part-time handyman—a little carpentry, a little landscaping, simple plumbing repairs, and some painting. He was not considered that bright, but he had a gentle, affable manner. He barely finished his final year at the vocational school. Classroom stuff bored him. Working with his hands was fun. He dreamed of someday owning his own construction company.

Rob was the youngest of three boys born to Joan and Joe Carleton. His father was a self-employed painter who died of lung cancer when Rob was nine years old. The oldest son became the man of the house. Rob became the precious baby, the object of mom's need to protect and preserve what was left. Her Rob was indeed pampered. By the end of adolescence, it took his brother's prodding and his own embarrassment to loosen the strings.

After a few casual meetings in the nursing home, Rob felt a stirring. Sarah Smith was not just a pretty, shy, soft person, but a real woman. Neither of them was in a rush. They arranged to meet for coffee in the staff kitchen as many mornings as they could. Next came lunch, and after that Rob got up the courage to ask her out to a movie.

Sarah was still living in a condo with her mother Melanie and her mother's latest husband, Tex. After all the early years of coolness and resentment, the two women had reached an accommodation. Sarah paid a generous monthly amount toward expenses, and Melanie valued her companionship during Tex's long hauls as a truck driver.

Sarah wanted Rob to meet her mother, and Melanie agreed to a dinner invitation at their apartment. Tex was on the road, so the two women had plenty of opportunity to size up the serious and ardent young man. Melanie liked him instantly. She said he was simple and gentle. Her only reservation was his ambition. Could he provide for her? Or was he stuck as a handyman forever? Otherwise the first meeting went well.

The two young folks added other activities to their repertoire. Dancing, bowling, roller skating, walks on the beach, and drives to Boston. They genuinely liked each other and that affection grew. Before they knew it, they were genuinely in love. Mutual admiration had turned into desire. Hugs and goodnight kisses became more fervent. Sarah had never felt this way before. For so many years, she had rejected the sight of her own body. Now she was excited with the rushes and tingles.

Rob proposed marriage the night before Sarah's birthday. As she was reading the greeting card, he pressed the little jewelry box into her hand. She was overwhelmed. Her joy was unbounded. She laughed and cried all evening. They agreed to tell their parents immediately and set a six-month schedule for the wedding.

The ceremony and the reception were simple. A nuptial mass and a small reception at the Veterans of Foreign Wars Hall in Lynn. Sarah looked radiant. Rob sported a wide grin throughout the day. The guests shared a common sentiment. These two were meant for each other. They were good kids.

Together they could afford an apartment a mile away from the nursing home. Melanie adjusted to the loss of her daughter better than Joan Carleton. Joan missed her baby but was smart enough to not interfere with the newlyweds. Rob was grateful. He made sure of weekly visits to his mom during the first few months. Sarah encouraged it.

The two of them had saved up a down payment for a forty-year-old two-family house by their third anniversary. Rob was now working twenty hours a week for a home builder and gave his notice to the nursing home. It was time to move on. Sarah cried at first at the loss of her coffee klatch partner. But she was also proud of her man. He was heading in the right direction and he loved his new work.

As with the courtship, their sexual relationship developed slowly. Sarah had to discard so many misconceptions and fears about physical love. Years of unnecessary distortions were replaced by the comfort and security of her tender lover. They learned together to give and take.

They often talked about having children. Sarah wanted to wait. With some difficulty, she explained to Rob that she wasn't quite ready to be a mother. She was now dealing with issues that were not part of her earlier therapy. Deep inside of her, she realized that the passive abandonment by her own mother had a lot to do with it. Gertrude, her grandmother, had played mother quite well, but Sarah never quite got over her resentment of her own mother. And the guilt feelings over her reciprocal rejection of Melanie continued to haunt her.

In an effort to rid herself of the emotional unfinished business, she went to her mother to talk about the possibility of having a baby. It was a big mistake. Melanie's response was cold and callous. She laughed and said to hold off as long as she could. Kids just complicate your life and tie you down.

A year later, she became pregnant but only carried the baby for three months. She fought off the feelings of guilt and inadequacy. But even with Rob's support, she drifted into the old familiar feelings of depression. She began to lose time at work and stayed in bed for hours on weekends. Most important, she stopped eating. The nursing supervisor where she worked came to the house and convinced her to see a female psychiatrist in Danvers. Her previous counselor at Children's Hospital had moved out of state.

With Rob and Joan's backing, she finally went to the doctor. Within a few weeks, the antidepressant medication kicked in and she felt much better. She also developed a genuine trust with the doctor and looked forward to their weekly counseling sessions. Rob was relieved. He had never seen his wife in such a condition and he felt so helpless.

Sarah returned to work. She was delighted with the welcome she received from patients and staff. She was stronger. She realized that the one major influence in her determination to recover was her love for her husband. He was the one constant in her life. He had never hurt her. He had never betrayed her.

Ruth Reardon

Ruth finished the first year of medical school at the end of June. She and Dana Broderick were married in mid-July. Between final exams and the big event, she supervised all the details of her upcoming wedding in her usual well-organized way. Rita was a big help. The two of them reveled in the last-minute shopping in Boston and the frantic changes to be made with the caterer and the florist.

The wedding went well, despite a slight mist hovering over Marblehead Harbor. Joe was lucky to book the yacht club dining room before the pandemonium of upcoming race week. He spared no expense. The length of the guest list was limited only by the number of tables available.

The newlyweds chose Disney World for a honeymoon. Money was tight. She wasn't working and Dana was waiting for his first promotion at the biotech firm in Cambridge. They leased a small apartment next to the MBTA commuter line in Melrose.

The in-laws got along pretty well. His mother was a grammar school teacher and his father a soon-to-be-retired fire department lieutenant in Marblehead. During the first year, Rita called Ruth a couple of times each week. Chummy but not intrusive. The newlyweds managed to break bread at each in-laws once a month. Ruth and Dana were good company for each other. So many years of friendship gave them a solid base for the biggest test of anyone's life, the ability to share it.

Their delayed sexual intimacy made it all the richer and more trusted. What they couldn't express in words of everyday interaction flowed effortlessly in the language of that deeper, more meaningful intercourse.

Their parents respected the laid-back, casual style. The two kids were made for each other. Smart, sensible and caring. They were truly extensions of each other's family, not just accidents of a misguided immature passion.

The demands of medical school led them to hope for a delay in starting their family. It worked until the early months of her internship at the Boston Floating Hospital. She delivered Martha Jean in July of the following year. Her residency program was put on hold for six months. By that time, she decided to switch from pediatrics to emergency medicine.

Dana's career was going quite well. By the time the baby was born, he had changed companies and was now a junior executive in a Route 128 genetics research company. He was making quadruple his original salary and loved his work. They saved enough money over the next two years to buy a new house in Lynnfield, again allowing both commuting access to their separate places of work. Ruth needed less than a year to complete her residency training at that point.

Shortly after their sixth anniversary, she gave birth to Dana Jr., and after a six-month leave of absence from her Boston job, she took a position at Salem Hospital in the emergency room.

Ruth and Dana at no time took their marriage for granted. The occasional fussing and squabbles never got out of hand. Each gave a little and gained a lot. Both grew comfortable as partners and parents.

They called it a second honeymoon, a two-week trip to England and Scotland for their tenth anniversary present to each other.

Alan Reardon

After graduation, Alan spent a month on Cape Cod. He stayed with a classmate at his family's summer home in Hyannis. Still no job, still no future. Out of desperation, he answered an ad in the local newspaper for a position at Barnstable High School. They were desperate too. He got the job of assistant freshmen football coach and also agreed to teach one English course per week.

His summertime buddy went to New York to law school, and the family homestead closed down for the winter. He was forced to rent a cute little Cape-style house in Mashpee and braced himself for the long, lonely season ahead. Cape Cod in the winter shifts from high speed to idle.

He loved working with the raw, young talent on the football field. But preparing his English classes was much harder. He felt awkward in front of the kids. Approval had always been lavished on the high school football star because of his physical talents. Now his brain and his mouth were the tools of success, and he had genuine doubts about his performance as a teacher.

The varsity coach asked him to double date with a friend of his fiancee, another teacher in the Falmouth school system. Two weeks later, they were sharing his apartment. They proceeded to make wild passionate love, day and night, for the next couple of months. She then visited her mother in Plymouth at Christmas and returned to say that she was quitting her job and moving back home. Mom had been diagnosed with breast cancer and was all alone.

After surfing the local bars on weekends, Alan managed to arrange a few bed-and-breakfast encounters. By the end of the school year, he felt a need to head back home. He was tired, flat, and lonely.

The Reardon house was crowded. His stepbrother Mike had reoccupied his old room while he recovered from a nasty divorce. A high school buddy welcomed him into his condo next to the Boston Yacht Club. He needed someone to share the expenses.

This was more like it. Marblehead in the summer. The North Shore Riviera. Yacht races, long beach days, and party, party, party. For Alan, one gigantic Cheers bar after another. Everyone knew his name. And then it was over. Labor Day again.

Rita and Joe sat down with him one night in August and talked about his future. He was annoyed, but he wasn't. They really did care. By the end of the evening, he told them that he had applied to three business schools in Boston for the second semester. He would retire from his job on the Cape if he was admitted to one of them. He felt that he just couldn't stand another entire winter there. He received an acceptance to Boston University Business School by mid-October. He gave his notice to the high school principal on the Cape and spent the holidays at home.

Boston looked better than ever. He was going to a college on the banks of the Charles River, even though it wasn't the proper college on the other side of the river. Graduate school was different. No fooling around. Very serious people. No sports and no sports heroes at that level. He soon got into it. He put his love life on hold. The closest he came to a date during the winter months was at morning coffee breaks at a Commonwealth Avenue deli. Carol Branch was in two of his classes and they struck up a casual relationship at the deli. She was perky and blunt. Once or twice a week, they would meet to grab a quick cup and analyze the clothes, hairdos, and personalities of their teachers. Carol's fiancé was a senior at Northeastern University in the engineering course.

They didn't mean for it to happen. But it did. One snowy winter day, Carol's car got plowed in. She asked him for a ride to her mother's house in Somerville. Mother was scheduled for gallbladder surgery the next day. The storm turned into a real blizzard, and their day turned into a riotous series of mishaps that almost found them marooned in a tavern in Cambridge.

In chronological order, the events of that day went like this. His car got sideswiped by a snowplow, immobilizing the left front wheel. From the safety of a nearby tavern, they emptied their pockets on futile rescue calls. After a few beers, they witnessed the disintegration of the bar's front window courtesy of a sliding pick-up truck. Next they took a cab to mom's apartment only to find that the cab could not get through the snowdrifts. They had to walk eight blocks. When they arrived, they found out that Carol's mother, in a panic state, had gone to her sister's for safety.

After the laughing and the shivering stopped, they both took a steaming hot bath (separately). They then sat in the parlor watching sitcoms and sipping hot tea. She took mom's bed and he tried the couch that evening. They were both bone tired. However, they were not tired enough to go to sleep right away. Within an hour, they both took mom's bed.

The wedding reception was at the Yacht Club in mid-October of that year. It was a gala. The Branches were totally outnumbered. Joe and Rita insisted on paying for the whole affair. Carol and her mother were not in any financial position to argue. The guest list included high school and college classmates of both parties and family and friends. Carol was indeed popular. The consensus of the guests was that Alan was a lucky guy to get Carol. Only a few said the reverse.

They took out a lease on a third-floor apartment on the Fenway. Both hooked up with entry-level positions in town. Alan was assigned to the

Marriage

BankBoston marketing department, and Carol became an assistant to the director of Macy's human resources division.

The first few months were exciting. They loved playing house. Friends were still plentiful in the Boston area. Carol was a cook and hosted one dinner party a week. Friday and Saturday nights were reserved for other kinds of parties. Carol was also an antique nut. On Sunday afternoons, they usually traveled far and wide to flea markets and antique shops. Alan finally drew the line on the third cute little wicker rocking chair—just no room in the apartment.

Each job required some traveling. Once a month, she needed to attend a meeting at Macy's headquarters in New York. The climate of bank mergers required feverish efforts to hold on or acquire new accounts. Alan's assignment, along with his boss, was to travel throughout the country putting out fires or trying to save failing bank affiliates.

No matter how busy they were, Alan and Carol found time to just sit on the sofa before bedtime to sip some wine and dream young people's dreams before a flickering scented candle on the coffee table. Reviewing the events of the day, sharing the little triumphs and tragedies, talking about old-time family stuff was what they did. They split the holiday family obligations. Thanksgiving in Somerville, Christmas in Marblehead.

During the late winter months, the traveling increased. Every week one or the other was gone for a few days. Alan returned one night from Texas to find his wife crying. She told him that her sister from Cape Cod had stayed over one night and told stories about the Don Juan from Marblehead. He was ashamed and angry. What was past was past. Carol heard the words but felt betrayed. Her own father had run away before she had started grammar school.

They talked about their marriage and the toll that the business trips were taking. Each had signed a one-year contract. By the end of the summer, they would be free to look elsewhere. A small business together in the suburbs seemed the right choice. Insurance, real estate, anything, as long as they worked together.

In May, Alan was sent to Miami. He was tired of the job and tired of Carol's constant reminder that he be a good boy. He met a Harvard football buddy at the Fontainebleu Hotel and spent a couple of nights soaking up some beers. The second night they bought drinks for a couple of Dolphins cheerleaders. Peter took one back to his hotel. Alan politely excused himself and went home alone. He tossed and turned most of the night. What was he thinking? She was gorgeous and oh so ready. In the old days, he wouldn't have wasted a minute. He thought of Carol and the changes that were taking place. Ever since her sister talked it hadn't been the same.

She was no angel either. At business school, she was reported to have been a real party girl. And what about dumping her fiancé so quickly after their snowstorm romance? What was she doing tonight?

Carol wasn't home when he arrived from the airport. The note said, "Mom's sick again. Staying over in Somerville for a few nights. Call when you get in. Chicken in the fridge. Hope you missed me."

He didn't call until the next night. Now it was her turn to be angry. She came home within an hour and they had a major argument. He was tired of her suspicions and she was tired of his trips.

The argument took a nasty turn when he presented her with a matchbook that he found lying on the kitchen counter. The logo was "Sparky's Lounge" in Copley Square. Since she didn't smoke herself, he challenged her as to why it was there. She explained that she had gone there for a going away party for one of her fellow workers. She needed a ride home and her boss drove her home. Alan was in such a mood that no answer would have been acceptable, and the two of them slept separately that night. They tried to patch it up over the next few weeks, but it just didn't seem to work as it had before.

Alan's job was constantly on his mind. He was just plain fed up. He had never felt so tied down in his life. Never had a full-time responsibility. The summer playground jobs required no heavy lifting. In fact, they were opportunities to get together with his gang and fool around on the playground. The traveling was becoming tiresome, the paperwork boring. And the demands of his penny-pinching boss were aggravating him. He could hardly wait until the early fall when his contract came to an end.

Carol worried about the growing coolness between the two of them. They rarely went to bed at the same time. Hello and goodbye kisses turned into cool pecks on the cheek or none at all. No more late-night snuggles on the couch. He preferred watching the news and she had her book. Carol wondered if they needed outside help. He adamantly refused. Two intelligent people ought to be able to work it out.

The company scheduled one final trip before the summer. Alan was booked at the newest hotel in Las Vegas. A new corporate rule required that employees on the same mission share hotel rooms instead of a wasteful one-person-to-one-room tradition. His jolly friends who met them in Las Vegas from their base in Los Angeles worked out a special scheme that headquarters had not anticipated. The Californians suggested a coed system. After an evening of mix and match at the bar, Alan was paired with a tall, muscular blonde named Mitzi. She was a champion beach volleyball athlete and brought to their boudoir an athleticism that left even the Harvard jock exhausted.

More than that, Alan was genuinely smitten with this woman. The suntanned beauty with the Doris Day face had a brain, a good brain. After college, she had acquired an MBA at UCLA and was moving up the ladder quickly.

They parted company on the last day, saying all the right grown-up clichés that would match the traditional Hollywood wisdom. "Chin up. No crying. We shared some wonderful moments. Some day we may meet again. No regrets."

Within a day, phone calls were exchanged between Los Angeles and Boston. Alan faked a business trip to California in late July to see his new woman. In August, he told Carol it was over. He had fallen in love and there was no turning back. She cried and threw some things around the apartment. She insisted that he leave the apartment immediately.

Joe and Rita were disappointed, but not surprised. Friends from their yacht club had mentioned during the summer rumors about Alan's reputation at BankBoston. One of the rumors had it that his business trips were costing the company money. Alan beat them all to the punch. He notified his employers just before the contract expired that he would not renew his end of it. He left for Los Angeles before the no-fault divorce was final.

CHOICE

Holly Diamond

The attraction was natural and innocent. Two strangers on opposite softball teams. Both good looking, athletic and competitive. He liked her spunk and her strong inviting body. She was struck by his dark, well-chiseled features and his macho facade.

Like so many of their friends, they just started living together. No big deal. No pressure. No legal ties. Just fun and games. Either one could pull out at any time. Lots of sex, booze, drugs and laughs. Life was good.

Rick let it be known right from the beginning that he would not change his ways. He insisted on the rights of bachelorhood. Cleaning, cooking and laundry were women's work. That was how he was brought up. Why change now? Included but not openly flaunted were certain inalienable freedoms. The freedom to work when he felt like it, the freedom to go to sporting events without her, the freedom to drink with his buddies on a regular basis and even the freedom to pick up another chick once in a while.

Holly let it slide. Who knew how long their ride would last? She was ready for a relationship, she was hungry for one, any kind of relationship.

She had suffered such loneliness and despair since her breakdown, then came the pregnancy.

Rick was furious. This wasn't part of the deal. Get rid of it! But Holly couldn't bring herself to get rid of it. He dove head first into a pool of booze and drugs, but nothing changed. It wouldn't go away. He did not want the responsibility. He wasn't ready. Holly threatened to leave him. She couldn't take the sickness and the hassle at the same time. Whatever unmeasured affection, whatever loyalty or respect existed in Rick's heart surfaced. He just couldn't let Holly go. He agreed to a wedding.

Once the knot was tied, Rick reverted to his selfish, immature behavior. He still needed his woman to take care of him, but didn't need a third party in his life, especially one that needed his care.

During the pregnancy he refused to listen to her complaints of nausea and fatigue. At the end, he openly insulted her about her weight gain and misshapen body. The jokes at the pub ceased to be funny. The other guys called him "diaper dad." "She's really going to tie you down now, Rick. You'll need a real job now, Papa."

Holly's breakdown shortly after her delivery was perhaps predictable. The necessary love and support from her husband were missing. She had no close friends or family and the most natural resource, a mother for herself, was absent.

A new mother needs a certain amount of mothering. It is an instinctive yearning for caring and sharing that only another woman can supply. Friends, female relatives, and even maternity ward nurses may offer this timely boost. But if all of these supporters were missing, one person would probably be enough. That is the new mother's own mother. This does not diminish the need for a husband's support, but it is simply not of the same intimate, nourishing quality.

Holly felt a painful longing to be reunited with her own mother. The coldness and finality that separated them was terrible. All of this coupled with the realization that Rick was more of a child than a husband drove her into a deep depression.

Research into the causes of postpartum depression has established the fact that a number of issues are at play. One of them, however, is the weakened body. Hormone levels are measurably lowered following the birth of the baby, including thyroid and endocrine systems. Not only that but the blood-making organs are asked to respond to the blood loss, which takes some time. In general, there is a total ache and weakness to the body itself. There is also the issue of the patients ability to cope with change in the form of an additional child to be responsible for.

If a woman has enjoyed sufficient measures of love and support throughout her life, she will likely withstand the trauma of childbirth. Women who have coped with significant problems and overcome them are also likely to weather the storm. But those who have been either overprotected or underprotected are vulnerable.

The serious depression that may follow childbirth is not a disease. It is an event, a painful and debilitating event with possible long-term consequences. Most women recover, particularly in modern times with timely and proper treatment. They are usually able to resume their marriage and lifestyle and accept the role of mother as their strength returns. For some, however, the event leaves emotional scars. And the wounds do not heal cleanly.

Before the discovery of antidepressant medications a generation ago, the use of electroconvulsant treatment was common. The results were usually dramatic in a positive sense. However, quite often an indefinable residue of emotional blunting occurred. Not uncommonly, future pregnancies and childbirth resulted in repeated breakdowns. Today, the combination of medication, support, and counseling offers more assurance of a healthy recovery.

The marriage ended in divorce within a year. Holly and Rick were wedded but never truly married. Rick particularly had no intention of keeping the promises he spoke at the wedding. He had little or no conception of commitment other than to himself. At first, Holly wanted it to work. She needed it to work. Her family relationships had dissolved. In truth, she wasn't surprised or totally unhappy when it didn't work.

Now she had a person she could call her own, however. Little Louis was hers and hers alone. She determined that she would survive the marriage and the breakdown and make a life for both of them.

Sarah Smith Carleton

At first, no one in the nursing home noticed the two young folks who took their midmorning coffee break together. They were both quiet, polite, steady workers. Gradually the word spread, however. The couple were going out together. Good for them. Two nice kids who minded their own business and kept their mouths shut. The announcement of their engagement surprised no one. It was easy to wish them well.

Sarah had come a long way. She was painfully shy and unsure of herself when she arrived at the nursing home on the first day. The supervisor was quite perceptive and kind. She took her under her wing and gave her simple assignments. Praise and encouragement followed. Gradually, she mastered her chores and felt good about it. As with the counseling she had received at the Children's Hospital, the knack of setting goals and reaching them was the key to solidifying her confidence.

Confidence was not such a big issue with Rob. Having been babied and protected by his widowed mother, he possessed an abundance of it. His problem was to shave it down to a realistic self-worth. That he did by simply doing his best as the chief handyman at the nursing home. When he and Sarah had met, he had no great ambition to do much else.

The engagement was uneventful, except for the gradual joining of two grateful persons. Leisure time was shared. At no point did one or the other take over and demand to do one thing or another. They drifted through shopping malls and food pavilions and bought little. Movies were a regular pastime. Hours at the beach in summer and more hours leaf peeping in October were part of their modest pleasures.

If the wedding was simple, then the marriage was not. It turned out to be simply beautiful, not by accident. Each of them was extremely sensitive to the needs of the other.

The first bump in the road was Sarah's miscarriage. She and Rob had discussed her uncertainties about the role of motherhood. The unresolved issues of her childhood resurfaced. The sadness, madness and badness bubbled and boiled inside her. She was both sad and angry over Melanie's absence during her childhood. Slowly she lost herself in the maze of guilt over her rejection of Melanie in preference to Grandmother Gertrude.

Whatever physiologic forces lead to miscarriages, the emotional determinants are contributors. Obstetricians are well aware that the emotional stability of a pregnant woman is vital. To be sure, there are babies who are born to women whose personal lives are chaotic. Other women who may be abused, abandoned and treated quite badly may sail through the nine months without a ripple. On the other hand, a person who on the surface seems to have it all together may spontaneously abort. The determining factor seems to lie somewhere in the depths of the psyche. For whatever reason, if a woman has enough ambivalence or mixed feelings about being a mother, that coupled with the interaction of gestational hormones may order the body to reject the fetus.

Sarah worried about her readiness to be a mother. That worry turned into a serious descent into a clinical depression. She recovered and was stronger for it. Her love for Rob was a major factor.

Ruth Reardon Broderick

Ruth and Dana brought little emotional baggage to the marriage. No major traumas or tragedies to overcome. Their parents did not spoil or deprive them. On both sides of the parent-child relationship, there was genuine trust and affection.

That did not completely immunize them against change and challenge, however. Each had the opportunity to rebel, to go with the flow, and snub their nose at authority. To a degree, each one of them tried it during their adolescent years.

Married life was less a challenge than another opportunity to keep growing. The responsibilities of career and parenting were handled with common sense and hard work. The quality of their marriage was not measured as the sum of two committed adults; it was much more. As partners and parents, the two became one in a precious, almost mystical, sense. If one hurt, so did the other. So also did they share joy, disappointment, successes and failure.

By their tenth anniversary, Ruth and Dana were secure in their love and respect for each other.

Alan Reardon

Alan drifted into and out of college with a gnawing sense of insecurity. The one thing he relied on was his ability to score both on the athletic field and in bed. Women were a comfort and thus a commodity. As a commodity, they could be purchased for a reasonable price: his charm and good looks.

But something was wrong. On Cape Cod, he discovered that he was also a commodity. He could be seduced and abandoned. No loyalty, no respect. Sayonara!

He chose to reestablish some career goals and adopted a more responsible outlook on his life. Along came Carol Branch. They fell in love and gambled on the intensity of their infatuation to carry them beyond the wedding vows. It was not enough. The long separations drew them apart, geographically and emotionally. The ghosts of her missing father rekindled suspicions that grew into obsession.

Alan did not have the will or interest to salvage the union. She could not fill his needs anymore. He wondered if anyone ever could. He found a temporary fix in Las Vegas. The voice inside him would not go away. Only now instead of "What's it all about?" he heard "What's with you, you jerk?"

Substance Abuse Problems

At this point, it is helpful to review the most costly, disruptive and prevalent behavioral disorder in modern society, drug and alcohol abuse.

Thousands of books and articles are available offering theories as to cause and prevention. Millions of dollars are spent annually by governments all over the world to provide research, education and law enforcement efforts in the control of the traffic of substances. The saddest feature, however, is the growing number of young children who are victims of unscrupulous predators seeking wider distribution of their deadly chemicals.

It is only in the latter part of the last century that addictive problems were included in the mainstream of psychiatric discussion. For centuries, alcohol and drug abuse was considered either a simple problem of bad habits or a defect in one's moral fiber. This has led to much confusion as to what it is all about. Even now, there are those who claim that alcohol and drug abuse are human diseases, while others insist they are a matter of choice and will power.

Let me offer a few simple ideas about this subject using observations and terminology that we are already familiar with in this book.

At the beginning, we explored the vital role of two fundamental emotions: anxiety and depression as the cornerstones of our response to life's changes and challenges. As we followed the Smith and Malone families from the door of the hospital until now, we have watched these two emotional constants spawn a variety of behavioral patterns. Most of these developed into maladaptive behaviors to which we attached diagnostic labels.

But throughout the growth, development, and expansion of the Smith and Malone families the impact of addictive behavior on each family has been quite clear. Billy Smith's parents both had significant problems with drug and alcohol. Billy himself used and sold drugs. Terry Brennan, Holly and Anne Diamond, and Alan Reardon used alcohol or drugs to excess. Each had a different taste and style in the use of these substances. All were using chemicals, however, for the same purpose: to dampen and even silence the pain of unbearable anxiety and depression.

Over the forty years that I have practiced psychiatry and written prescriptions, which I would estimate to be in the amount of over two hundred thousand, I have found that ninety percent of those prescriptions were for the purpose of bringing relief to two basic disturbances, anxiety and depression. The official pharmaceutical designation for the medications I prescribed were anti-anxiety and antidepressant medications. Thus it should be clear that whether the medication is self-administered or by legitimate prescription, the two target emotions are the same.

The person who becomes seriously involved in the repeated use of illicit drugs, such as marijuana, cocaine, or heroin, and the person who develops a persistent and escalating use of alcohol is attempting to medicate themselves with chemicals that are often more effective than legitimate prescription drugs. But there is a hitch. The medications that are self-administered may cause physical harm and even death. They may ultimately destroy families, careers, friendships, and the integrity of one's soul.

I suggest that the why of drug and alcohol abuse begins with an effort to kill pain, emotional pain. If this is a why, then what about the how? How does a person advance from the first drink, smoke, snort, or needle to full addictive dependence? There is no single answer. But as we look back at the families and extended families of the Smiths and Malones, one thing is clear. The process of addiction is gradual. It takes time.

Let us look at least three stages and use the more common pathway to alcohol dependence as the model. Perhaps not a single family has escaped the heartache, the embarrassment and the helplessness that accompanies their connection to an alcoholic relative.

It all starts with a single drink. The drink leads to pleasure and relaxation, often in the company of friends and family. This is all innocent and, in a manner of speaking, healthy. Used this way, alcohol is not bad. It is a helpful tool in relaxation and socialization. It is the magic elixir that allows us to unwind and relax with others. It promotes sociability. It reduces tensions and inner turmoil.

But for some, social drinking is not enough. At this point, they may graduate into a more intensive variation of this stage. Larger quantities of alcohol and more frequent bouts of intoxication gather the attention of family and friends. At first it appears funny. Friends may giggle and recall last night's party with some impish joy. The person who is losing control begins to stand out. In time, however, if this pattern continues, the cute little words like being "smashed" or "pickled" turn into a worrisome judgment. He's just "plain drunk."

If this person fails to recognize and correct the dangerous direction of their drinking pattern they may move into stage 2, which I would call alcohol abuse. When this happens, the regularity and the quantity of alcohol consumption begin to affect the drinker's lifestyle and the people around them. Poor job performance, inattention to spouse and children, neglected hygiene soon follow. Inappropriate outbursts mark a definite deterioration of personality and control. Confrontations by friends and family are more common. This is a crucial moment. For if the person fails to accept the certain well-intentioned advice to desist the habit of drinking and refuses to believe and trust their closest of friends and family, then they are well on their way to total dependence on the substance.

Alcohol dependence is the final stage. There are many scenarios within this stage. They range from the totally reckless social behavior to the hollow shell of the streetcorner wino clutching the brown bag with the liquid poison inside. The alcohol-dependent person surrenders all their belongings. To hell with spouse, kids, friends, job, God. Screw the world. I'm hurting and no one cares. Leave me alone. Just give me a bottle.

This total retreat from responsibility and any meaningful interaction resembles in some ways the retreat of the schizophrenic. Whereas the schizophrenic is forced involuntarily to leave a world they simply cannot cope with, the alcoholic leaves a world where they once functioned with the give and take of love, relationships and purpose. The new world of their making is a world that is a surreal, shallow cocoon where self-pity and blame of others sustains them. Instead of using the chemical to cope with losses and changes, they fill themselves with the flammable material of alcohol that in the brain saturates the healthy cells and adds to a massive depression. Madness and sadness eventually take over, but instead of trying to resolve and cope with this, the alcoholic wears these feelings on their tattered sleeve as an emblem of martyrdom. They dwell on the badness of life and on the badness of people. But always the badness is externalized. You are bad, not me.

Let's return to the debate. Is alcohol dependence a disease or a weakness?

I believe that the third stage of either drug or alcohol dependence is truly a disease. The key factor is the helplessness of the adult. The stranglehold of the chemical in the brain and in the body renders such a person incapable of recovering without outside help.

Fortunately, there is a lot of help today. Most communities in this country are equipped with medical facilities to begin the detoxification procedures and then guide the person through proper programs. Ultimately, however, the person must choose to follow this direction and recover from the addiction.

Once free of the chemical shackles that go with drugs and alcohol, such a person may make a measured decision and choice regarding their future. It all sounds so easy, but it isn't. For within this last and final stage of alcohol or drug dependence, there may emerge within certain persons an attitude toward their life and toward the people in their life that truly leads them into a regression and a relapse. This signals a true intention to abandon whatever lifestyle they enjoyed. Only repetitious relapses and painful medical consequences bring some people back to a decision to save their life rather than give it up.

Chapter Five: The Middle Years

CHANGE

High noon! And nowhere to hide.

The middle years are the inventory years, the reflective years, the what's-life-all about years, the what-has-happened-in-my life years, the what's-happening-now years, the years of fear and doubt and uncertainly about what will happen to my life before I die. And there are many days when it feels good just to be alive.

The middle years are the years of unavoidable confrontation with our mortality, with life and death. The middle years represent another change and another challenge. Only this time the decision is not whether to grow up, but whether to keep growing up while the body starts to grow down.

The middle years are the years without warning and sadly without much preparation. No one is really ready. There are millions of words written about the physiologic involution called the menopause. A few words about the existential limbo that awaits. One does not hear about it at home or in school or in church. Those who have been through it hesitate to revisit it and those who have not cannot imagine the experience.

Living through the middle years requires enormous amounts of patience, perseverance, hope, faith, love, courage and humor. But despite all the support and kindness of friends and family, it is at times a most solitary, lonely business.

In the chapter on adolescence, I mentioned the concept of "unsureness" as the predominant experience of the first major "change of life." For the middle years, "aloneness" is the terrible burden. Aloneness is not the same as being lonely or alone. One may feel lonely in the midst of a crowd. The lonely person yearns for someone who is missing, someone who brings comfort support and love. And when that person is rejoined, the loneliness ends. Being alone is just that. No other person present. But being alone does not necessarily bring loneliness.

Aloneness is the burden of the middle years. It is that unique feeling that despite trusted people being present or within reach, the emotional struggle must be resolved within our selves. Only the person afflicted can decide what to do with their thoughts, feelings, what to do with their life. Total responsibility without sharing that responsibility. And no one can really understand what is being felt. It is no wonder that there is a high rate of suicide during the middle years. Suicide is a choice, a desperate choice. The result is death where there are no more changes, challenges, or choices.

Midlife issues thus call our existence into question and, once again, we are forced to make a choice about that existence. Only now the stakes are high, the choices truly being life or death. We must choose to go forward with our life until a natural death or retreat from that life and emotionally begin to die backwards, slowly but surely.

To choose life means to weigh the importance and worth of life and to reconcile the courageous determination to continue to grow and give of life with the firm belief that there is a purpose to life and a life after death. To give up on life, however, means to play it safe, to retire prematurely from life, to seek the elusive comfort of depending on others rather than oneself. Rejecting responsibility for one's life yields to constant expectations of being cared for by others.

The phenomenon of dying backwards mentioned above means that the child within the adult takes over and seeks protection from the uncertainty and pain of life. Future changes and losses are not accepted anymore. Any change is avoided and detested. When one starts the emotional dying then real death must be denied at all costs. It is something that is too overwhelming and inconceivable. Time inexorably extends beyond the middle years, and the person who starts avoiding life soon begins to despise the clock and the calendar. Their personality shrinks into disillusionment, bitterness and hopelessness. In the olden days, this sad predicament was best pictured by a person sitting in a rocking chair draped with a black blanket or shawl around their shoulders. The people around them used the polite term "their decline."

⁓

The middle years are generally referred to as "the change of life." Another frequently used term is menopause. These terms are not the same. Menopause is an experience, specific to women, whereby certain body chemicals called hormones begin to shut down the childbearing potential. It usually begins in the early forties and can last several years. More on that later.

The change of life experience, in distinction to the menopause, is shared by both men and women and involves a confrontation with oneself regarding one's lifestyle and purpose in life. Each person's encounter with

The Middle Years

these issues is different. Some enter the midlife experience as early as the late thirties, and others are spared until their fifties.

I have referred to adolescence as the first change of life. Recall the duration of the experience, at least a half-dozen years. It takes even more time to endure and resolve the ordeal of the middle years, and the time span is related to each one's individualized struggle. As with the first change of life, the matrix within the emotional, spiritual, and physical changes takes place in that private world of our own personal existence. The everyday events of our lives become the locus of an incredible drama.

On that stage, five specific facets of our life are challenged. The most common midlife issues are the body, the job, the marriage, the family and God.

The Body

It isn't fair! Why us? Women have a far more difficult time as the reproductive system decides to call it quits. Just as the mysteries of the menstrual cycle shocked and distressed the young girl at pubescence, the barrage of unwanted menopausal symptoms come crashing down ready or not. Hot flashes, nausea, fatigue, cramps, erratic periods, irritability, frustration, and mood swings all ebb and flow without warning, without a predictable end point.

The same questions raised thirty years before reappear. What's happening to my body? Is something wrong? Am I sick? Do I have cancer? Why me? Why didn't someone tell me? At the end of it all, a plus and a minus. For most women, the cessation of the menstrual cycle is welcome, but the knowledge that Mother Nature has declared an end to childbearing presents some doubts and questions about one's future role as a woman.

Other questions arise also. What about the vulnerability of the body so suddenly altered? This may lead to a preoccupation with one's health. The concern over readjusted reproductive hormones is understandable. Osteoporosis and cancer of the breast, uterus and ovaries are statistically more likely to occur in the postmenopausal years.

Anxiety over what bad things might happen and depression over what's been lost are the predictable, natural emotional responses as they have been since birth. The pattern of each menopausal experience depends on the impact of the changes and the emotional stability that a woman brings to this experience. We will explore the various patterns in the Challenge section.

Men do not experience the drastic changes of female menopause. Nevertheless, they also receive warning signals about their body's fragility. Slower reflexes, diminished physical stamina and softening muscles drive men away from the mirror and into fitness programs. As with women, the first set of eyeglasses to accommodate the normal aging of the eye muscles occurs in the forties.

Men are slower to recognize the signals, partly because the signals are less intrusive and partly because of the masculine avoidance of vulnerability. But Mother Nature finds a way. The shocking news of a friend's death from a heart attack is an attention-getter. The actual experience of a heart attack or a transient stroke leaves no misunderstanding about the male body's limitations. The wise man will seek and follow his doctor's advice. Diets, weight loss programs, and fitness activities reduce the fears and anxieties of premature aging and death.

But life will never be the same for men and women confronted with major insults to the body that previously had not given them any trouble. Some decide to take out a new lease on life and swallow the medicines, endure the therapies, and discard dangerous habits. Others allow the slightest infirmity to create a host of fears and doubts that feed on each other and ultimately create an attitude of helplessness and hopelessness.

Thus, the inevitable physical changes of midlife are accepted by some as yet another challenge and by others as proof of life's list of insufferable burdens.

The Job

What am I doing here anyway? There's got to be a better job somewhere. So many years! Same place! Same people! What do I have to show for it all?

The harness begins to chafe. This is the time of life when men and women balk at the daily routine of work. For some, it is a legitimate wake-up call to shake loose the coils of inertia or apathy and truly find a better position. But for others, quitting work without sufficient reflection may lead to a variation on the theme of musical chairs. At the end of the game, there may be no job.

Often the impulse to change one's job is a reaction to the frightening web of changes going on in the other four areas of midlife. The more helpless and trapped one feels, the more driven one becomes to control something, to make a decision, to make a change. A protest against life's cruel demands. The danger, however, lies in mistaking the anxiety and depression of midlife for a specific unhappiness related to the job. Such confusion can affect the coal miner as well as the corporate executive.

The worker who is career-oriented is particularly vulnerable, for such issues as pride, self worth, success are so intertwined in the meaning of a job that the buffeting winds of midlife are ignored. One's job is one's career, and one's career is equated with one's worth, and one's worth or the illusion of same may be all that keeps one alive.

The scenario of musical jobs can be exhausting and the toll in lost income and lost self-esteem only compounds the effort to stay free from the whirling vortex of change and loss.

The Marriage

Not uncommonly the silver wedding anniversary falls within the middle years, and not uncommonly the marriage comes to an end. The midlife issues exact a heavy toll on a shaky union. Statistically, the divorce rate around the 25th anniversary is the third highest peak.

Why? No single answer. But four factors have been identified as contributors: the deterioration of the marriage bond, the empty nest, the swirling emotional and physical changes, and finally women's ability to survive economically outside the marriage.

If the couple work through the first year hurdles, the working phase of marriage begins. How to adjust to the arrival of children, money pressures, two-parent employment, home ownership, school choices, parent participation, family of origin obligations. These real pressures test the mettle of the couple whose idyllic romance seems so long ago. But like so many tests, the opportunity arrives to build on the marriage or slip away from the commitment.

In the chapter on marriage, we touched on the success of the wedding promises being directly related to the spouse's ability to convert subconscious expectations into reachable goals. Neither party can ever satisfy the unfulfilled yearnings of the child within the adult partner. Marital bonding is accomplished by giving up unrealistic expectations and working hard to fashion a union built on selflessness. Giving rather than taking is the priority.

If this does not happen, then the corrosive power of impossible demands gradually leads to living together but not loving together. To those friends and family outside the intimacy of the relationship, a facade may be temporarily shown. But a gradual deterioration of the relationship affects the behavior of the children first and ultimately sours friendships and family ties. Some unhappy couples call it quits early on. But a surprising number grimly struggle to get the kids through high school and college before choosing divorce.

The empty nest syndrome is a term that has outlasted some of the cute clichés that came out of the Pop Psych movement. It is a major event in the midlife experience, as we shall see shortly on the subject of family changes. The marriage is affected directly. For the loss of interaction and communication between parents and kids forces the couple to reassess the state of their bond as they realize that they are the only ones at home.

Once more change invites a challenge, and once more challenge invites a choice. The choice is to reinvest in the marriage or not.

As we noted earlier, this is an ongoing challenge. Partners need to remarry each other approximately every five years in order to survive. If the marital glue is diluted into a thin paste of tolerance and the understanding that we will merely "stay together for the kids," then a breakup is inevitable. If the couple see the children moving out as a natural evolution of the family and if their love has continued to grow, then they will turn toward each other for more of the same.

Likewise the committed couple buffeted by involutional physical changes and emotional challenges may build an even tighter bond during these stormy years. But the couple who have lost the love and respect for each other will likely perceive the major cause of midlife as coming directly from a sterile relationship and subsequently blame the other for all of their woes.

A major factor in the midlife divorce rate is the wife's opportunity for economic independence outside the marriage. Despite continuing inequities in salaries and job opportunities, women nowadays are far better equipped than their mothers and certainly their grandmothers to sustain themselves financially without their husbands. This same exposure to the business and cultural changes of the last century has left women bolder and less guilty about divorce and the yearning for that elusive "meaningful relationship."

Thus, the middle years provide a stage on which those sacred promises spoken in sincerity and innocence so many years ago are tested in a drama without a script, without a director and without a supporting cast. The couple is ultimately alone to remarry each other or unmarry.

The Family

Two parts: family of origin and family of a marriage.

During their forties, each person becomes aware, sadly, that their elders are dying—grandparents, aunts and uncles, older cousins, and in many instances parents. The annoying reminders of our mortality through the menopausal experience and male sense of body slowing combine now with the stark image of a family funeral. This sharpens the sting of vulnerability. The ranks are thinning out. There were always older people ahead of us, leading the way through life. Though not always totally loved or respected, the older folks somehow insulated us from the march of time and from the confrontation with our own death.

Now, we are pushed forward to the front ranks in the big parade of life. There is no one to copy or blame. Children and grandchildren replace us in the back rows. We are expected to take responsibility for leading the

The Middle Years

family now. We are the wise men and women, the soothsayers, the leaders of the clan. What a time to inherit the throne. The time of hesitancy and doubt. Some days life seems so hard, and leadership responsibilities are not welcome. Just getting through the daily routine is the main goal.

We are forced to look anew at our forebears. They are no longer measured with the petty resentments of our youth, where at times we seethed over the unjust privileges and authority of the big folks. A new found admiration arrives.

How did they get through it all? Did they doubt? Did they question? Did they want to run away? What helped them? What kept them steady? I wish they were still around. I would ask them.

The second family issue for those who are married and have a family is the slow, steady natural separation of family members as discussed in the last chapter. Life's inevitable changes, though expected, are difficult to accept, especially when changing winds are blowing all around us.

Many parents speak of the special sorrow of the first and last child leaving home. It is not that the others are less valued. It is more the symbolism of the event. The first child to go off to college or get married cuts deeply into the sense of family unity. The event is sadly disruptive, but it also sends a warning of future losses to family harmony. The last child to leave closes the door on a treasured time of life.

In the section on marriage, we examined the enormous importance of remarrying each other. Parents can never replace the special fabric of family life when the kids were at home, but they can reinvest in the love and friendship that shaped that magnificent experience.

God

Last, but by no means least, on the agenda of midlife struggles is one's unavoidable confrontation with existence. The same questions that were raised by the adolescent and young adult return. Only now the context is that frightening point in life where changes and losses compete with each other in a ceaseless barrage of emotional bumps and bruises.

In young adulthood, the most important question is the "why" of our existence. The reason that most people choose to live and grow is that they find some purpose to their life. For many, it resides in the goodness and value derived from being with other people, family and friends. It is a "now" thing, supported and sustained by teachings and beliefs learned in earlier years. The faith of our fathers and mothers gives us direction and hope and encourages us to continue on. During those early years, the question of life after death is pondered and worried about, but it is still an abstraction compared to the busy flow of events in everyday life. For some, this is not the case and death is a real choice, whether by reckless behavior or by their own deliberate hand. Faith and hope become unreliable companions at this early stage.

The midlife struggle is different. One problem is the palpable awareness that death is inevitable and closer. The other is the vacuum-like sense of aloneness that wraps the midlife soul in a blanket of helplessness and doubt.

"My God, my God, why has thou forsaken me?" In the Christian tradition, these words were spoken by the God-Man Jesus Christ at the time of his execution. This event and these words capture the agony of every human being during the middle and later years. The sense of desolation and abandonment screams for answers. One's God seems remote and deaf to the cries. The sense of aloneness deepens and the search for a meaning to life at times seems to be futile.

It is high noon and one is all alone to decide the future course of life. To continue the search and to rekindle and embrace a personal philosophy of life takes enormous courage and faith—faith in oneself as well as one's God.

The choice to live and to continue on with life is not usually made in solitary meditation or on some Tibetan mountain. It is made in the bustle of everyday life. It is made by getting up each day while not feeling too good and going to work. It is made repeatedly by interacting with close friends and even strangers. It is made by developing a whole new set of values. It is made by establishing priorities which begin with loving loved ones more. It is made by being grateful for what one has rather than resenting what one has not. It is made by enjoying the simple pleasures of life.

One must wrestle with these issues for months and years. A quiet, private personal struggle to make sense out of life and death, a ceaseless search, a heroic quest, a wondrous journey. But out of this trial and tribulation comes an unshakable confidence. One truly owns oneself, one totally is in control of oneself. And one will never again be trapped in the terrible darkness of high noon.

But as with previous changes and challenges, there is always another choice. If one does not find one's God by forgiving oneself for the doubts, if one does not let go of the unrealistic expectations of other people in one's life, the consequence is to wander aimlessly without a compass, without a star and without a light that can dispel the darkness.

The remainder of life will be marked by bitterness. And the old familiar ghosts of anxiety and depression will set up permanent residence in the creakiness of the old rocking chair and the chafing fibers of the dusty shawl.

CHALLENGE

Billy Smith

They lived together for two more years. But the AIDS virus got in the way. Harold hosted a deadly organism that found other victims through sexual intimacy. That single fact permeated the subconscious mind of both lovers. At first, they practiced so-called safe sex, aimed at avoiding the transmission of fluid. In time, the preparations led to a lack of spontaneity and ardor.

Harold was the first to comment. Billy acknowledged his fears and said his own needs were not being satisfied. Harold was horrified. Billy then admitted to several liaisons and insisted that he be allowed freedom to continue them. Harold pleaded for a return to the love and loyalty he deserved. After a series of ugly confrontations, Billy left Harold and moved in with another partner.

Harold overdosed and died three months later. Billy was shaken. He experienced a deep depression that became unendurable without the magic balm of marijuana and cocaine. For the first time in his life, guilt feelings penetrated his conscious mind, and he was brought to the edge of suicide several times. Billy then sought relief in a reckless marathon of sexual encounters with little regard for his own safety. But it wouldn't go away. He finally lost his job at the hospital and retreated totally into the netherworld of drugs and alcohol. Only habitual use of heroin quenched the crushing sense of despair. His lover finally insisted that he leave the apartment, and when Billy refused, he tipped off the police who raided the place. Billy did a four-year stretch at Walpole Prison and was transferred to Bridgewater Hospital after being diagnosed with HIV disease.

His sister Sarah visited him on the occasion of his fortieth birthday. He was then in another state hospital but he was dying. She hardly recognized him—gray matted hair, dirty beard, and hollow eye sockets. He weighed a little over a hundred pounds. Through a frail, cracked voice he thanked her for coming, but asked her to leave within the hour. He was too tired. Before she left, she told him she would keep him in her prayers. Billy thanked her and held on to her hand. He promised to do likewise. He said the chaplain had taught him how to pray. Sarah would always remember his final comments through a thin, weak smile. He said that his conversion was forty years too late.

Sarah Smith Carleton

The birth of Christine Marie was a wonderful event after the many tries, and Sarah and Rob were delighted. Sarah was now thirty-five and her biological clock was ticking down. She had suffered her third miscarriage three years earlier and had been bitterly disappointed. If the birth of Christine was a gain in her life, then she was just about to suffer two more losses before her fortieth birthday: Billy Smith's death and her mother's confinement to a nursing home with early Alzheimer's disease. Her mother-in-law, Joan Carleton, was a savior. She became a surrogate mother for Sarah just at the right time. Sarah needed her so badly.

The middle years came too quickly. Sarah had apprehensions about the menopausal experience. Her entry into womanhood thirty years earlier had been a frightful time, and now she was exiting from a stage that had been sometimes frightening, sometimes awkward, and only lately fulfilling.

By her mid-forties, Sarah had a solid grip on herself as a wife, a solid grip as a mother, but was still quite shaky as a daughter. The hot flashes, cramps, fatigue and irritability became more persistent. Then came the vaginal bleeding. Her gynecologist ruled out cancer or other diseases, but advised that she have a hysterectomy.

The trauma proved too much. As she lay in her weakened postoperative state, her thoughts drifted to the bizarre experience of her preadolescent struggle. She felt the terrible fears return. Once again, psychiatric intervention allowed her to interrupt the downward spiral. Medication plus brief counseling helped turn the bout of depression around. In her therapy session, Sarah was able to distinguish the unfinished emotional business of her early childhood from the real challenges of the middle years. With the help of her psychiatrist, she took stock of what she had going for her, rather than brood over irretrievable losses.

Her marriage to Rob headed the list of good things. She determined to reinvest in that marriage. She managed to sort out the confused feelings about her own daughter who was now preadolescent, and rather than be spooked by the memories of her own confusion at that stage of her life, she chose to get closer to Christine and to stick by her.

Sarah started to let go off the wasteful churning in her mind of madness and sadness and guilt. For too many years, it had crippled her and engulfed her. The loss of her brother and mother almost brought it back but she would not allow it.

When Christine started high school, Sarah began working as a volunteer at her old nursing home. It felt good. Even though the original staff had changed, she felt comfortable. She still had something to offer. Money was not the issue. Rob was successful as a contractor. They now lived in a sprawling estate in Saugus. Rob's mother Joan was invited into their home after she developed diabetes and loss of vision. Sarah truly loved this woman and felt that it was payback time for all that she had done for her.

The Middle Years

The marriage was back on solid ground. On the occasion of their thirtieth anniversary, they took Christine and Joan on a cruise to the Caribbean. Christine was now a grammar school teacher in Melrose.

The middle years' struggle brought Rob and Sarah closer to their religious beliefs. They attended services more regularly and had easy conversations about the blessings they had received from their God.

Holly Diamond

Holly had the best intentions after she and Rick divorced. But faced with no family back-up, no job, no husband, and no expertise in caring for a tiny baby, she stumbled badly. Waitressing jobs with flexible hours were available, no experience necessary. That drew her into the cocktail scene again, and soon she was in over her head with after-hours drinking. A string of babysitters quit out of protest about her late arrivals home from work.

Within a year, she had lost four jobs and been arrested twice for driving under the influence. She was sentenced to a two-week rehabilitation hospital and a judge requested that Social Services take her child for what he felt was neglect. Little Louis was never returned to his mother. She started living with a guy she met at the state rehab program, and soon they were both back to drinking.

Cocaine parties became regular routines. At the age of thirty-eight, she had done two stretches at Framingham Women's Prison for possession and trafficking. On each occasion, she suffered a bipolar regression, which was managed in the medical ward. On the second occasion, she assaulted a nurse with a pair of scissors.

By the age of forty, Holly was living in the Salem Shelter for the Homeless. On her way back to the shelter one night in a drunken stupor, she was hit by a car and suffered severe fractures of the upper and lower left leg. This required an above-the-knee amputation. She remained in the rehabilitation hospital for three months, and by the time she was discharged she was eligible for Social Security disability and offered low-income housing in Salem.

She wrote to her mother Anne several times but received no reply. Her father Cliff had retired to Florida, but did make sure he visited her on his infrequent trips north. Her son Louis was now settled in to a stable family in Wakefield and visited only around the Christmas holidays. She saved all the newspaper clippings about his successful high school hockey career. She often wondered about the irony—had she passed on a special ice skating gene?

As time went on, she had more to ponder. Refusing any prosthesis, she rendered herself in a more weakened condition and ultimately fell one night and required the assistance of police to get her to the hospital. She had fractured the opposite hip and as a result was placed at the Salem Willows Home for the Permanently Disabled four blocks from where she had grown up.

She was now fifty-two, alone, and crippled. Her depression turned into a chronic attitude of desolation and despair, and she was not the most popular person in the home.

Ruth Reardon Broderick

Ruth Reardon knew the drill. How often she had offered advice and prescriptions to other women. At the age of forty-three, the menopausal symptoms arrived. She felt lousy. Perhaps the most amazing part was her changeable moods. The once feisty teenager could now become an insufferable bitch around the house and even in the emergency room. Dana soon learned not to laugh. As ornery as she could be, they usually caught themselves after working hours, smoothed over the intemperate behavior of the day.

Their oldest child, Martha, had graduated from Radcliffe and was a social worker in Boston. Dana Jr. followed his mom into the field of medicine. He had been accepted at Tufts Medical School and was quite excited. Ruth and Rita stayed in close touch. Hardly a week went by without a lunch or shopping trip. Joe and Rita had bought a condo on the beach in Naples, Florida. The whole family held their breath after Rita's routine mammogram. The nodule that was found proved to be negative. It was that time of life. Going through the physical changes of midlife made all of the family aware of the infirmities of aging. Ruth started every conversation over the phone with "How do you feel, Mom?"

Ruth moved off the front lines of the emergency room into a more administrative job. The truth was that she felt a bit burned out. As assistant chief, she welcomed the switch to the meetings and scheduling.

Dana became Chief Financial Officer of his third company. Their combined incomes made life secure and comfortable. The kids threw a gigantic fiftieth birthday party for both of them at the yacht club. A joyous occasion. They headed into the next decade a bit bruised from the challenges of the forties but committed to each other and their family. They were still very much in love.

Alan Reardon

Alan stayed in Southern California for three years, soaking up the sun and romping with the sun bunnies. His fling with Miss Volleyball U.S.A. was brief. She was indeed smarter than he thought. She enjoyed the bed part, but grew tired of his drinking and snorting. He latched on to a job in Silicon Valley after a series of go-nowhere positions around Los Angeles.

The Middle Years

Within a year, he was transferred to the East Coast equivalent of the high-tech industry, Route 128 around Boston.

He stayed in Marblehead with Joe, Rita and Jessica for about one year. He was grateful, actually, for the home cooking. But there was more to it. It was their home values. No airs, no pretense, no phoniness. They were the real thing. They didn't preach or teach. He was their son. They enjoyed hearing about his job and friends but never pried. Alan could even talk to his stepsister, Jessica, no longer the strange, silent creature that he recalled. She had a job. And she was a beautiful woman. Rita once asked if he knew of a nice boy whom she could meet. Alan actually tried to arrange a double date but she backed out at the last minute.

As the year came to an end, he got restless. The old hometown wasn't the same. Most of his friends were married or had moved out of Marblehead. The legends of high school heroes all but dry up after ten years. He shuddered to think of the approaching zero year birthday. The big 3–0. Alan had met a woman at work. Before leaving Marblehead for his new Waltham apartment, he brought her to meet Rita and Joe. Janet McHale made a good impression on his parents. So much so, that after he returned from taking her home, they insisted on staying up for a while to chat.

They wasted no time. They told him that he had struck gold. She was not only bright, engaging and gorgeous, but she had balls. Alan laughed at their bluntness. They recalled for him a couple of incidents earlier in the evening where she appropriately offered him a put-down for what was a bragging type of behavior. They wanted to know more about her, but he didn't know much more. She was third-generation Irish and the fourth and last child of parents who were in the teaching profession. Dad was a math teacher at Boston College and Mom a grammar school teacher. The late evening chat ended with some warm hugs and a reminder that he wasn't getting any younger. The field was thinning out, they said with a smile.

Janet McHale refused Alan's invitation to move into his apartment. She threatened to break off any further dates. After a few weeks, he realized that his parents were right. This woman was different. They were married the following summer.

During the engagement, the two of them had time to think about what it was that attracted them and what it was that brought them some concern. They were independent people. The two parts of Alan were at war with each other. The little boy resented the rules of courtship and the maturing young man welcomed her insistence on curbing his appetite. She, on the other hand, loved him but was not overawed by his reputation or good looks. She had turned down better offers. Perhaps what really got to her was an instinct to protect him against himself and help him to grow.

He really didn't have that far to go. Just a few more pinpricks in his puffed-up ego and he would be just right.

What helped them through the first couple of years was their robust sense of humor. It softened the occasional rifts over piddling things. They played off each other easily with their spontaneous remarks that were often light and funny. They were also the hit of office parties and social gatherings for the same reason.

Janet gave birth to Alan Jr. three years after the wedding. She left the firm for her maternity leave, but it turned out to be a permanent leave. Alan's income was more than enough to support the family at that point in their marriage. They bought a house in Concord and settled in happily.

Fatherhood wasn't as bad as he expected. He felt a genuine love and affection for the little guy. Somewhere in the deepest reaches of his mind, he recalled the presence of his real father, Eddie. Being held, carried, dressed, and talked to by a gentle man.

Robin was born three years later. She looked like her mother and she had her mom's temper. Alan and Janet were happy with themselves and their kids. Except for the usual cuts and bruises, their life moved along quite well until Alan hit an emotional stone wall a month shy of his forty-fifth birthday.

As he would later recall, it probably started the previous year. His uncle Paul Malone called to notify him of his father's death. Eddie died in a car crash in San Francisco. No details. No big funeral. His fourth wife had him cremated a week before she notified the family on the East Coast.

Alan couldn't shake the old feelings of longing and disappointment. A few months later, he visited a teammate from Harvard at Mass General. Cancer of the lung. At his own annual physical exam, the doctor discovered high blood pressure. Diet and exercise were recommended.

Alan began to ruminate, first on his own mortality and then on the fragility of his life in general. Illness and death were real possibilities. That led him to deeper thoughts on life itself, its purpose, and its transient nature.

Things became tense at home. Janet was just beginning her hormone therapy for menopausal symptoms. The two of them were wrestling with separate demons, and the marriage did suffer. In his younger days, Alan would avoid unpleasantness with sex and booze. Now there were times when he yearned to truly shake loose from his problems. Just get away.

Work became a chore. He had risen to the level of vice president for research and development. However, the number one guy was only five years older. More than once he asked himself if he should go somewhere else. Alan Jr. was stumbling through his early adolescence and was a genuine pain in the ass. Robin was close on his heels. He insisted that Janet stop serving red meat and sweets. Alan became diet conscious. He dropped twenty pounds in six months. They both became health and body nuts. Their love life lacked warmth and spontaneity. Silently, each blamed the other.

Try as he might, he couldn't take his eye off the buxom young secretary down the hall. The company Christmas party found the two of them laughing and joking and at times smooching rather inappropriately. As he lay in bed that night with Janet, he became terribly guilt ridden but also felt a suffocating sense of entrapment.

Driving home the next evening, it hit the fan. Alan experienced a crushing panic attack, preceded by a frightening urge to turn his car away from home and drive as far as he could and not come back. He broke out in a cold sweat. The shame and guilt poured over him. Suddenly he pulled the car over to the side of the road and vomited.

What was happening? He had never experienced this before. He felt like running and hiding. But where? Something had snapped inside. His world was falling apart. He dimly recalled a similar experience when his father Eddie walked out the door. Why now?

He suddenly turned off at the wrong exit and headed for downtown Concord. He just couldn't go home like this. He had to pull himself together. The Minuteman Tavern was up ahead about a half a mile and he figured that a quick shot and a beer would do the trick. But as he approached the car kept going. A drink wasn't the answer. The panic would not go away. He felt like his nerves were plugged into an electric socket and he could not stop the shaking inside. Where could he go? And then he knew.

It was beginning to snow, just light fluffy stuff, but enough to make it slippery. Strangely, the swish of the wind shield wipers steadied his nerves. At least something was going right. He slid into the empty parking lot of the downtown Catholic Church.

Thank God the door was open. The only light was the flicker of a few votive lamps up front near the altar. Just as well. He wanted to stay unnoticed in the darkness. His whole body was shaking. He focused on the statue of Saint Joseph and then it all came out. He cried so hard and so long that he felt terribly weakened. He completely lost track of time. He must have sat alone in the church for about an hour. He prayed as he had never done before.

What had gone wrong? Why was this happening? What could he do? Please God, help me.

His mind was racing in all directions. But through it all, he found himself returning to the image of his mother. He recalled being just a tiny boy.

Dad hadn't been gone for more than a month. Each night she would come into his bedroom before he fell asleep, turn down the blanket and sit on the edge of the bed. She would lean over and sing one of her many traditional Italian songs. Her voice was low and soothing and beautiful. He could hear her now. His favorite, "I have but one love. This love I give you."

Before he left the church, he prayed to the Blessed Mother of God for help. The shaking and the crying had diminished. As he was buttoning up his coat, he heard the large door at the rear of the church open and then bang shut. A little old lady shook off the mantle of snow from her shoulders and walked feebly to the altar. She lit a red votive light and knelt down to pray. What was she praying for? What could bring such a frail person out on a night like this? It must be something important. He had a sudden urge to walk up and join her and hold her hand. Instead he slipped off the bench to leave, making a squeaking sound as he did so. She turned inquisitively in his direction and gave him a warm, generous smile.

Janet was on the verge of hysteria when he trudged through the door around seven o'clock. She had called his office twice. The first time to ascertain that he had left, and the second to ask if he had returned. The six o'clock news did not record an accident and that gave her some comfort. She followed him nervously upstairs and asked what was wrong. He turned away and headed for the bathroom.

She waited. When he came out, he looked totally drained. They sat on the edge of the bed and he immediately grasped her hand and held it tightly. She waited for him to speak. Tell her something. What terrible thing had overcome him. He began to cry. Now it was her turn to panic.

"Alan, please tell me what is going on. For God's sake, tell me. Nothing can be so bad that we can't face it."

She put her arm around him and held him tightly. For the next thirty minutes, he recalled the events of the last two hours. She was dumbfounded. So strange, so bizarre. No one in her family had ever gone through anything like this. She asked if he wanted something to eat. The kids had already eaten. He declined and said that he was just so exhausted that he needed to lie down. She fetched his pajamas, turned down the covers and shut off the light. Before she left she leaned over and kissed his forehead gently.

"We'll beat this thing, Alan. We'll beat it together. I need you so much. You are my love, my one and only love."

Alan could not bring himself to go to work the next couple of days. His confidence was completely shot. The shaking was gone, but he couldn't sit still. He needed help and he needed it soon. Instead of calling Dr. Joe or his sister, he phoned a classmate from Harvard who was now a cardiac surgeon.

The Middle Years

The friend gave him the name of Dr. Paul Gordon who lived and practiced in neighboring Lexington. Alan asked if this psychiatrist was a quack and his friend laughed and told him that he was in for a surprise.

That he was. The good doctor lived in a hundred-year-old house on the back side of a twenty-acre corn and hay farm. The rutted road in was barely plowed and the frozen furrows made his BMW bounce like an Army jeep.

Alan wondered if it was a hoax. On the back wall of the house was a weathered sign that said "Office." The waiting room smelled of barn. The decor was early pioneer. The doctor must be in. He could smell the wonderful sharp aroma of hot coffee.

According to their local pediatrician, Dr. Paul Gordon had retired from active practice on Beacon Street in Boston and moved to his parents' homestead after his oldest brother died. It had been in the family for ninety years. His own wife had died of colon cancer the previous year. Apparently, he had been a successful psychiatrist with staff appointments to Mass General Hospital and Harvard Medical School. The only warning offered by the pediatrician was, "Watch out. He's different."

A big meaty handshake drew him gently into the dimly lit den, crowded with large comfortable leather chairs. A rolltop desk was shoved against one wall and was buried beneath a shamble of papers and books. The only other piece of furniture was on the opposite wall. It was a small, hand-hewn kitchen table upon which the coffee machine delivered its delicious smell.

Three things stood out: the man's size, his disheveled patch of snow-white hair, and his wonderful smile. He moved his six-and-a-half-foot frame over to the table and returned with two steaming mugs of black coffee. No cream or sugar offered.

"What can I do for you, son?" was the opening line. Alan let it all out. He reviewed the stunning events of a few days ago and broke down. Not a word from his listener. When he had finished the doctor rose himself slowly, walked over to him, handed him a box of Kleenex and returned to his chair. Still not a word.

Alan blew his nose and burst out laughing. He said, "I heard you shrinks could be odd, but is this all you are going to do for me?"

Paul Gordon leaned over toward him and said, "No. That's not all I'm going to do for you. This is the nice part. Coffee and Kleenex. So you better relax and enjoy it while you can. Because after this comes the hard part. I intend to whip your ass into shape so that when we are finished you won't ever drop another tear on my precious furniture."

At this point, both men sat back and roared with laughter.

"Son, let me tell you what you are up against. It's you. Now, what I've got to hear about from you is not what happened the other day but how this forty-five-year-old man got so screwed up. And you're not leaving this house today until you start filling me in. I have the rest of the afternoon off. How about you?"

Alan was shocked. In the movies the fifty-minute hour was sacrosanct.

"Let's not waste time. Come on with me over to the back end of the farm. I've got to tend to a busted fence. So button up your coat and give me a hand. Come on! Time's a wasting."

They reentered the warm office an hour later and drank some more coffee. In the meantime, Alan did in fact trace back the highlights of his life as he could recall since the earlier days. The manner of questioning by Dr. Gordon was totally disarming. He revealed more about his life to him than he thought he ever knew.

"It's been a hard day, Alan. And it's getting dark. I want you to go home and get some sleep tonight. Also, I have a prescription for you which is for a mild tranquilizer. I want to see you next week, same day, same time, and we'll sort out a few more things and set up a game plan."

He trusted this guy. Alan was both exhausted and relieved by the end of the day. Before leaving he commented on a dozen framed photographs on the far wall which were action photos of football games. Dr. Gordon smiled and said that they were all games that he had played in. High school, Harvard, and even the New York Giants for a two-year stint.

True to his word, he spent the next session sorting out and setting up a game plan. No farm chores the second week. It was snowing hard. Dr. Gordon explained that there would be three parts to his treatment of Alan. Part one was identifying the problem, which meant sorting out causes of the painful feelings. The second part moved on to an agreement on a game plan which would include a few more sessions and also the use of tranquilizing medication as well as a possible antidepressant pill. The third part was the toughest. The action part.

The doctor asked Alan to come over to the kitchen table and gaze at a half-finished jigsaw puzzle. He said that the first thing one does is to get the outer square fixed before working on the inner puzzle. The straight edges come first. That way you know the size of the problem at hand. He returned to his chair and asked Alan to do the same. He explained that part one was like the jigsaw puzzle. The straight edges of Alan's problems were his age and to a large extent his problems fit into that dimension. Where was Alan with his life at this point? He explained that the problems of midlife were not the same problems of a little child or an older person. He listed the classic changes and challenges of midlife and gave Alan a perfect score for having fallen prey to these unsuspecting attacks on his sense of stability. The marriage, the family, his health, his job, and his reason for living.

They took a long coffee break and just talked about sports. When they returned to the problems at hand, Alan asked why if it was so common to all persons that other people didn't go through the God-awful experience that he had a few days ago.

His psychiatrist explained that there was no simple answer. Two things seemed to make a difference in terms of one person's ability to weather midlife pressures. The first was the amount of unfinished emotional business each person brought into the middle years. The second was how much true change and loss was experienced during those years. They explored the first area together.

The doctor talked to him about two parts to the unfinished emotional business. The first part had to do with actual losses in his life that he had not resolved, and thus carried with him as lingering depression coupled with a certain amount of uncertainty and anxiety. The second part of the unfinished business had to do with how he coped over the years with the different changes and challenges that came his way. This was somewhat of an embarrassment for Alan since the doctor went directly to his artificial way of dealing with things as an adolescent and young adult. He explained that his athletic fame and popularity replaced some real solid growth and maturity early on. Along those lines, he carried the theme up to Alan's sordid sexual affairs with little or no control and no respect for the other person. On the good side, he talked about his sincere turnabout when it came to marrying Janet McHale.

As for "now" stresses, they discussed the fact that the midlife challenges and changes were not that overwhelming and that no one of them should have caused such a disruption. The doctor focused in on the unresolved grief that Alan had for his father's early departure and the rekindling of those emotions when he found out that he had died and left his life again.

Their third session a week later did not take that long. This was the time to make a treatment plan. The plan was the product of earlier explorations. Dr. Gordon explained the task before his patient. The level of anxiety and the dreadful feelings of loss and helplessness would not and could not go away overnight. They would only go away with Alan's own efforts, and those efforts would be extended over a period of months and possible years.

"What do I do?" Alan asked.

"Simple, my son. You do nothing but what you're supposed to do."

His explanation was almost as direct as the statement. The first task was counting his blessings, mainly the good things in his life, and holding on to them. The doctor helped him to count his blessings. Alan's first comment had to do with his wife and his marriage. They explored the issue of reinvesting in the marriage and truly giving back to his wife some of the great gifts of loyalty and love she had offered him. Now more than ever, Janet needed her husband, especially as she was struggling with her own midlife issues.

Next came the kids. They both laughed as they talked about the unfair circumstance of two generations going through different changes of life in the same household. Nevertheless, Alan did focus on the need to put the kids almost ahead of his own problems at times and try to develop some patience in helping them get through their first change of life, adolescence.

Dr. Gordon paused and said, "These are the two biggest challenges, Alan. Your choice will be to stay with your loved ones, despite how you feel. The little boy inside you will tempt you to cut out and lick your own wounds. Your father did it before you, and there will be a mighty temptation to repeat what he did, despite the fact that you never forgave him. Do not run away."

He urged Alan to continue the list of things that were important in his life. The job came next. More than forty hours a week was spent out of the home away from the family, and the job was indeed a serious stage on which Alan's flight-or-fight dilemma rested.

"Your job will become a painful prison to you over the next several months. You will not have a day when you will not wish to leave and go somewhere else, feeling that there is a better opportunity. This is folly. Because this is the time when many people start playing musical jobs in an effort to remove the chains of boredom and dull routines. You will not be a good judge at this point because you are feeling so lousy. So stick to your job as you stick to your family. There may come a time when an honest reappraisal of another job opportunity may be more valid."

Dr. Gordon paused and let these statements sink in and then continued. "Now let me tell you the cost and the prize that go with this effort. The cost will be daily amounts of emotional pain for a significant period of time. The pain will be the product of wanting to chuck off the responsibilities on the one hand or be faithful to them on the other. Remember your problems did not arise overnight. They were a long time coming. Just as you experienced in the car the first night, you will feel a tremendous tug-of-war inside you.

"You may lose some weight and you will lose an awful lot of sleep. You will not enjoy life so much for awhile, and you will go to bed early to shut out the whole damn mess.

"But one day you will begin to feel better. Much less shaking, crying and wondering. You will start to laugh a little more and you will know that you are winning the war. The prize is yourself. You will begin to like and respect yourself more. You will have earned the right to really love and appreciate others. And you will never visit this hell again."

Alan sat for several minutes before responding.

"Dr. Gordon, I know you are right. But where am I going to get the strength to do this?"

"Alan, you already have what you need inside of you. Despite that angry little boy raising hell, there is a grown man still running your life. You started to really grow up fifteen years ago when you married Janet. You made a choice then to stop the screwing and drinking. This is the next chapter. But there is something else you are going to need. And that his your higher power, your God."

Alan's expression softened. "What about that?"

"Alan, I am not a minister or a theologian, but I do know that the midlife changes and challenges include serious questions about one's purpose in life and whether there is a life hereafter.

"Return to the values of your youth. Review and remember the messages taught by your parents. Reconnect with the God of your younger days and pray hard for the strength to pull this task off."

"Where will you be in all of this, Dr. Gordon?"

"I'll be right here planting corn and pitching hay, and if you want, I'll take a little time out once in a while to kick your butt and keep you on the right path."

That night Alan brought Janet out to dinner to discuss what he called his "second job." As she heard him summarize the session, she broke down and cried. Alan reached across the table to join their hands and told her that he never been so scared in his life and he had never been so hopeful. She told him how proud she was, how much she loved him, and that together they would make it.

Jessica Reardon

She loved her job at Children's Hospital. A full-fledged social worker, and all the letters after her name to prove it. Jessica was sincere, caring, and thorough. The kids and the parents loved her. They were her second family. She collected piles of thank-you notes from patients and patients' families. She volunteered at the Peabody Museum one day a week as a guide and sang in the church choir. Symphony orchestra tickets were her other outlet. No male companionship, however.

Her life was indeed well regulated, and she worked to keep it that way. But the reproductive hormones had other ideas. The hot flashes were an annoyance at first. Then came the cramps, some nausea and sweats. She read up on the menopausal problems in magazine articles, but became confused and more frightened. She thought of talking to Rita but was ashamed. She had never talked to anyone about her periods. Deep inside was a lingering fear that death was associated with it. Her thoughts occasionally wandered to the bloody horror of her mother's death so many, many years ago.

Rita became concerned over her withdrawal and her deepening mood swings. When she broached the subject to Jessica, she snapped at her stepmother and said it was none of her business.

After Dr. Joe Reardon's retirement party, he and Rita took an extended trip to China and the Far East. Jessica insisted that she would be fine at home. But inside was a pounding fear that something would go wrong. They chose the month of February for their trip. This was Jessica's least favorite month of the year. For years, she recoiled against the cold, the isolation, the snow and the darkness.

A blizzard whipped across Marblehead harbor two days after they left. Jessica panicked. The phone lines were down and she was without electricity for eight hours. The first night, she lit two candles in her bedroom and crawled under the covers. She woke a few hours later to the howling wind and the flickering shadows from the candles. She let out a scream. In her mind, she was transported back to the death scene of her mother. Indeed she was there again, complete with the bloody sheets, as her changing menstrual cycle was ill timed. When she failed to show up at work for three days, her boss dropped over. No answer. Before she left, she peeked in the parlor window and saw Jessica lying on the rug, stark naked in a fetal position. From the Salem Emergency Room, she was again transported to McLean Hospital. Only two members of the original staff remembered her. However, the antipsychotic medication began to kick in within three days and she was released a week later. Joe and Rita cut short their trip. Jessica returned to work by the end of March with a good deal of hope and enthusiasm.

The changes and challenges of midlife were not completely over for her. But she had rallied once again from the dissolution of her mental defenses. She determined to look forward and not backward. She was grateful for the good things in her life, namely family and a job. She thanked God for giving her the strength to begin anew.

CHOICE

It's a toss-up. Adolescence or midlife. Which is worse? Which is the more uncomfortable, disruptive, confusing and discouraging change of life experience? There is no agreement. Each person would have a different

The Middle Years

response. But there is no question about which stage of our existence demands clear-cut choices.

In our teen years, we are led or pushed along a developmental conveyor belt called school. To be sure, some kids choose to drop off that belt and embark on a journey of protest or nonconformity. But for most teens, the choices are limited to clothes, friends, rock stars, and on a more serious level, what to do with sexual urges, and finally whether to go to college or get a job.

When confused or reluctant about those choices, adolescents tend to blame others, such as parents or teachers. In midlife, however, there is no one else to blame. We must stand alone and decide for ourselves to push on with our lives or not.

The Smith and Malone families traveled different roads, as did their extended families. How they handled earlier changes and challenges most definitely influenced the outcome of their individual midlife encounters.

Billy Smith died before the middle years. The terrible trauma of his early childhood, plus the legal confinement in late adolescence and adulthood, led him to narrow choices regarding lifestyle. His sister discovered as his life was ebbing that his final choice was to recognize a God and put his faith in a better life after death.

Sarah, on the other hand, responded to professional help at the end of her adolescence and chose to shake off the chains of sulkiness and her eating disorder. Along with her husband, Rob, she worked hard to be a wife and mother, and by midlife, had a pretty good grip on who she was and what her life was about. But the residue of her dysfunctional upbringing seeped into her consciousness and, coupled with the midlife changes, dragged her down again. Once again, timely professional help allowed her to recover and rejoin her husband and family.

As a child, Holly Diamond relied on two parents and a pair of skates. By the time she reached her forties, there was nothing left. Plus, her child had been taken away from her. Her mother never reentered her life, and her father had retired to Florida. Her choices by midlife were indeed limited. The desolation of her life after the leg amputation led to alcohol and drug dependence. The fractured hip that followed stripped her of all the freedom she had had to live her life on her own. In the chronic disease hospital in Salem, she was consumed till the end of her life with bitterness and helplessness.

Dr. Ruth Reardon Broderick handled the midlife changes pretty well. She was a strong and well-adjusted woman by that time. And she still had Rita and Dana by her side. The menopausal symptoms had been anticipated and were bearable. She loved her job in the emergency room but cut back from the stressful hours to a lighter job. She had a deep faith in her God and ultimately found ways to strengthen her beliefs.

The one area that caused her problems was coping with the natural family erosion. Both of her maternal grandparents had died before her mid-forties. Her own father seemed to have dropped off the face of the earth. His youngest brother, Uncle Terrence, was dying of lung cancer. She thus became more conscious of Rita's aches and pains and for a while became obsessed with the depletion of the older members of the family. She and Dana talked humorously about the thinning of the front ranks of the family. Together she and her husband emerged from the troublesome middle years stronger and more secure.

Jessica Reardon was not as well prepared. The midlife storm almost passed her by. Were it not for the mysterious body changes, she might have weathered the whole thing. But the menopausal symptoms intruded on her well-regulated lifestyle and drew her back into a world she thought was behind her. The child within took over briefly, breaking down all the barricades she had built to avoid another psychotic regression. Her body image had always been her most vulnerable spot, and the hormones fired up the old memories of devils and death. She welcomed the efforts of the hospital staff and was relieved that she could survive once more the strange malady that now seemed to visit her much more infrequently.

Alan Reardon caught the full brunt of the midlife challenges. For a while, he had been nurturing doubts and misgivings about his life that slowly moved him into the storm itself. But he was unprepared for the sudden onslaught. Soon he found himself caught in the quicksand of crippling anxiety and depression. And the more he struggled, the deeper he got. As frightened as he was, he was also angry. Something had blindsided him, and that was unfair to a former athlete. Who was to blame? And there was no answer.

Dr. Paul Gordon was the right man at the right time. The sign on his wall told it all: "NON FECUM TAURI." No bullshit. Dr. Paul had seen it and heard it all. The midlife trap. Waiting to ensnare the unprepared. After a few solid sessions, Alan found that he had regained some confidence and was ready to take on the tasks outlined by his psychiatrist. But during those first few weeks, He bounced and flailed within the invisible walls of what Dr. Paul Gordon called the "anxiety triangle," made up of anxiety, panic and phobias.

The Anxiety Triangle

At this point let us take a closer look at the phenomenon of the anxiety triangle, since the experience of anxiety, panic and phobias is so commonplace.

As we recall from the earliest pages of the book, anxiety is defined as an irrational fear that something bad is going to happen. I don't know what it is and I can't prevent it. Unlike the dilemma of the anxious newborn, the midlife version brings an extra twist. The extra twist is the feeling that not only is something bad going to happen, but I may even be to blame for causing it.

That was exactly the experience that Alan Reardon went through on the first horrible night. The second part of the anxiety triangle is the panic attack. The devastating sense of being totally immobile and defenseless. One's brain seems to fibrillate and the heart wants to jump out of the chest. The sweat glands pour out warm sticky goo, and the muscles are paralyzed temporarily. This event seems to last an eternity, but in actuality, usually has a lifespan of no more than a few minutes.

From this experience, the building up of phobias follows. Phobias appear to be a defensive reaction to avoid falling into any further experiences of panic. A phobia may be defined as an irrational fear of being somewhere or with others whereby one may fall into a serious anxiety or panic attack. Some of the more recognizable phobias are claustrophobia (fear of closed spaces), agoraphobia (fear of open spaces), and social phobias (fear of being with people or in crowds).

Phobias are derived from the awful feeling of the panic attack and serve to fix the attention of the person on any possible site or situation where another panic attack could take place. The most common sites in our society are elevators, shopping malls, bridges, airplanes. The situations most prevalent for phobias are crowded rooms or large audiences where one is expected to speak or perform.

In our modern society, the problem of phobias, panic attacks and anxiety is enormous. More and more people seem to complain of moments in their life when they feel crippled by these emotional catastrophic events. A vast amount of literature is available on the subject, but an in-depth look at the causes and treatments is beyond the scope of this book.

Despite all this, there is, I feel, a sad and unfortunate appreciation by mental health professionals of what it takes to truly overcome this terrible problem. There can be no lasting freedom from the problems of the anxiety triangle without simple, determined hard work on the part of the patient. All the talk and pills can take the sufferer just so far. But the only way to reestablish a sense of control and ownership of one's life is to doggedly face the phobias themselves and to truly dispatch the ghosts one by one. One must conquer the fears by facing them in an active way to prove that one's behavior will not be restricted. This may take years to accomplish. But as Dr. Paul Gordon said, the prize is well worth it: one's self-esteem and the control of one's life and one's soul.

The same game plan offered to Alan Reardon works to reduce the sadness, madness, and particularly the badness of midlife depression. As Alan gained his confidence by setting goals and reaching them, the distorted remnants of hurt and loss acquired over a lifetime began to shrivel.

The midlife experience offers the clearest picture of the devastating power of anxiety and depression as the two slip in on the wings of change and challenge. And to the great credit of our human spirit, we do have the choice of whether to give in to these challenges or not.

Posttraumatic Stress Disorder

Having just reviewed the many stresses of midlife, it might be helpful to explore a different kind of stress. Such stress results from direct trauma inflicted by other persons or by errant forces of nature.

Posttraumatic stress disorder (PTSD) has become a widely discussed mental health issue since the return of veterans from the Vietnam War. In my early training years at the Boston Veteran's Administration Hospital, I encountered many survivors of World War II and the Korean Conflict who bore the emotional scars of combat or internment as prisoners. Man's inhumanity to man has been universally exposed by concentration camp victims.

In my own practice over the past forty years, I have treated relatively few persons who have been severely traumatized by war, either combatants or civilians. The same for victims of natural disasters such as earthquakes, hurricanes, etc. Thus I lay no claim to expertise on the subject.

Nowadays, in mental health circles, there is much confusion and even disagreement as to which experiences should be included in this diagnostic category. Of some concern is the use of the term posttraumatic stress disorder by patients, professionals, and the media in such a broad and all-inclusive way that it has lost its original meaning.

PTSD is claimed by a growing number of applicants to our clinic at Salem Hospital. When asked to describe it, many patients struggle to define its origin or effects. A most upsetting response is that some other health professional told them that they had it. And the most discouraging reply is that it is a necessary diagnosis for an application for disability assistance.

Nevertheless, let me try to differentiate trauma-induced stress from the stresses of everyday life. Up until now, we have explored the natural stresses of growing older and growing up—coping with change and challenge and making choices. These events take place in our daily lives where family and friends affect the quality of our existence for better or worse. The important thing to note is that none of these people dedicate themselves to consciously hurting us.

For the victims of war or natural disasters, it is the opposite. Either armies or out-of-control forces of nature bring incredible disruption and suffering. Aside from the immediate mind-numbing effects many such victims carry throughout their lives, there is a lingering fear that the disaster will repeat someday. In addition, they must endure the anxiety and depression that accompanies all changes and losses.

Trust or lack thereof is perhaps the most burdensome result of serious trauma. As a protective measure, the mind of a seriously abused person stands guard against a repeat of the hurt. Once again, depending on the degree of the insult, survivors may walk through the remaining years of their lives never able to completely trust certain people or the world around them.

As for treatment, certain programs are available in many communities. For the most part, they are for victims of rape, battering, stalking and assault. The immediate goals are protection and intervention. Some offer longer-term treatment to help reestablish safe boundaries and to pick up the shattered pieces of disrupted lives. Psychiatrists may be of help with medications and hospitalization if necessary.

Chapter Six: The Latter Years

CHANGE

Retirement

It's over now. Getting up every day. Work! No excuses. Winter, summer, spring, fall. Rain, snow, sun. The joys and the jokes. The fuss and fun. The boredom, the hopes, the friendships, the enemies. The loyalties, the jealousies. The money. And finally the gold watch. Nowadays, the gifts are more simple, more personal. The retirement dinner is giving way to the smaller after-hour cocktail party or even luncheon.

Most people spend at least a quarter of their lives away from family and friends working for money to support themselves and their loved ones. Work is a necessity. Work is a habit, a time-consuming habit, that suddenly ends. Now what?

Retirement brings a mixed bag of emotions. The big reward for one's labor is more free time. But at the same time, one is reminded that there are fewer years left than one has spent working. The joints are a little stiffer, the walk a little slower, the eyes a little dimmer. Thus we arrive at the next significant phase of life. The next change and the next challenge.

The retirement years bring a different kind of challenge. We are not faced with the previous challenges regarding college or work, sex or abstinence, to be or not to be, marital commitment or divorce, to live or die at midlife. The challenge of retirement is not how to face life but how to enjoy it knowing that there is less of it left.

The first enjoyable change is the freedom from the old routines. However, a certain number of people find it difficult to abruptly stop the daily habits of a lifetime. The prevailing customs of upward mobility and job switches make this less of a problem. The one company, one job phenomenon is fading. Thus, deeply rooted loyalties to a company or to co-workers are less painfully severed.

If the suddenly liberated retiree has a problem adjusting to all this newfound time, then so does the spouse. At first there is an awkwardness. The important daily routines of home life are threatened. Grocery shopping, volunteer meetings, exercise classes, and lunches compete with the unsure game plan of the new daytime guest. Because so many of these activities are solo enterprises, the retired spouse feels left out. Thus, a necessary period of adjustment.

For the married couple accustomed to compromise and change, this solution may be easy. New daily and weekly routines can be developed. But for the couple who have not kept up the readjustment process over the years, this new change may expose a continued unwillingness to compromise. Divorce is not likely at this point—too many years together. What is more likely is a slow drifting apart into an intolerant cohabitation.

It is during the retirement years that the fruits of an intact marriage are especially important. As we saw in the last chapter on midlife, the role of friends and family begins to change. Death and sickness force us to realign our alliances with friends and older acquaintances. The marriage of the kids may bring a sense of accomplishment and acceptance of new acquaintances, but it also may bring the ache of some loneliness and a feeling of rejection.

Marriage thus becomes the one solid institution, the one relationship that does not need to fade or diminish in its importance. If the couple turns to each other again in recognition of the natural and necessary yearning for love and support, the promise of the golden years is more reassuring.

Another bonus is the rediscovery of the family, especially the children of the children. Grandchildren are very special. Grandparents truly do have all the fun and do little work. Grandchildren pump life into a life that by all that is natural begins to slow down. They play, laugh, cry, jump and hug. They see their grandparents as friends, playmates and advocates in the ceaseless battle against parental oppression. Being part of the conspiracy is wonderful; the alliance, pure joy.

In closing the experience of the retirement years, a word about the two basic emotional responses to change and challenge: anxiety and depression.

As we already know, these two elements are the fundamental ingredients in all emotional adjustments to life. As we have witnessed, the tremendous challenge in dealing with life's demands produces behavioral patterns of a wide variety. The core of it all is the inevitable feeling of anxiety when faced with new and unknown experiences. As we all have seen repeatedly, the reluctance to let go of what is familiar produces depression.

When one faces the challenge of retirement years, anxiety and depression are likely to be experienced in their purest form. By that I mean the coping mechanisms of our childhood and young adulthood are out of style, not available. There are fewer behavioral choices to hide our fears at this point in life. The unsure and anxious teenager found solace hiding in the herd. And the gang itself chose cultural icons that were both satisfying as well as protective of each awkward member. T-shirts, logos, earrings, hip talk, hard rock, MTV—there is not much of a market in the golden-years age group for these symbols of unanimity. Sex, booze and drugs offer transient anti-anxiety and antidepressant relief to the groping, searching and unsettled young adult. Eating disorders, bipolar disorders, schizophrenia, obsessive-compulsive disorders are developed in the youthful years. But the volcanic ash of these maladies has long since cooled by the time the retirement years arrive, and the smoldering tensions in the soul of the young adult and middle-aged person become inactive by the time we leave the job.

For those who still have not accepted themselves or life's challenges, for those plagued by the uncertainty of death, anxiety will be a constant companion, but now the most available manifestation of this affliction is withdrawal. Withdrawal from people, places and things, anything that threatens to invade the false security of the uncertain self.

The term agoraphobia is now commonly used. Simply put, it means the fear of being out in space, the fear of the outside world, the fear of leaving one's illusory fortress. If one succumbs to this fear, the path of isolation and emotional shrinkage is endless. Family and friends are of value only in sustaining the retreat backwards into a childlike existence. And then ultimately, family and friends are rejected.

Depression walks hand-in-hand with anxiety and produces an attitude of hopelessness, helplessness, bitterness and entitlement. This is sad and unnecessary. But as we shall soon see, only we are ourselves can really turn it around.

The Final Years

The retirement years drift slowly and inevitably into the latter years. There is no exact day or date to mark this change—perhaps the late seventies or early eighties.

The body parts start to wear out, regardless of the triumphs of modern medicine. An anatomic notice is served that we are slowing down. The skeletal structure points the way. Brittle bones succumb to slippery surfaces. Fractures and ligament strains may lead to immobility and possible surgery. Allowing this forced inactivity invites respiratory, circulatory, and even dietary alterations. The most vital organ, the heart, announces that there are only so many beats left and the two major afflictions, coronary artery disease and congestive heart disease, become a worry amid other infirmities.

What about the emotional response to the latter years? As mentioned in the last chapter, our personalities are not likely to change at this stage of life. A lifetime of coping with change and challenge leaves each one of us with a distinctive character, a recognizable style and even a predictable behavior. This predictable response to change implies the possession of values and an automatic defense of these values. This brings us once again to a discussion about an often ignored part of our mental apparatus: our attitude. As we discussed before, an attitude is a habit of thinking, usually driven by our perception of life and ourselves in life. Now the attitudes of a lifetime combine to lead us into the latter years in a manner where we may truly live each day with a sense of security and certainty or with a sense of grave anxiety and fear of death.

The first serious questions about life's meaning occur in late adolescence. In young adulthood, the "if-to-be," "who-to-be," and "what-to-be" questions must be answered. Depending on those answers, a unique, personal set of values is formed along with our character, and this in turn shapes our attitude to life itself. By the latter years, our attitude becomes a permanent guiding force in dealing with everyday events. Basically, attitudes at this time of life fall into two categories: positive and negative. Our attitudes at this point in life will determine how much anxiety and how much depression we will have to endure.

Those who have lived with a positive view of life will accept what comes their way with a certain patience and grace. Personal pain and discomfort will not isolate them from a concern for others and a value of life itself. A positive attitude is selfless. It recognizes the need for people, especially friends and family. It treasures relationships; it nurtures the closeness and love that will help us endure. Physical pain and personal loss may temporarily dim the glow of a positive attitude, but the fire burning deep in the soul is not likely to be extinguished at this final stage of life.

On the other hand, a negative attitude is a terrible burden for the owner and all who come in contact with that person. The little child within the adult takes over, entitled and demanding. Any discomfort is an injustice, and someone out there has to atone. Relief is expected for the misery of life, and others have to provide that relief. The complaining child screaming inside the shrinking body of the aging adult resembles the infant in the crib. "I" and only "I" exist. All others exist to serve me.

Anxiety over what lies ahead is a daily companion, a dreaded companion, for the person who expects all from others and who has surrendered total responsibility and control of their own life. Depression, likewise, dampens their every thought and feeling as the curses ring out over the injustice of it all.

What about one's attitude toward death? Early in the chapter on adolescence, we learned of the first serious inquiry of the human soul for meaning. The distractions of daily adolescent turmoil preempt a meaningful search at that time. Such a search reappears in the young adult years when we are forced to deal again with the issues of life after death. The "if-to-be" question will not go away.

The midlife struggle once again revisits this issue. It includes not only a search for meaning to life but demands a decision to go on with life or not, a time to reinvest in one's belief in a supreme being and a hereafter or the choice of hopeless abandonment of such beliefs. Even at these crucial moments, some people in the middle years manage to avoid the issues. These people continue to live out their lives by focusing only on the now, particularly looking for the pleasures of life while denying the pain.

Finally, we have the final years, with certain death approaching. The distractions now are few, and avoidance of the issue of life after death is impossible. In these final days, those whose whole life was built on hope, love and courage have a decided edge. For at each stage of their life, they gambled and won. Each challenge was accepted and the choice was to go forward.

For those people, the choice was richly rewarded. They continue to make a choice to live life to the fullest to the end with the firm belief that life for them will go on and on.

CHALLENGE

Aging takes its toll. Having following the original Smith and Malone families from the birth of Billy and Ruth, we now arrive at a point where not all have survived. In this chapter, we will walk with the remaining members from the early retirement years on into their last years of life.

One thing will be apparent. Although the changes and challenges will be less surprising and more manageable, the choices themselves will be limited to daily activities, rather than life-altering decisions. One does not change one's stripes at this stage of life. We are what we are. Our personalities, values, habits and attitudes are pretty well fixed. As we will see, this last journey is made so much better by truly investing and appreciating one's faith, family and friends.

Sarah Smith Carleton
The first big challenge for Sarah was letting go of her only child, Christine, to marriage. She was completing graduate studies at Salem State College.

She had only been dating for six months, but insisted that he was the right guy. Rob helped Sarah through it. This time she did not break down because of the momentous change in her life. At first, the newlyweds rented in Saugus and then bought a new home in Topsfield. In time, they produced two grandchildren, Becky and Sam. Sarah doted on them. As they grew, she attended all their recitals, plays and ballgames. She loved the role of grandmother.

Around his sixty-fifth birthday, Rob sold the business somewhat reluctantly. He loved the hands-on part, but his arthritis had forced him back into the office. The two of them joined a senior citizens travel club and began seeing the world. Amazingly, Sarah's old fears of flying had disappeared. A surprise fiftieth anniversary party was held at Christine's house within a month of Sarah's seventy-fifth birthday.

Sarah and Rob were grateful to the family but also to each other. Life had not been easy for them. Their love and loyalty had endured and would continue to do so.

Ruth Reardon Broderick

Dana Jr. married in his late thirties after establishing a solid law practice. His wife was three years older. After two miscarriages, she delivered a girl who had Down's syndrome. They and their families were affected mightily but rallied to support the newest family. Ruth was particularly generous with her time and medical talents, and even cut short her hours at the hospital to be available. She and Dana bought a condo in Arizona after their retirement and divided up their time into six months at each home.

Her mother Rita survived Dr. Joe Reardon by four years. She died in a nursing home at the age of ninety-two. Before going to the home, her stepdaughter, Jessica Reardon, took complete responsibility for her care at home.

Ruth and Dana lived into their nineties, still firm in their love and blessed with a solid sense of humor. They attended daily mass almost till the end. When they stopped driving, they hired a taxi to take them to and from church.

Jessica Reardon

She had never asked for much in her life. Life had been built around her family, her job, and her leisure activities. Thus, it was hard to see her folks get older and even harder to retire from Children's Hospital. Quietly, Jessica began to fill the available hours with new activities. She joined a Bible study group and lent her voice to a North Shore Chorale. At first, she minded the long winter months alone without the company of Rita and Joe. She finally agreed to spend one month each winter at their condo but took the train. She was still petrified of flying.

The Latter Years

She came close to breaking down when her father died, but rallied with the support of Ruth and Alan. After twenty years being medication free, she finally agreed to see a psychiatrist and benefited from his support and medication therapy.

Rita had shown signs of dementia prior to Joe's death. It worsened dramatically afterwards. Jessica devoted herself entirely to her stepmother's care, insisting that a nursing home was out of the question. For her it was payback time. She had been given so much. When Rita finally went to the nursing home, Jessica visited her daily.

Jessica had come such a long way in her life. She suffered the pain and recurrent torment of the one true mental disease. Throughout her life, however, she made the choice to keep growing up until the end of her life. A woman of great courage.

Alan Reardon

Alan emerged from the torment of this midlife crisis a much stronger man. Slowly but surely, he exorcised the devils carried by the sad and bitter little boy inside. He and Janet renewed their love and commitment to each other and lived out their retirement and final years with joy and gratitude. Their children and grandchildren were a source of great pride and comfort.

Alan chose not to run away at a critical time in his life. The emotional struggle that ensued and the success of the ordeal guaranteed his children and their children a much happier life.

CHOICE

Choice is perhaps the most bothersome word in the English language. For choice demands responsibility, but in truth life demands that we make choices. To be sure, there are times when we would like to avoid making those decisions.

As noted in the beginning of this chapter, the big, important choices about the direction of one's life have already been made by the time our families arrive in the later years. These later years truly reflect on how choices that are made affect the last few years of our life on this earth.

The Smith and Malone families and all who are gathered into their lives represent some of the more common experiences of all our lives. Each member of these two families was given a different preparation for their adult years. And some were much better prepared than others. Perhaps the most important lesson to be learned from all of these lives is the important responsibility of parents and elders in preparing each child for the changes, challenges, and choices of later life.

Conclusion

As stated in the Introduction, my hope in writing this book was to take the mystery and confusion out of emotional illness. As a wise person once said, "Truth is not complicated, only our understanding of it."

What I have presented is my best effort to share with you the lessons taught to me by my many patients. This is not a textbook of psychiatry or psychology, nor an encyclopedic description of all known diagnoses. It is intended to introduce the reader to the more common afflictions that we human beings suffer in our journey from birth to death.

Let me return to the words in the introduction: Very few people truly go crazy. Most other emotional problems are man-made. What we can cause, we can prevent.

My earnest hope is that by better understanding the roots of mental illness, particularly the vulnerability of the child, we can prevent the unnecessary pain and suffering of later life.